Gramsci and Educational Thought

T0341595

Educational Philosophy and Theory
Special Issue Book Series

Series Editor: Michael A. Peters

The *Educational Philosophy and Theory* journal publishes articles concerned with all aspects of educational philosophy. Their themed special issues are also available to buy in book format and cover subjects ranging from curriculum theory, educational administration, the politics of education, educational history, educational policy, and higher education.

Titles in the series include:

Patriotism and Citizenship Education
Edited by Bruce Haynes

Exploring Education Through Phenomenology: Diverse Approaches
Edited by Gloria Dall'Alba

Academic Writing, Philosophy and Genre
Edited by Michael A. Peters

Complexity Theory and the Philosophy of Education
Edited by Mark Mason

Critical Thinking and Learning
Edited by Mark Mason

Philosophy of Early Childhood Education: Transforming Narratives
Edited by Sandy Farquhar and Peter Fitzsimons

The Learning Society from the Perspective of Governmentality
Edited by Jan Masschelein, Maarten Simons, Ulrich Bröckling and Ludwig Pongratz

Citizenship, Inclusion and Democracy: A Symposium on Iris Marion Young
Edited by Mitja Sardoc

Postfoundationalist Themes In The Philosophy of Education: Festschrift for James D. Marshall
Edited by Paul Smeyers (Editor), Michael A. Peters

Music Education for the New Millennium: Theory and Practice Futures for Music Teaching and Learning
Edited by David Lines

Critical Pedagogy and Race
Edited by Zeus Leonardo

Derrida, Deconstruction and Education: Ethics of Pedagogy and Research
Edited by Peter Pericles Trifonas and Michael A. Peters

Gramsci and Educational Thought

Edited by
Peter Mayo

A John Wiley & Sons, Ltd., Publication

First published as Volume 41, Issue 6 of *Educational Philosophy and Theory* except for *Antonio Gramsci and his Relevance to the Education of Adults* which was published in Volume 40, Issue 3.

Blackwell Publishing was acquired by John Wiley & Sons in February 2007. Blackwell's publishing program has been merged with Wiley's global Scientific, Technical, and Medical business to form Wiley-Blackwell.

Registered Office
John Wiley & Sons Ltd, The Atrium, Southern Gate, Chichester, West Sussex, PO19 8SQ, United Kingdom

Editorial Offices
350 Main Street, Malden, MA 02148-5020, USA
9600 Garsington Road, Oxford, OX4 2DQ, UK
The Atrium, Southern Gate, Chichester, West Sussex, PO19 8SQ, UK

For details of our global editorial offices, for customer services, and for information about how to apply for permission to reuse the copyright material in this book please see our website at www.wiley.com/wiley-blackwell.

Library of Congress Cataloging-in-Publication Data

Gramsci and educational thought / edited by Peter Mayo.
     p. cm. — (Educational philosophy and theory special issue book series)
  Includes bibliographical references and index.
  ISBN 978-1-4443-3394-7 (pbk. : alk. paper) 1. Gramsci, Antonio, 1891–1937.
2. Education—Philosophy. 3. Educational sociology. I. Mayo, Peter, 1955–
  LB775.G742G73 2010
  370.1—dc22

                           2010000774

A catalogue record for this book is available from the British Library.

Set in 10pt Plantin by Graphicraft Limited, Hong Kong
Printed in Malaysia

01   2010

Contents

Notes on Contributors

Peter Mayo is Professor and Head, Department of Education Studies, University of Malta where he teaches/researches in the areas of sociology of education, adult education, comparative and international education and sociology in general. He is the author of *Gramsci, Freire and Adult Education* (Zed Books 1999, translated into five other languages), *Liberating Praxis* (Praeger, hbk 2004, Sense, pbk 2008, AESA Critics Choice Award 2005), *Adult Education in Malta* (DVV International, 2007) and, with Carmel Borg, *Learning and Social Difference* (Paradigm, 2006). With Carmel Borg and Joseph A. Buttigieg, he co-edited *Gramsci and Education* (Rowman & Littlefield, 2002) and produced, with the former, *Public Intellectuals, Radical Democracy and Social Movements. A book of interviews* (Peter Lang, 2007). He co-edits the book series on 'Postcolonial Studies in Education' (with Antonia Darder and Anne Hickling Hudson) for Palgrave Macmillan and edits the book series on international adult education for Sense Publishers.

Deb J. Hill is a Political Philosopher of Education at the University of Canterbury at Christchurch. She is the author of *Hegemony and Education: Gramsci, post-marxism and radical democracy revisited* (Lexington Books, US, 2007). Her interests lie in critical theory and the dialectical thought that underpins it.

John Holst is currently an associate professor in the Department of Leadership, Policy and Administration at the University of St Thomas in Minnesota, USA. He is the author of the book *Social Movements, Civil Society, and Radical Adult Education* (Bergin & Garvey, 2002) and articles that have appeared in several journals including the *Adult Education Quarterly*, the *International Journal of Lifelong Education* and the *Harvard Educational Review*.

Thomas Clayton is Professor and Chair of the English Department at the University of Kentucky, USA. He is a language policy scholar, and he has written widely on educational language policy and English language spread, particularly in Cambodia. He is also interested in Gramsci and the process of hegemony relative to language and education.

Peter Ives is an Associate Professor of Politics at the University of Winnipeg, Canada. He is the author of *Gramsci's Politics of Language: Engaging the Bakhtin Circle and the Frankfurt School* (University of Toronto Press, 2004; Winner of the Klibansky Prize 2004–5) and *Language and Hegemony in Gramsci* (Macmillan/ Pluto Press, 2004). His current research investigates the relationships between language and democracy.

Margaret Ledwith is Professor of Community Development and Social Justice at the University of Cumbria. Her commitment is to social justice through popular education. For many years, she worked in grassroots community development, building a critical approach to practice founded on the ideas of Antonio Gramsci and Paulo Freire.

Uwe Hirschfeld was born in 1956 in Kassel, Germany, and studied social work, education and political Science (Dr. rer. pol.). Since 1992, he has been Professor of Social Work at the Protestant University of Applied Science, Dresden.

Rosemary Dore Soares has a PhD in History and Philosophy of Education, and is an Associate Professor in Philosophy of Education in the Faculty of Education of the Federal University of Minas Gerais (UFMG), Brazil. She has published *Gramsci, o Estado e a escola* [Gramsci, the State and the School] (Unijuí Ed., 2000) and is coordinator of research on philosophical and pedagogical references of the organization of the school in Brazil and in Italy, and the project 'Observatory of Vocational Education and Drop Out in Brazil'.

Foreword

As the editor of this book Peter Mayo has provided an appropriate context in which to view the excellent contributions to this monograph in the year of Gramsci's anniversary. I remember inviting Peter to edit the original special issue of *Educational Philosophy and Theory* when I visited Malta for the International Network of Philosophers of Education Conference in 2006 (http://www.ucm.es/info/inpe/). As Editor I was pleased to be able to offer Peter the opportunity to display the best of Gramsci's scholarship in the field of education and also to meet with him and his colleagues at the University of Malta, including Kenneth Wain, Carmel Borg and others.

Peter Mayo rightly emphasizes that Gramsci's prison writings constitute an educational project based on the valuable concept of hegemony that Gramsci develops as an essential part of the sociology of capitalist society enabling an understanding of the manufacture of consent by the powerful through the institution of cultural values. I have nothing to add to what the contributors have made clear in their individual chapters and applaud the new scholarship on Gramsci's educational project—its origins, its enactment in the context of the party, its applications to 'global English' and women's 'ways of knowing, its contribution to the envisioning of the project of socialist education in Brazil.

Gramsci's analysis of Fordism and education in the age of Fordism has a new relevance with the global recession, the neoliberal meltdown and end of the ideology of automobilism. In 1934 in insightful notes in the *Prison Notebooks* Antonio Gramsci defined 'Americanism' as 'mechanicist', crude, brutal—'pure action' in other words—and contrasted it with tradition. He attempted to demonstrate how Fordism was destructive of trade unions leading to a crisis in high wages, hegemonic at the point of production and the production of new Taylorized workers. Fordist production entailing an intensified industrial division of labor, assembly line flow of work with increasingly specified tasks by management, increased the potential for capitalist control over the pace and intensity of work and led to the displacement of craft-based production in which skilled laborers exercised substantial control over their conditions of work.

Now arguably, the time has come again to analyze, understand and enact a new politics that has come to characterize late capitalism and the new subjectivities demanded by post-fordist regimes that are conducive to an emerging globally integrated capitalism and which increasingly rest on aspects traditionally considered central to education—knowledge, learning, research, collaboration, and collegial peer review. Gramsci brilliantly details the social and educational subjects that were so essential in the first phrase of Fordism and today Gramsci's challenge to educational thinkers is to analyze and determine the contours of the educational subject of knowledge capitalism, the nature of political struggles centering around symbolic manipulation and appropriation, copyright and the production of intellectual goods, the rise of the new global information utilities, and the new international class formations of what contemporary Italian theorists call 'cognitive capitalism' (Lazzarato, 1996, 2001; Caffentzis & Silvia Federici, 2007; Terranova, 2000) defined by what Antonio Negri and Michael Hardt call 'immaterial labour'. Based on Marx's notion of 'general intellect' Lazzaroti (1997) suggests:

> All the characteristics of the post-industrial economy (present both in industry and at a territorial level) are heightened within the form of 'immaterial' production properly defined: audiovisual production, advertising, fashion, the production of software, photography, cultural activities etc. The activities of this kind of immaterial labour oblige us to question the classic definitions of 'work' and of 'workforce', because they are the result of a synthesis of varying types of savoirfaire (those of intellectual activities, as regards the cultural-informational content, those of manual activities for the ability to put together creativity, imagination and technical and manual labour; and that of entre-preneurial activities for that capacity of management of their social relations and of structuration of the social cooperation of which they are a part). This immaterial labour constitutes itself in forms that are immediately collective, and, so to speak, exists only in the form of network and flow.

Hardt and Negri (2000) identify three kinds of 'immaterial' labour: 'Informaticized' industrial labor that has become a service to the market; analytical and symbolic labor—knowledge work both creative and routine; production and manipulation of affective labor that involves human contact, and includes bodily labor. On this basis education itself can be seen as an example of immaterial labour, leading to other forms of symbolic work—both creative and routine.

I would like to record my thanks to Peter Mayo and his contributors for such a penetrating and scholarly collection.

Michael A. Peters

References

Caffentzis, George & Federici, Silvia (2007) 'Notes on the edu–factory and Cognitive Capitalism' at http://eipcp.net/transversal/0809/caffentzisfederici/en

Gramsci, Antonio (1971) 'Americanism and Fordism', *Selections from the Prison Notebooks*, trans. Q. Hoare and G. Nowell Smith, New York: International Publishers pp. 277–318.

Hardt and Negri (2000) 'Postmodernisation, or The Informatisation of Production', chapter from *Empire*, at http://www.marxists.org/reference/subject/philosophy/works/it/negri.htm

Lazzarato, M. (2001) 'Towards an Inquiry into Immaterial Labour', at http://www.makeworlds. org/node/141

Terranova, Tiziana (2000) 'Free Labor: Producing culture for the digital economy', *Social Text*, Spring, at www.btinternet.com/~t.terranova

Introduction: Antonio Gramsci and Educational Thought

Peter Mayo

I write this Introduction at a time when several organizations throughout the world are winding up or have just wound up their series of activities commemorating the 70th anniversary of the demise of Antonio Gramsci. Gramsci has been granted iconic status in many countries, where every tenth anniversary of his death does not pass unnoticed, given the several activities and seminars held in his honour. Gramsci enjoys one of the widest influences in social theory, except perhaps in his own country where he represents a classic case of *nemo profeta in patria*. Of course one comes across the usual activities carried out by the Fondazione Istituto Gramsci, including a two-day conference in Rome in April 2007, which drew scholars from different parts of the world. The local council (Comune) in his home town of Ghilarza understandably also carried out a series of activities to mark the anniversary year. This notwithstanding, one gathers the impression that Gramsci is much more revered outside Italy—in Germany, France, Canada, the USA, the United Kingdom, Finland, South Africa, India and Latin America, for example—than within his homeland. His image in Italy seems to have suffered following the fall of the Berlin Wall and the transmutations that occurred within the former Italian Communist Party Gramsci helped found in 1921.

This book, however, seeks to pay tribute to this great political figure and social thinker of the 20th century. It comprises chapters from different parts of the world including New Zealand, Brazil, the United States, Canada, Germany and England. It complements another publication which I co-edited (Borg *et al.*, 2002) in that it draws on the work of authors with which we three editors of the 2002 book were not familiar at the time of planning that volume. I was very careful therefore not to include in this book authors who had contributed to the 2002 book. The issues tackled are various. Deb Hill provides an in-depth philosophical discussion on the Hegelian and Marxian influence on Gramsci's 'philosophy of praxis' arguably the central phrase in his prison writings originally intended as a work '*für ewig*' (for eternity). The connections between Gramsci's thought and Marx's theory of consciousness and dialectical mode of thinking are carefully teased out here. This piece complements the work of Paula Allman (2002) around the subject.

Gramsci's entire project in the prison writings, centring on the notion of hegemony, of which he does not provide a systematic exposition, is an educational project—education in the broadest sense possible. Education is central to the workings of hegemony in which every relationship is a pedagogical relationship. In other words, to do justice to Gramsci's writings that are of relevance to education, one should tackle Gramsci's work holistically (Borg *et al.*, 2002) and not confine oneself to the tract on schooling, or more precisely 'the Unitarian school', found in Notebook 4 and revised in Notebook 12. Gramsci's pre-prison writings are also of great relevance here, together with some of his letters, since Gramsci accorded different forms of education, including adult education, great importance, considering their organization to be a key task of the Modern Prince that is the revolutionary party. This constitutes the subject of a well-informed chapter by John Holst, an attempt to see the several 'altre vie', which Gramsci explored for education, within the context of party work. As Holst underlines (see also Holst, 2001), it is fashionable these days to dilute or camouflage this aspect of Gramsci's thinking to render his ideas suitable for contemporary and possibly liberal appropriation.

And yet despite the wide range of educational activities which Gramsci explored both outside and inside prisons (recall his contributions to the development of the Scuola dei Confinati—prison school—at Ustica when awaiting trial, the Club di Vita Morale, the Institute of Proletarian Culture inspired by the Proletkult and the correspondence party school) quite an interesting debate arose, in the educational literature of the late 1970s and 1980s, around his notes on the Unitarian School. This was mainly because of the publication of Harold Entwistle's (1979) well-researched book (covering most aspects of education tackled by Gramsci) with its provocative title *Antonio Gramsci. Conservative schooling for radical politics.* This book sparked off quite a debate around Gramsci's conception of schooling in reaction to the *Riforma Gentile.* For this reason we are including, in this volume, a highly informative piece by Thomas Clayton, concerning Gramsci and the actual pedagogical ideas of Giovanni Gentile, the leading Italian idealist philosopher who, together with Benedetto Croce, is widely regarded in Italy as having kept Italian philosophy rooted in idealism (some argue derogatorily that he rendered Italian philosophy quite 'provincial' in this respect) through which it therefore developed a strong anti-positivist stance. Gentile, of course, became Italy's Minister of Education (Pubblica Istruzione) during the Fascist period and, as the title 'Riforma Gentile'(the Gentile Reform) indicates, was responsible for the scholastic reform that Gramsci criticised. Clayton (2006), the editor of a very revealing volume on some international reinventions of Gramsci's ideas, seeks to 'do justice' to Gentile in this well researched piece.

It would be amiss to discuss Gramsci's political and educational ideas without giving due consideration to one of the major preoccupations in his thinking, and the area of his specialization (*indirizzo*) at the University of Turin: language. Gramsci's writings on language have been the concern of several leading Italian scholars including Tulio de Mauro (the great linguist who served as Minister of Education in Italy in the Amato Government). Peter Ives is arguably one of the leading contemporary writers on Gramsci's notion of Language and Hegemony as testified by his two books on the subject (Ives, 2004a,b). I am pleased therefore to be able to include a contribution from him with respect to the Hegemony of Global English. For the concept of hegemony, as Ives has been at pains to indicate, featured prominently in the linguistics debate to which the young Gramsci was exposed at the University of Turin as a student of the acclaimed Matteo Bartoli who once hailed the young Sardinian as the archangel destined to defeat the grammarians.

Gramsci's influence is however felt in a variety of areas, including feminism (see Holub, 1992) and community development (see Ledwith, 2005). Margaret Ledwith provides us with a Gramscian analysis of community development from a feminist perspective drawing on her own work as a practitioner in the field. Furthermore we notice the various discussions in the educational literature on the relevance of Gramsci's thought for different aspects of education in specific continents or countries. Uwe Hirschfeld from Dresden is, together with Ursula Apitzsch, Armin Bernhard and Andreas Merkens, among the most prominent German scholars writing on Gramsci and education, working collaboratively with one of the major German publishing houses that promote Gramsci's work: Argument Verlag. Hirschfeld provides us with an interesting discussion, translated from the original piece in German, concerning Gramsci's relevance for social pedagogy, an important area of educational, social and cultural work throughout Germany. Furthermore, as indicated earlier on and in other volumes, Gramsci has a major following in Latin America especially, as indicated by Morrow and Torres (1995), in the field of popular education. He is also influential in the debates about schooling and Carlos Nelson Coutinho (1995), one of the leading Brazilian Gramscian scholars, states that he has been very influential in the work of Brazil's ruling Partido dos Trabalhadores (at least in its early years). Rosemary Dore Soares (2000), who authored a book on the subject of Gramsci, the State and Brazilian education, provides us with a very revealing and insightful piece on the subject.

The range of subjects tackled and the international representation found in this book make for a very variegated and rich compendium of writings on Gramsci's relevance to educational thought. It should make a strong contribution to the ever growing international literature on Gramsci and education.

References

Allman, P. (2002) Antonio Gramsci's Contribution to Radical Adult Education, in: C. Borg, J. A. Buttigieg & P. Mayo (eds), *Gramsci and Education* (Baltimore, MD, Rowman & Littlefield).

Borg, C., Buttigieg, J. A. & Mayo, P. (2002) Introduction. Gramsci and Education. A holistic approach, in: C. Borg, J. A. Buttigieg & P. Mayo (eds), *Gramsci and Education* (Baltimore, MD, Rowman & Littlefield).

Clayton, T. (ed.) (2006) *Rethinking Hegemony* (Melbourne, James Nicholas Publishers).

Coutinho, C. N. (1995) In Brasile, in: E. J. Hobsbawm (ed.), *Gramsci in Europa e in America* (Italian edition edited by A. Santucci) (Roma—Bari, Sagittari Laterza).

Dore Soares, R. (2000) *Gramsci, o Estado e a Escola* (Ijui, Rio Grande do Sul, Editora Unijui).

Entwistle, H. (1979) *Antonio Gramsci. Conservative schooling for radical politics* (London and New York, RKP).

Holst, J. (2001) *Social Movements, Civil Society, and Radical Adult Education* (Westport, CT and London, Bergin & Garvey).

Holub, R. (1992) *Antonio Gramsci. Beyond Marxism and Postmodernism* (London and New York, Routledge).

Ives, P. (2004a) *Gramsci's Politics of Language. Engaging the Bakhtin Circle and the Frankfurt School* (Toronto, University of Toronto Press).

Ives, P. (2004b) *Language and Hegemony in Gramsci* (London/Halifax, Pluto/Fernwood).

Ledwith, M. (2005) *Community Development. A Critical Approach* (Bristol, Policy Press).

Morrow, R. A. & Torres, C. A. (1995) *Social Theory and Education. A critique of theories of social and cultural reproduction* (Albany, SUNY Press).

1

A Brief Commentary on the Hegelian-Marxist Origins of Gramsci's 'Philosophy of Praxis'

DEB J. HILL

Introduction

> The true fundamental function and significance of the dialectic can only be grasped if the philosophy of praxis is conceived as an integral and original philosophy which opens up a new phase of history and a new phase in the development of world thought ... If the philosophy of praxis is not considered except in subordination to another philosophy, then it is not possible to grasp the new dialectic, through which the transcending of old philosophies is transcended and expressed. (Gramsci, 1971, p. 435)

There has been a great deal of speculation about the 'integral and original philosophy' which Gramsci here names the 'philosophy of praxis'. As Haug has suggested (2000, p. 11), several functions are potentially united in Gramsci's use of the phrase. Not only does it serve a pragmatic purpose as a linguistic camouflage to appease the prison censor: more importantly, it functions in a metaphorical fashion as a 'substantive programmatic concept' to inaugurate Marx's own distinctive form of thought. With regard to this latter role, Haug claims that what it ushers in is a 'coherent but non-systematic thinking' which not only 'grasps the world through human activity' (p. 11) but also 'addresses the whole' from below 'with a patient attention to particularity' (p. 12).

I fully concur with Haug's prognosis, and in this chapter want to explore the specific nuances of what Gramsci above names 'the new dialectic'.[1] The dialectic, as will be outlined, was Marx's specific 'mode of thought' or 'method of logic' as it has been variously called, by which he analyzed the world and man's relationship to that world. As well as constituting a theory of knowledge (epistemology), what arises out of the dialectic is also an ontology or portrait of humankind that is based on the complete historicization of humanity; its 'absolute "historicism"' or 'the absolute secularisation and earthliness of thought', as Gramsci worded it (Gramsci, 1971, p. 465). Embracing a fully secular and historical view of humanity, it provides a vantage point that allows the multiple and complex effects of our own conceptual heritage to be interrogated in relation to our developing 'nature' or 'being'.

As I demonstrate in this contribution, reading Gramsci's pre-prison and prison notebook legacy entails understanding the specific nuances of this Hegelian-Marxist vantage point. In particular, it entails understanding the problem that Gramsci's writings attempted to articulate: namely, the impress of capitalism's economic and extra-economic aspect upon humanity's own relational and valuational capacity. Just as this problematic formed the basis of Marx's analysis of capital, as I wish to highlight here, Gramsci's work was similarly directed at combating the specific and alienating form of subjectivity fashioned by the logic of capital. As I emphasize throughout this chapter, the struggle against capital must therefore be seen as an 'onto-formative' struggle—a challenge to grasp the powers of self, given the dispossession of these powers under a capitalist mantle. In this respect, the legacy of both Hegel and Marx is manifest in the depth of Gramsci's comprehension of what he termed this 'educative-formative' problem. It is precisely the legacy of this Hegelian-Marxist radical philosophical critique, as I argue below, that is signified in his continuing commitment to the 'philosophy of praxis' and the historical-dialectical principles that underpin this worldview.

After initially backgrounding the conjunction between Hegel's theory of epistemology and ontology and highlighting the criticality of an historical-social view of the subject that arose out of this analysis, I want to suggest that these same Hegelian propositions formed the basis of Marx's own historical and dialectical vantage point. In the course of this discussion, I want to draw attention specifically to the fact that Gramsci's concerns are consistent with his acceptance of the problem Marx charts in relation to capitalism and the problem of capitalism as an inherent counter-ontological force. This involves understanding its tendencies towards the fetishism of human productive capacity, broadly understood. Here, whilst I wish to argue that the concept of 'labour' or 'work' certainly signifies the manner in which mankind interacts with the environment to fulfil its various needs, it is a concept that must be interpreted correspondingly as 'effort' or 'activity' that is ontologically formative of agency. In the final section of this chapter, I intend to showcase how Gramsci's relentless advocacy for self-education was simultaneously an urging to free minds from the existing capitalist mode of thought and inevitably from their own fetishization.

Historical-Dialectical Thought in Hegel and Marx

Common to the history of Gramsci studies has been a tendency on the part of many early commentators to vilify Hegel's contribution to Gramsci's ideas, on the grounds that Marx's work offers a necessary 'corrective' to Hegel's idealism. Interestingly, however, in more recent times, a growing number of Hegelian and Marxist scholars alike have begun to stress the advantage of reading Hegel and Marx in a more congruent fashion (Arthur, 2004; Beiser, 1993; Burns & Fraser, 2000; Fine, 2001a,b; Fraser, 1997; Houlgate, 1998; Kedourie, 1995; McCarney, 2000a,b; MacGregor, 1984, 1998; Rockmore, 2000; Sayers, 1998; Wood, 1993). Despite the fact that such a move appears to sit at variance with many of Marx's overt proclamations about Hegel's usefulness with respect to his own evolutionary ideas,[2] the fruit of this reinvigorated Hegelian-Marxist scholarship has been a wealth of books, articles and chapters that re-examine their relationship. For reasons of space, I want to focus specifically on the historicization of philosophy in Hegel and explain how this vantage point forms the ground for his dialectical style of thought, which Marx later adopted. This discussion is an important prelude to my later analysis of Gramsci's own historical and dialectical portrait of humankind: his view of the onto-formative character of 'being' that underpins his allegiance to 'praxis'.

As Beiser (1993) and others have maintained (Arthur, 1986, 2004; Houlgate, 1998; Pinkard, 1996; Sayers, 1998; Smith, 1993), Hegel's examination of Kant's theory of knowledge took the form of a critique of the validity of the *a priori* categories of conceptual investigation which Kant had employed in his own interrogation of the nature of the world and our understanding of ourselves within it. As a direct response to the manner in which Kant's categories of understanding were seen to be themselves abstract creations of a fundamentally ahistorical approach towards philosophy—which thus bypassed an investigation of the dynamic and fluid nature of thought itself—Hegel posited his own categories of 'being' and 'nothing' in an attempt to explore afresh the interconnected nature of thought and the objects—self and other—it sought to capture therein (Hegel, 1807/1977). In so doing, Hegel firmly married epistemology with ontology insofar as he argued that thought could never exist as a stand-alone entity separate from the subject from whom it emanated. In this respect, he thus changed the meaning of philosophy itself. By its very nature, it had to constitute *the* most self-critical enterprise among all other forms of thought. No longer could philosophy be content to exploit pre-existing suppositions. Accordingly, it became critically self-conscious and historical in Hegel's hands (Beiser, 1993; Houlgate, 1998; McCarney, 2000a,b; Pinkard, 1996).

The net result of this interpenetration of 'knowing' and 'being' is what has been named Hegel's historical-dialectical vantage point. As alluded to above, it is a vantage point that moves scepticism unapologetically onto centre stage by its refusal to confer certainty to our various and assorted knowledge claims. Given that the only knowledge we can ever have of the external world is mediated by what Hegel calls 'formations of consciousness', which constitute mere interpolations of reality, reality is always only 'known' through a fixative process of 'abstraction' (Ollman, 1976, 1993; Pinkard, 1996). To put this yet another way, we are only ever able to gain a *semblance* of reality, this being a mere *representation* or a *mediated impression* of what lies beyond our human and historically situated field of vision.[3] Knowledge can only ever be knowledge of 'appearances' by this view. Far from our reasoning therefore being braced by timeless and eternal truths, it becomes a very human and historical entity as a result. Pinkard (1996) aptly summarizes the consequences of Hegel's thought:

> The dialectical history of self-consciousness is thus also a history of rationality itself. All forms of reason-giving must also be treated as 'appearances', and the historical nature of rationality consists in the way in which forms of life develop practices for evaluating and criticising other practices but also develop practices for reflecting on the practices of evaluation themselves.
> (p. 12)

To Marx as well, this active sense of sceptical self-comprehension was of primary significance in distinguishing philosophy *as* philosophy. Agreeing with Hegel's critique of the 'management' or 'containment' of thought inherent in previous Cartesian logic,

Marx perceptively grasped the importance of dialectics in restructuring thought to understand the myriad particulars that form the moving landscape of reality/history. In this regard, he acknowledged the revolutionary nature of Hegel's attempt to capture what history is: a dynamic process of motion, temporal fluidity, development and change. Following Hegel, he saw that it was only by refocusing on reality itself that the inadequacy of the classificatory and categorizing processes we impose upon particulars becomes visible to our consciousness. In effect, this practice reveals the fragility of the universal claims we are apt to make, alerting us further to the importance of contradiction and dissonance in reconstructing the thought/reality nexus. Like Hegel, Marx saw that it was precisely the presence of such 'contradiction'— these 'antimonies', as Hegel preferred this dissonance to be called—that revealed the true extent of the mediation process that reality/history underwent.

As intimated above, what becomes clear from this account is how Hegel's dialectic outlook implied that all abstractions (conceptions about the world and our place within it) needed to be subjected to constant scrutiny and rigorous audit *based on real world experience*. Justifiably in my view, it is on the basis of this recognition that several commentators have duly argued the increasing difficulty of making a compelling case that Hegel therefore advanced a demonstrably 'idealistic' viewpoint (Arthur, 1986, 2004; Beiser, 1993; Burns & Fraser, 2000; Fine, 2001a,b; Fraser, 1997; Houlgate, 1998; Kedourie 1995; McCarney, 2000a,b; MacGregor, 1984, 1998; Rockmore, 2000; Sayers, 1998; Wood, 1993). Because of the nature of his dialectical historicism, far from elevating the *conceptual* at the expense of the *concrete*, his overall theoretical stance was one that was in fact vehemently *opposed* to any such forced separation (Beiser, 1993; Hudis, 2000; Kitching, 1988; Ollman, 1976, 1993; Pinkard, 1996).

Hegel's work can in this way be seen to offer a fundamentally non-reductive way of viewing the world. Within this perspective, matter can never exist independent of thought, for example, just as thought can never be seen to exist suspended in a vacuum, independent of matter. Resemblance and likeness similarly are not over-exaggerated to the point of negating the crucial differences that co-exist between objects (Arthur, 1986, 2004; Beiser, 1993; Fine, 2001a,b; Houlgate, 1998; McCarney, 2000a,b; Sayers, 1980; Smith, 1993). In short, dialectical thought strenuously opposes any such tendency to paralyse reality by dogmatic or formalistic ('one-sided') thinking. Dichotomies are thus 'united' yet at the same time held to be discrete ('not-united') by the all-embracing reach of this perspective. Particulars are analyzed as particulars whilst being acknowledged simultaneously as parts of a larger and dynamic whole (totality/reality).

One final word about the dialectic is required: insofar as it negates any distinction between the conceptual and the concrete—or between the internal relation of ideas and the external relation of facts, as some have put it (Rubinstein, 1981)—it has often been referred to as 'a philosophy of internal relations' (Ollman, 1976, 1993, 1998) or 'the algebra of revolution' (Rees, 1998). As the former phrase appropriately suggests, everything is seen as being referential or relational with respect to everything else. In particular, mind and the meanings generated therein do not stand apart from the social context in which meaning gains purchase, contrary to the view of much psychological theory (Lefebvre, 1940/1968; Rubinstein, 1981). As Rubinstein's excellent work on the overlaps between Marx and Wittgenstein's thought show, 'meaning is a property of the system of collective social practices' (p. 185). The dialectical approach affirms that we cannot properly understand ideas separately from the practices that induce such meanings and from the larger context in which these are imbricated. Ideas both articulate and animate social practice (Lefebvre, 1940/1968; Ollman, 1976, 1993, 1998; Rubinstein, 1981; Sayers, 1998).

The above is obviously only a brief and understandably much abridged account of key aspects of Hegel and Marx's shared historical and dialectical standpoint. To the extent that the argument in this chapter rests on perceiving how Gramsci's 'philosophy of praxis' expresses his allegiance to this non-reductionistic and historical/social way of viewing the world, it is nonetheless an adequate overview of the nature of the revolution in thought that inspired future generations of thinkers of Gramsci's ilk. In this respect, it is important to note how Marx's view of human nature represented a *critique* of traditional forms of enlightenment humanism. Far from advancing the existence of universal and timeless character traits, as many 'modernist/humanist' theories of personality and character development imply, it is a perspective that projects a fluid and changing account of society and subjectivity and the way in which it derives its own 'nature' by virtue of its concrete and day-to-day living (Beiser, 1993; Kitching, 1988; Ollman, 1976, 1993, 1998; Pinkard, 1996; Rees, 1998; Rubinstein, 1981; Sayers, 1998, 2003). A word is now in order to consolidate these points.

Marx's Onto-formative View of Human Nature

The implications of Hegel's characterisation of the problem of knowledge, as noted above, are that our claim-making activities are ultimately self-referential; that is, they emanate 'inwardly' from the authoritative practice of a temporally and historically specific, social community. This is a fully secular view of humanity just as it is a view that also stresses the active and material aspect of mankind's historical existence. As intimated by this line of thought, the concept of 'labour' for Marx neatly captured the spirit of the Hegelian subject-object conjunction. Importantly, it brought into focus what actually animated the category of 'being' itself—it was precisely man's 'work' or 'activity' or 'effort'. As Ollman (1976) has characterised Marx's meaning, 'activity is the actual movement of man's powers in the real world [and] the living process of objectifying those powers' (p. 97). To this effect, Marx marked his debt to Hegel thus:

> The outstanding achievement of Hegel's *Phenomenology* ... is, first, that Hegel grasps the self-creation of man as a process ... and that he, therefore, grasps the nature of *labour*, and conceives objective man ... as the result of his *own labour*. (Marx, 1844/1963, p. 202. Emphasis in original)

Indeed, in any reading of Marx it is imperative to understand how this deeper sense of self-creation is being appealed to simultaneously in his analysis of capitalism and its substantive effects upon human possibility or 'becoming' (Arthur, 1986, 2004; Ollman, 1976, 1993, 1998; Rubinstein, 1981; Sayers, 1998, 2003). 'Labour' does not refer simply to the toil involved in man's productive engagement with the environment. It refers to the self-production of mankind and the self-creation of the conditions that define human existence. Humanity's 'nature' is self-fashioned, and it is by virtue of this capacity that Marx identifies the distinctive quality of its species-being. Mankind therefore distinguishes itself by its productive activities inasmuch as production is defined in an extended sense to embrace this richer idea of 'activity'. Activity, in this regard, defines not just production of the means of subsistence but self and social production correspondingly. It is this insight that led Marx to conceive of labour ultimately as 'the essence, the self-confirming essence of man' (Marx, 1844/1963, p. 203).

Society and the individuals who constitute that society are therefore squarely onto-formative within Hegel's phenomenology, as they are in Marx's. The social formation develops its own 'nature'. In Hegelian fashion, Marx therefore does not consider productivity to be simply the *expression* of some inner human essence—the visible sign of some god-given or innate capacity. Rather, he sees the productive activity of mankind as constituting the very *character* of one's humanity. Evidence of this stance is affirmed repeatedly throughout Marx's writing. In *The German Ideology* (1846/1939), for instance, he wrote: 'As individuals express their life, so they are. What they are, therefore, coincides with their production, both with *what* they produce and *how* they produce' (p. 7). In *Capital* he commented: 'By thus acting on the external world and changing it, [man] at the same time changes his own nature' (Marx, 1867/1961, p. 177).

Rather than history therefore being depicted as some external force operating upon us and to which we must passively submit, Marx projects a thoroughly humanised and dialectic view of history that advances human purposive activity as the motor force of cultural evolution and progress. Indeed, it is this account of mankind and its creative powers that comprises Marx's 'philosophy of praxis'. In direct contrast to traditional ways of viewing the world whereby humanity is forced to discriminate between its subjective presence and the objective world beyond it, the adoption of an historical-dialectical vantage point ensures the rejection of this inherent matter-mind dichotomy. No longer is there a diametrical opposition between humanity and nature but instead a wholeness and a unity. Such a 'unity of distincts' or 'unity of opposites', as this conjunction has often been named, typifies the abandonment of the old categories of explanation and method and the embrace of alternative ways to explain our material and relational existence.

In true Hegelian fashion, therefore, Marx rejects the excessive degree of abstraction that sees subjects divorced from their social context and the products of their own creation. Instead, he directly repositions them as the makers of that context; of their own history. As intimated in my discussion above, philosophy itself becomes human-ized, synonymous as it is with mankind's *consciousness of concrete self-presence* within his thought. Instead of acting as a limitation on presence and action—as a hindrance to humanity realising its own productive powers—thought (philosophy) becomes liberated, 'self-aware' and concretely active. This release of philosophy itself from the previous strictures that narrowed its utility made it 'independent and original', as Gramsci would later comment (Gramsci, 1971, p. 398). The Hegelian-Marx innovation that he so enthusiastically celebrated was this concrete projection of mankind's presence upon the world. This was what Gramsci's own philosophy projected: mankind's consciousness of its own active potentiality.

By this historicization of humanity's own nature, Marx actually asserts the primacy of a new form of rationality; one in which the old normativity or 'common sense' way of responding to the world is challenged and replaced with a critical and conscious awareness of the weakness of the abstractions we have chosen to describe the nature of the world and our place within it. What we constantly witness within Marx's work is thus a continuation of the challenge that Hegel initiated—a challenge against the basic units constitutive of thought, inquiry and analysis and how these operated to represent the world normatively in his own time. As Ollman has shown so well in his extensive investigations into Marx's use of the dialectic (1976, 1993, 1998), Marx's words must be understood as 'place-holders' or 'markers' that signify the presence of this new historical-dialectical orientation.[4] This is the reason why, Ollman explains, Vilfredo Pareto once characterized Marx's words as functioning 'like bats'; that is, in one instance one might see a bird, yet in another, a mouse (Ollman 1976, p. 3). Such confusion arises precisely because Marx assigns traditional words a new and 'liberated' meaning conducive to his dynamic, dialectical vantage point.

Once we begin to understand the nature of the challenges to our thinking that this perspective represents, we can begin to 'read Marx' in a manner consistent with the historical view of human presence that sits at the centre of this interpretation of 'being'. This is the reason why his usage of the term 'philosophy' both supersedes and exceeds all previous meanings. Moreover, it is also the reason why ascribing normative meanings to the other terms he employs—like 'science', for example— will result in the inevitable misinterpretation of his perspective. Unless ordinary and everyday words such as these are interpreted dialectically, the profound nature of the challenge that Marx inaugurated is likely to be completely lost from view. What needs to be recognized within his writing, above all else, is this 'against the grain' style of 're-abstracting' words so that they emit a fuller, richer picture of the moving, changing and concrete reality they seek to describe. As I will suggest in my subsequent discussion of Gramsci too, one cannot understand *his* ideas unless there is a similar recognition of the conjunction between this Hegelian-Marxist dialectical-historical perspective and Gramsci's own novel usage of language.

Capitalism As a Counter-ontological, Fetishizing Force

From the account offered above, it is important to appreciate that Marx's challenge to conventional forms of thought focussed on what he perceived as the 'congealed' way in which mankind regarded its own material and social existence through customary language usage. Instead of words expressing the dynamic, interconnected nature of humans and their own concrete and social forms of production—their production in relation to their own 'subjectivity' as well as in relation to their environment— Marx noted how the economic logic inherent in capitalism tended to render invisible these material and social relations as *products of human manufacture*. In simple terms, this negation of mankind's productive self-activity amounted to a denial of the potential power of humankind to reassess its own 'nature' and to change this nature accordingly. It was precisely the excessive abstraction of 'man in general' associated with this engineered politics of 'self-forgetting' that he highlighted within his writing.

To the extent that Marx's target therefore became that form of thinking that led to the mystification of mankind's own sense of 'self-production' or 'self-activity', capitalism presented itself to him as the epitome of a socially-destructive and fetishizing force, paralleled in its toxicity only by religion and empirical science. Although he labelled all such forms of speculation 'ideological', the consequence of these forms of conjecture nonetheless took a very definite material form: each constructed a transhistorical and metaphysical view of 'generic man' which represented the transmutation of real relations into a general and abstract form. Rather than constituting forms of thought that revealed the definite mode of life of concrete subjects in definite historical epochs—which included a comprehension of those very clear limitations imposed by each epoch on self-activity also—what each in fact promoted was a contrived and fabricated view of 'eternal man' and 'human progress', and a fetishized view moreover of the products of human creation.

The illusory nature of the 'freedom' celebrated by these speculative modes of thought was equally objectionable to Marx, just as it was the issue that provoked his constant petitioning for the use of dialectical-historical investigation to counter such fiction. The universal, transhistorical principles of rights and justice that were associated with the individualistic portrait of mankind that capitalism promoted, suggested a degree of freedom that was wholly incommensurate with the strictures ultimately imposed upon its 'freely' contracting subjects. Whilst man was therefore depicted as an independent being, seemingly at liberty to form his own relationships, the competitive, antagonistic 'exchange-for-profit' relations that capitalist economics unapologetically endorsed ensured the celebration and reward of highly competitive and mutually antagonistic social practices. Indeed, it is this shift in the value relationships inaugurated by capitalism that lie at the core of Marx's conception of class relations. The universal struggle of individual against individual that capitalism cultivated represented the loss of humanity's inherent ability to determine the value of what he referred to as its own 'living labour'. It was the coalescence of these sentiments that he sought to convey in *The German Ideology* when he wrote:

> [In capitalism] the productive forces appear as a world for themselves, quite independent of and divorced from the individuals, alongside the individuals; the reason for this is that the individuals, whose forces they are, exist split up and in opposition to one another, whilst, on the other hand, these forces are only real forces in the intercourse and association of these individuals. Thus ... we have a totality of productive forces, which have, as it were, taken on a material form and are for the individuals no longer the forces of the individuals but of private property. (Marx, quoted in Sayer, 1987, p. 45)

As a number of writers have begun to emphasize in their own accounts of Marx's ideas (Allbritton, 1999; Arthur, 2003, 2004; Knafo, 2002; Postone, 1993; Sekine, 1998), his wholesale condemnation of capitalism was precisely because of its unapologetic function as a counter-ontological or de-ontologizing power. Instead of mankind developing an ever-greater sensitivity to its own historical and self-determining 'nature'— and thus gaining an ever-expansive critical capability to express its own modes of living—humanity became *ipso facto* an instrument of production. With relations based on mutual hostility rather than mutual recognition and substantive social engagement, capitalism ensured a divided society, so much so that in fact the dominance of independent identity inevitably smudged any recognition of the dependence on the totality (society) that had necessarily framed that identity. As a reaction to this 'witchery', Marx devoted significant critical energies to an intensive re-examination of the way in which economic abstractions distort the internal relations that actually exist between human beings. It is precisely the irony and perversion exemplified in this inversion of human capacity to 'become' that Marx sought to expose in his various discussions about ideological fetishism and its alienating effects (Ollman, 1976, 1993, 1998; Sayer, 1987; Sayers, 1998, 2003).

Given that the crucial and pivotal aspect of Marx's thought is that human self-activity *is* history, to misconstrue the nature of history meant plainly to forfeit the ability to determine one's future. To this end, works such as *The German Ideology*, *Capital*, and the *Grundrisse* were essentially works that provided a counter-cultural (counter-historical, counter-scientific, counter-economic) rendering of the subject. In contradistinction to the 'common sense' portrayal of the individual and society generated by the dominant historical, scientific and economic narratives of his day, Marx's refocus on the actual living presence and practice of real human beings in making history was deliberately orchestrated to unmask these privileged forms of contemporary explanation as themselves fetishized products of human ideology. Evidence is littered throughout Marx's writing of his intense exasperation with a variety of these fetishisms. Arguably one of the best examples appears in his work, *The Holy Family*. Here, in keeping with his continuous attempts to unmask the nature of the human drama at the base of history, he rallies against a naive conception of history as something which is inanimate—something 'alien', like a 'thing'—and entirely separate from the human dynamic that in fact animates its production. To this effect, he wrote:

> History does nothing; it 'does not possess immense riches', it 'does not fight battles'. It is men, real, living men, who do all this, who possess things and fight battles. It is not 'history' which uses men as a means of achieving— as if it were an individual person—its own ends. History is nothing but the activity of men in pursuit of their end. (Marx & Engels, 1844/1975, p. 93)

To summarize these points, and the ones offered previously, Marx's philosophy of praxis in many ways represents a dynamic and active philosophy of mankind's living presence and productive movement within the material world. Unless humans grasp their own 'self-presence' within their material and ideological landscape—that is, the presence that stands behind what they have constructed as *their* history, *their* politics, *their* economics, *their* education, and the institutions furthermore that have become associated with these terms—they will remain forever blind to the actual substance— the human origin—of these constructs. In Marx's estimation, the more we are unable to envision the extent to which self-presence governs our lives, the more such abstractions would continue to remain significant and enduring obstacles to our future cognitive and material practice.

Knowing that what we esteem both conceptually and pragmatically within our society has been the result of human determination is the necessary starting point identified by both Hegel and Marx; the point where we might begin to reclaim this lost sense of identity. In this respect, it is important to understand how the concept of 'consciousness' within the thought of both writers becomes importantly a reference to mankind's *self*-consciousness—that is, to the significance of our comprehension of our own 'productive capacity' or 'onto-formative' nature. With Marx especially, as I have shown above, this historical-dialectic vantage point is synonymous with a non-reverential attitude towards the verities of the present in order to detect the multiple forms of ideological governance which alienate humankind from the products of its own making. Put simply, the 'ideological' is identified with the 'pathological' within Marx's writing. It is equivalent to 'that which corrodes our capacity for self-determination'—and does so precisely *because* it has assumed various institutionalized and fetishized forms. When viewed in this way, dialectic thinking is ideological-materialist critique that concomitantly *enables* future practice. It permits us to posit for ourselves new modes of self, social and material practice.

Those who have read Gramsci will know only too well the parallels between his thoughts and these: that his consistent advocacy to 'know the laws governing the mind' (Gramsci, 1990a, p. 13) meant understanding that the qualitative measure of human civilization emanated from its own philosophical preferences and the practices that these simultaneously endorsed. This was an orientation that clearly involved the historicization of contemporary thought and practice as the most effective means to undermine the general tendencies towards the normative acceptance of what Gramsci would often refer to as 'vague and rampant superstition'. To this effect, his own campaign of reflection and critique targeted what he called the multitude of 'limiting ideas' (Gramsci, 1975, pp. 71–72) which effectively sterilized thought and created a culture of passivity in its sway. His analysis and commentary was an exemplification no less of his own concrete, dialectical practice, as I now want to highlight in the final section of this chapter.

Gramsci's Historical and Dialectical Campaign against Capitalism

Gramsci's early journalistic activity was the medium through which he began to articulate this 'philosophy of praxis' and to identify the various sites upon which the proletarian counter-cultural struggle needed to be fostered. As page after page of his political and cultural commentaries attest, civil society had assimilated and naturalized a certain political outlook that fortified capitalism (Gramsci, 1971, 1975, 1985, 1988, 1990a,b, 1992, 1994, 1996).[5] What Gramsci's ongoing commentaries therefore represent are, significantly, his concerted attempt to map the myriad of factors that had contributed historically to the failure of his society to cultivate a social (socialist) consciousness. What this archive equally demonstrates is Gramsci's acute understanding of how the inorganic and anti-dialectical manner in which thought and its manifestation in the structural organization of society normalized class division, rendering it natural and impenetrable as an outcome. His diverse reflections and subtle cameos on culture and politics represent Gramsci's profound grasp of the reach of capitalism's power and its deleterious impact on mankind's transformative, onto-formative capabilities.

Gramsci's ensuing bid to initiate a dialectical rejuvenation of culture to foreclose the fetishizing practices that conditioned humanity's associational and valuational preferences is obvious right from his early attacks on the reification of concepts such as 'culture' and 'intellectual'. In one of his most celebrated articles (Gramsci, 1990a, pp. 10–13), for example, we see him objecting to the 'common sense' view of culture as an externalized entity that appeared to stand entirely independent from the intentional actions (labour) of concrete individuals. Here he challenges the traditional asymmetry that had arisen between the two concepts of 'culture' and 'intellectual', arguing that both cultural activity, as well as intellectual functioning, was a 'natural' feature of human life. Urging his colleagues to reject these fetishized interpretations of culture as 'encyclopaedic knowledge' and intellectual endeavour as the exclusive activity of a separate and 'superior' group of people, we see him begin to juxtapose these—and other inorganic concepts subsequently (e.g. education, state, party, democracy)—with dialectically reinvigorated ones. In this particular example, he wrote:

> We need to free ourselves from the habit of seeing culture as encyclopaedic knowledge, and men as mere receptacles to be stuffed full of empirical data and a mass of unconnected raw facts, which have to be filed in the brain as in the columns of a dictionary, enabling their owner to respond to the various stimuli from the outside world. This form of culture really is harmful, particularly for the proletariat. It serves only to create maladjusted people, people who believe they are superior to the rest of humanity because they have memorized a certain number of facts and dates and who rattle them off at every opportunity, so turning them also into a barrier between themselves and others. (Gramsci, 1990a, p. 10)

As he would later caution in one of his *Notebook* jottings (Gramsci, 1971, pp. 455–456), 'identity of terms does not mean identity of concepts'. By reappropriating the existing psychologically limiting terms and imbuing them with humanized, dialectical meanings, Gramsci was expressing his clear allegiance to Marx's 'philosophy of praxis'—a struggle, as I have intimated above, over the very terms and conditions of 'knowledge' and 'philosophy'.

Consistent with the Hegelian-Marxist importance of 'consciousness' as an awareness of 'self-presence' within history and a recognition of mankind's onto-formative capacity, Gramsci's relentless campaigning for self-education should likewise be read as the explicit means by which he theoretically and practically supported this struggle. The pervasive inability of individuals to discriminate accurately between those forces wholly within mankind's jurisdiction and those which constituted the whimsical play of 'fortune' or 'chance' in human affairs typified what he considered to be the pathological reach of fetishized and inorganic modes of thought. To reveal the inadequacies of religion, folklore, intellectualism and other such 'one-sided' forms of reasoning, Gramsci appeals directly in his later work to Marx's 'philosophy of praxis', describing it as a 'concrete' mode of reasoning that principally involves the juxtaposition of a dialectical and 'scientific' audit of reality against all existing normative (ideological, therefore counterfeit) accounts. Essentially a 'philosophy' based on 'a practise', Marx's philosophy is described correspondingly in precisely this manner; as the only 'philosophy' that is at the same time 'history in action' or 'life' itself (Gramsci, 1971, p. 357).

In keeping with these sentiments, Gramsci's own historiographical activity—of which his cultural and political notes are a perfect exemplar—should be taken to denote his active audit of history and experience; his own critical, intellectual 'labouring' to sift chaff from grain, 'permanent' from 'willed'. To the extent that the questioning of everyday and mundane assumptions equated to a deliberate and 'willed' intervention of the mind involving a movement away from a passive type of knowing to an active type of understanding, it served to enable 'active thought', which would in turn enrich or even displace 'given thought'. In other words, it forced to consciousness consideration of the normal. 'Common' understandings were thus released from their privileged location within an uninspected realm of the subconscious, their taken-for-grantedness openly exposed to the vicissitudes of reflection and revision as an outcome. What we are witnessing in Gramsci's extensive and ongoing commentary is, in effect, the practice of a 'counter-history'; a history he impregnates with the living presence of human beings. Insofar as history becomes the charting of human sensuous activity, it becomes nothing less than a history of the present, rewritten in light of this new 'self-consciousness'.

Much—if not all—of the friction that was generated between Gramsci and his socialist allies can invariably be traced back to his frustrations with his colleague's inability to conceive of Marxism as a coherent philosophy with a distinctive dialectical and historical outlook. In his opposition to Amadeo Bordiga for instance, the founder of the Italian Communist Party, the difference between them can be seen to lie directly in Gramsci's adherence to the *anti-subaltern* principles of action and organization that distinguished Marxism as a coherent philosophy and practice. To Gramsci's way of thinking, Bordiga's narrow and elitist view of the party and bureaucratic style of leadership implied the perpetuation of a psychology that simply replicated the differential treatment between leaders and led; the fundamental social divisions that Marxism sought to eradicate. His disagreement with Bordiga can accordingly be seen to centre on Gramsci's calls for the promotion of a new and popularly-inclusive conception of party—one in which the conviction that every person is a philosopher was duly acknowledged in the concrete provision for 'self-leadership' exemplified in the organizational makeup of the party.

Similarly, Gramsci's critique of Nikolai Bukharin's 'sociological' exegesis of Marxism centred on what Gramsci saw to be a complete misinterpretation of both the philosophical and practical premises of Marxism. Describing Bukharin's work as a 'sociology' that was only capable of capturing an abstract, scholastic Marxism, Gramsci portrays Bukharin's *Popular Manual* as yet another example of everything that was misunderstood about the historical and dialectical nature of Marxism (historical materialism) (Gramsci, 1971, pp. 425–472). In spite of Bukharin's best efforts to educate the mass by means of his *Manual*, we are left in little doubt about Gramsci's assessment of the merits of his work. As his commentary tellingly demonstrates, all that Gramsci saw Bukharin accomplishing was the rendering down of a complex, fluid reality into a simplistic, external description of phenomena according to criteria constructed on the existing model of the sciences (Gramsci, 1996, p. 155). In other words, Bukharin's sociological interpretation of Marxism was nothing short of a fetishized representation of Marxism. As such, Bukharin's error—along with others who nominally professed themselves Marxists—was invariably his inability to see himself as a product of the existing 'relations of force'. As Gramsci's notes clearly betray, it was Bukharin's lack of self-consciousness that inevitably made him oblivious to the fact that his own methodology was premised on a way of viewing the world that by definition perpetuated existing subaltern thought and practice.

In Gramsci's eyes, Bukharin was nothing other than a 'crystallized intellectual' (Gramsci, 1971, pp. 452–457) whose thinking was captive to the same aristocratic and traditional tendencies exhibited by one of Gramsci's most celebrated adversaries, Benedetto Croce. Neither thinker was able to theorize the role of existing philosophy in masking the source of the problems it professed to study and resolve—meaning that neither was capable of comprehending the essential elements of Marxism itself. As Gramsci describes the merits of the philosophy of praxis in his respective evaluation of both Bukharin and Croce, it was precisely Marx's ability to mediate the excesses of overly materialistic or overly idealistic interpretations of mankind's praxis that defined the essence and dynamism of the latter's theory. Taking human sensuous activity as its starting point, the philosophy of praxis alone offered a concrete understanding of human interaction—and therefore redress from the deficient rendering of a dynamic and shifting reality by such partial depictions of life and the living.

Suffice to say that much more could be said here about Gramsci's adherence to a Hegelian-Marxist vantage point than space permits. At this point, I would like to close this discussion by emphasizing that the Marxist-Gramscian philosophy of praxis epitomized a truly cognitive and morally defiant epistemology and practice. Having identified the multiple ways in which capitalism was etched onto history as a 'negative praxis' through language's normalizing effects—a process that entailed the decoupling of theory from practice and the dictatorship of all existing pathological abstractions—what Gramsci championed was alternately the repossession of a mode of thought, liberated from the impoverished portrait of human possibility that issued from capitalism's anti-historicist, anti-dialectical and anti-human agenda. The struggle to achieve a proletarian hegemony was a struggle to achieve what Gramsci described as a genuine social reformation; a *neohumanist revolution*, no less, in human thought and practice.[6]

Conclusion

It is worth reiterating my central thesis by way of a conclusion; that Gramsci's writings convey this Hegelian-Marxist story of human 'self-forgetting' and 'self-enlightenment' simultaneously. 'Forgetting' that history and knowledge and religion and suchlike are products emanating from mankind's own 'labouring' practices, the fetishization of these capacities—and their subsequent transition into objective (reified) entities, external from the control of will—converted them (falsely) into 'durable historical forces'. As we witness throughout the breadth of Gramsci's writing, concepts such as 'culture' and 'education' are targeted as prime examples of this 'self-forgetfulness'. Increasingly unrecognizable under capitalist logic as natural elements of human sensual activity—which both Marx and Gramsci described as a valorization or reduction of 'living labour' to 'productive labour' (see Gulli, 2002)—such activities are thus set apart from natural human practice and known subsequently only in this fetishized state (i.e. within a narrow economy of exchange). With this alienation duly legitimated and rendered normative in all forms of institutional and non-institutional organization, Gramsci's subsequent campaign of conceptual reappropriation (the de-commodification of that which had been fetishized) was no less than a struggle to institute a new *forma mentis*: a new way of conceiving man that allowed for a conscious and 'willed' extension of human onto-formative endeavour.

Notes

1. See also Haug, 2001.
2. This position is aptly summed up in the words of Robert Fine (2001b) who recently commented that 'if there is one way that we should *not* read the relation between Hegel and Marx, it is through Marx's own account of it!' (p. 73).
3. It is important to point out that Hegel's critique of Kant involved the acknowledgement of the existence of an external reality, independent of human thought. Hegel was therefore not denying the independent existence of the world. He was simply saying that our knowledge of that reality is mediated by the concepts mankind has developed to try to understand this world more clearly.
4. Lenin's remark on the nature of Marx's contribution to revolutionary theory is incisive in this regard. He wrote:

   > If one were to attempt to define in a single word the focus, so to speak, of the whole [Marx/Engels] correspondence, the central point at which the whole body of ideas expressed and discussed converges—that word would be *dialectics*. The application of materialist dialectics to the reshaping of all political economy from its foundation up, its application to history, natural science, philosophy and to the politics and tactics of the working class—that is what interested Marx and Engels most of all, that was where they contributed what was most essential and new, and that was what constituted the masterly advance they made in the history of revolutionary thought. (Lenin, 1973, p. 554).

5. Antonio Labriola is credited with imbuing Gramsci with his early Marxism. An Hegelian theorist himself, Labriola's *Essays on the Materialist Conception of History* (1903/1966) convey a strong Hegelian flavour.
6. Interestingly, Gramsci's praise of Machiavelli was directed towards the 'neohuman' reform which Gramsci saw that the latter advocated. The human contextualization of all existing form of philosophy and practical activity displayed in Machiavelli's thought played an instrumental role in Gramsci's reconceptualization of the nature of a truly representative and popular culture. See Fontana, 1993.

References

Allbritton, R. (1999) *Dialectics and Deconstruction in Political Economy* (Houndmills, Basingstoke).

Arthur, C. (2003) The Hegel-Marx Connection, *Historical Materialism*, 11:3, pp. 179–183.

Arthur, C. (2004) *The New Dialectic and Marx's Capital* (Leiden, Koninklijke Brill).

Beiser, F. C. (1993) Hegel's Historicism, in F. C. Beiser (ed.), *The Cambridge Companion to Hegel* (Cambridge, Cambridge University Press), pp. 270–300.

Burns, T. & Fraser, I. (eds) (2000) *The Hegel-Marx Connection* (New York, Palgrave).

Fine, R. (2001a) *Political Investigations: Hegel, Marx & Arendt* (New York, Routledge).

Fine, R. (2001b) The Marx-Hegel Relationship: Revisionist interpretations, *Class & Capital*, 75 (Autumn), pp. 71–81.

Fontana, B. (1993) *Hegemony and Power: On the relation between Gramsci and Machiavelli* (Minneapolis, University of Minnesota Press).

Fraser, I. (1997) Two of a Kind: Hegel, Marx, dialectic and form, *Capital & Class*, 61 (Spring), pp. 81–106.

Gramsci, A. (1971) *Selections from the Prison Notebooks of Antonio Gramsci*, Q. Hoare & G. Nowell Smith, eds & trans. (New York, International Publishers).

Gramsci, A. (1975) *History, Philosophy and Culture in the Young Gramsci*, P. Cavalcanti & P. Piccone, eds; P. Molajoni, M. A. Aiello-Peabody, P. Piccone, & J. Thiem, trans. (St Louis, MO, Telos Press).

Gramsci, A. (1985) *Antonio Gramsci: Selections from the cultural writings*, D. Forgacs & G. Nowell Smith, eds; W. Boelhower, trans. (Cambridge, MA, Harvard University Press).

Gramsci, A. (1988) *An Antonio Gramsci Reader: Selected writings, 1916–1935*, D. Forgacs, ed. & trans. (New York, Schocken Books).

Gramsci, A. (1990a) *Selections from Political Writings (1910–1920): With additional texts by Bordiga and Tasca*, Q. Hoare, ed.; J. Mathews, trans. (Minneapolis, University of Minnesota Press).

Gramsci, A. (1990b) *Selections from Political Writings (1921–1926): With additional texts by other Italian Communist leaders*, Q. Hoare, ed. & trans. (Minneapolis, University of Minnesota Press).

Gramsci, A. (1992) *Antonio Gramsci: Prison notebooks (Volume I)*, J. A. Buttigieg & A. Callari, trans. (New York, Columbia University Press).

Gramsci, A. (1994) *Antonio Gramsci: Pre-prison writings*, R. Bellamy, ed.; V. Cox, trans. (Cambridge, Cambridge University Press).

Gramsci, A. (1996) *Antonio Gramsci: Prison notebooks (Volume II)*, J. A. Buttigieg, ed. & trans. (New York, Columbia University Press).

Gulli, B. (2002) Praxis and the Danger: The insurgent ontology of Antonio Gramsci. *Cultural Logic*, retrieved 29 September 2004 from http//eserver.org.ezproxy.waikato.ac.nz:2048/clogic/2002/gulli.html.

Haug, W. F. (2000) Gramsci's 'Philosophy of Praxis', E. Canepa, trans., *Socialism and Democracy*, 14:1 (Spring-Summer), pp. 1–19.

Haug, W. F. (2001) From Marx to Gramsci, from Gramsci to Marx: Historical materialism and the philosophy of praxis, *Rethinking Marxism*, 13:1 (Spring), pp. 69–82.

Hegel, G. W. F. (1977) *Phenomenology of Spirit*, A. V. Miller, trans. (Oxford, Clarendon Press). Original published 1807.

Houlgate, S. (ed.) (1998) *The Hegel Reader* (Oxford, Blackwell).

Hubis, P. (2000) The Dialectical Structure of Marx's Concept of 'Revolution in Permanence', *Capital & Class*, 70 (Spring), pp. 127–143.

Kedourie, E. (1995) *Hegel and Marx: Introductory lecture*, S. Kedourie & H. Kedourie, eds (Oxford, Blackwell).

Kitching, G. (1988) *Karl Marx and the Philosophy of Praxis* (London, Routledge).

Knafo, S. (2002) The Fetishizing Subject in Marx's 'Capital', *Capital & Class*, 76 (Spring), pp. 145–175.

Labriola, A. (1966) *Essays on the Materialist Conception of History*, C. H. Kerr, trans. (New York, Monthly Review Press). Original published 1903.

Lefebvre, H. (1968) *Dialectical Materialism*, J. Sturrock, trans. (London, Jonathon Cape). Original published 1940.

Lenin, V. I. (1973) *Collected Works*, vol. XIX (Moscow, Foreign Languages Publishing House).

MacGregor, D. (1984) *The Communist Ideal in Hegel and Marx* (Toronto, University of Toronto Press).

MacGregor, D. (1998) *Hegel and Marx after the Fall of Communism* (Cardiff, University of Wales Press).

Marx, K. & Engels, F. (1939) *The German Ideology, Parts I & III* (New York, International Publishers). Original published 1846.

Marx, K. & Engels, F. (1975) The Holy Family, in: K. Marx & F. Engels, *Collected Works* (New York, International Publishers). Original published 1844.

Marx, K. (1961) *Capital*, vol. 1, S. Moore & E. Aveling, trans. (Moscow, Foreign Languages Publishing House). Original published 1867.

Marx, K. (1963) *Early Writings*, T. B. Bottomore, ed. & trans. (London, C. A. Watts). Original published 1844.

McCarney, J. (2000a) *Hegel on History* (London, Routledge).

McCarney, J. (2000b) Hegel's Legacy, in: T. Burns & I. Fraser (eds), *The Hegel-Marx Connection* (New York, Palgrave), pp. 56–78.

Ollman, B. (1976) *Alienation: Marx's conception of man in capitalist society* (Cambridge, Cambridge University Press).

Ollman, B. (1993) *Dialectical Investigations* (New York, Routledge).

Ollman, B. (1998) Why Dialectics? Why Now? *Science & Society*, 62:3 (Fall), pp. 338–357.

Pinkard, T. (1996) *Hegel's Phenomenology: The sociality of reason* (Cambridge, Cambridge University Press).

Postone, M. (1993) *Time, Labor, and Social Domination* (Cambridge, Cambridge University Press).

Rees, J. (1998) *The Algebra of Revolution: The dialectic and the classical Marxist tradition* (London, Routledge).

Rockmore, T. (2000) On Recovering Marx after Marxism, *Philosophy & Social Criticism*, 26:4, pp. 95–106.

Rubinstein, D. (1981) *Marx and Wittgenstein: Social praxis and social explanation* (London, Routledge & Kegan Paul).

Sayer, D. (1987) *The Violence of Abstraction: The analytic foundations of historical materialism* (Oxford, Blackwell).

Sayers, S. (1980) Dualism, Materialism and Dialectics, in: R. Norman & S. Sayers (eds), *Hegel, Marx and Dialectic: A debate* (Sussex, Harvester Press), pp. 67–143.

Sayers, S. (1998) *Marxism and Human Nature* (London, Routledge).

Sayers, S. (2003) Creative Activity and Alienation in Hegel and Marx, *Historical Materialism*, 11:1, pp. 107–128.

Sekine, T. (1998) The Dialectic of Capital; An Unoist interpretation, *Science & Society*, 62:3 (Fall), pp. 434–445.

Smith, T. (1993) *Dialectic Social Theory and its Critics: From Hegel to analytical Marxism and postmodernism* (SUNY series in radical social and political theory, Albany, State University of New York Press).

Wood, A. (1993) Hegel and Marxism, in: F. C. Beiser (ed.), *The Cambridge Companion to Hegel* (Cambridge, Cambridge University Press), pp. 414–444.

2
Antonio Gramsci and his Relevance to the Education of Adults[1]

PETER MAYO

In his scattered and often cryptic writings appearing as political pamphlets, journalistic pieces, cultural reviews, letters from prison and, most particularly, those notes from the same prison that were intended as the foundation for a comprehensive work *für ewig* (for eternity), Antonio Gramsci provides elements for a large all-embracing educational strategy. This strategy is intended to engender an 'intellectual and moral reform' of a scale that, in his view, would render it the most radical reform since primitive Christianity (Festa, 1976). Educational programmes targeting adults featured prominently in this all-embracing educational strategy. To appreciate the importance of the education of adults in this context, one should highlight some key features of Gramsci's social theory.

Gramsci and Marx

It is common knowledge that the root of Gramsci's theory is historical materialism. That Gramsci is indebted to Marx's own thought goes without saying, despite the fact that many of Marx's early writings were not accessible to him. After all, Gramsci is credited with having 'reinvented' some of Marx's concepts when discussing important aspects of his native Italy's post-Risorgimento state. One of his more enduring contributions is arguably that of having stressed the cultural dimension of revolutionary practice. He has thus made a significant contribution to various aspects of Marxist theory, including the debate around the 'Base-superstructure' metaphor. At the same time, one must not lose sight of his over-arching political analysis, lest one lapses into cultural reductionism.

Gramsci's works are embedded in a Marxian conception of ideology based on the assumption that 'The ruling ideas are nothing more than the ideal expression of the dominant material relationships, the dominant material relationships grasped as ideas; hence of the relationships which make one class the ruling one, therefore the ideas of its dominance' (Marx & Engels, 1970, p. 64). Not only does the ruling class produce the ruling ideas, in view of its control over the means of intellectual production (ibid.), but also the dominated classes produce ideas that do not necessarily serve their interests. These classes, that 'lack the means of mental production and are immersed in production relations which they do not control', tend to 'reproduce ideas' that express the dominant material relationships (Larrain,

1983, p. 24). After all, as Marx and Engels had underlined, '... each new class which puts itself in place of one ruling before it, is compelled, merely in order to carry through its aim, to represent its interest as the common interest of all the members of society, that is expressed in ideal form: it has to give its ideas the form of universality, and represent them as the only rational, universally valid ones' (Marx & Engels, 1970, pp. 65, 6).

Education and Hegemony

Although Gramsci did not have access to *Die Deutsche Ideologie*, from where the above quote is taken, his familiarity with many other works by Marx[2] led him to adopt such insights in his theoretical formulations. The above quote illustrates a feature of Hegemony, the term used by Lenin, Plekhanov and others and which also featured in the linguistics writings to which Gramsci, who studied the subject under Matteo Bartoli, had been exposed (Ives, 2004, p. 47). Education is central to his particular formulation of the concept of Hegemony. Hegemony refers to a social situation in which 'all aspects of social reality are dominated by or supportive of a single class' (Livingstone, 1976, p. 235). The emphasis here is on ruling by consent and not simply through force. Gramsci's politics were comprehensive, involving an analysis of class politics in a variety of its forms. As far as education goes, his was a project that extended far beyond an analysis and discussion of schooling and formal educational issues. One might argue that education, in its wider context and conception, played a central role in his overall strategy for social transformation since, in his view, every relationship of hegemony is an educational one (Gramsci, 1975, p. 1331; Gramsci, 1971, p. 350).

His entire political project is therefore an educational project. A process of intellectual and moral reform can only be predicated on such an expansive view of education. Gramsci scholar Joseph A. Buttigieg writes: '... the role of education in Gramsci's thought cannot be properly appreciated unless one recognizes that it resides at the very core of his concept of hegemony' (Buttigieg, 2002, pp. 69, 70).

The State and Civil Society

The agencies, which, in his view, engage in this educational relationship, are the ideological social institutions, constituting civil society, such as law, education, mass media, religion etc. Gramsci argues that, in Western society, the State is surrounded and propped up by a network of these institutions that are conceived of as 'a powerful system of fortresses and earthworks' which makes its presence felt whenever the State 'trembles' (Gramsci, 1971, p. 238; Gramsci, 1975, p. 866). As such, social institutions such as schools and other educational establishments are not 'neutral' but serve to cement the existing hegemony, therefore being intimately tied to the interests of the most powerful social groups, especially the bourgeoisie.

Implicit throughout Gramsci's writings on 'the State' and 'Civil Society' is a critique of educational establishments. Contained in his writings are elements for an analysis of the politics of education in the Western capitalist social formation.

Education is perceived as playing an important role in cementing the existing hegemony. It is crucial in securing consent for the ruling way of life, one that is supportive of and is supported by the prevailing mode of production. Compulsory initial learning, mandated by the Capitalist Italian State, during the years of Fascist rule, is problematised by Gramsci in his critique of the *Riforma Gentile* and the kind of streaming (tracking) it was intended to bring about. His critique of the Fascist regime's proposed separation between 'classical' and 'vocational' schools strikes me as being well within the radical tradition of opposing any kind of differentiation made on the basis of 'meritocracy' when, in effect, the whole process is one of selection made on the basis of class. Gramsci, however, does not limit himself to criticizing the contemporary reforms but offers alternatives that emerge from his vision of society.

Structure and Agency

Gramsci was no economic determinist. He was very anti-positivist, a stance that is also reflected in his view of language and linguistics and his criticism, following Bartoli, of the Neogrammarians (Ives, 2004, p. 47). As a matter of fact, his work is generally regarded as having marked a decisive break with the official Marxism of the time (cf. Diskin, 1993, p. 18). A strong sense of agency is conveyed throughout his writings. In an early article, entitled 'La Rivoluzione Contro il Capitale', the young Gramsci argued that the Bolshevik Revolution called into question the canons of historical materialism, a position from which he would move in his more mature years characterized by a deeper understanding of Marx's writings where the canons of historical materialism are not so 'iron like' as the young Gramsci would have us believe. One must bear in mind the particular phase in life in which the pieces by Gramsci that are cited have been written. Nevertheless it would be worth reproducing this quote from a much-cited work (often known in English as 'Against Capital') to capture his enthusiasm for the news of the October Revolution in Russia and to shed light on his earlier reception of Karl Marx's theory:

> ... facts have overthrown the critical schema within which the history of Russia was supposed to be confined, according to the canons of historical materialism. The Bolsheviks deny Karl Marx, and affirm explicitly by their deeds that the canons of historical materialism are not so ironlike as might be thought, and has been thought ... (the Bolsheviks) are not Marxists, that's all. (Gramsci, cited in Clark, 1977, p. 51; see Italian original in Gramsci, 1997, p. 43)

With respect to Gramsci's anti-positivism, Angelo Broccoli (1972, p. 28) argues that one of the reasons why the young Gramsci was attracted to the works of Benedetto Croce[3] was simply because the Neapolitan philosopher affirmed human values in the face of the sense of acquiescence and passivity conveyed by Positivism and which Gramsci associated with the mechanistic and deterministic theories of the Second International. As Giuseppe Fiori, arguably Gramsci's best-known biographer, writes,

> For Croce, man [sic] was the unique protagonist of history. His [sic]
> thought stimulates action—concrete 'ethical-Political' action—which is
> the creation of new history. (Fiori, 1970, p. 239)

This sense of agency can be discovered in his theoretical formulations concerning
Hegemony and the State. For Gramsci, hegemony is characterised by a number of
features. It is characterised by its non-static nature (it is constantly open to negotiation and re-negotiation, therefore being renewed and recreated). It is incomplete,
selective (Williams, 1976) and there exist moments wherein cracks can be detected.
All this indicates that there can be room for counter-hegemonic activity, which
can be very effective in specific circumstances. There are also excluded areas of
social life that can be explored by people involved in such counter-hegemonic
activities.

For Gramsci, the terrain wherein hegemony can be contested is the very terrain
which supports it, namely that of Civil Society which is conceived of as a site of
struggle. He argued that, because he regarded it as being propped up by the
institutions of Civil Society, the State cannot be confronted frontally by those
aspiring to overthrow it in order to bring into place a new set of social relations—
what he calls 'a war of manoeuvre'. The process of transforming the State and its
coercive apparatus must, to a large extent, precede, rather than follow, the seizure
of power (Lawner, 1973, p. 49) through pre-figurative work (Allman, 1988),
although this process cannot be fully achieved unless power is finally seized.

Jorge Larrain provides the important caveat that such pre-figurative work can
never result in 'total ideological domination' prior to the conquest of the state
since, as Gramsci maintains, 'class consciousness cannot be completely modified
until the mode of life of the class itself is modified, which entails that the proletariat
has become the ruling class' (in Larrain, 1983, p. 82) through 'possession of the
apparatus of production and exchange and state power' (my translation from
Gramsci, 1997, p. 161). While total ideological domination is not possible prior to
the conquest of the state, there is however much work to be carried out beforehand
to help generate the climate for change.

War of Position

People working for social transformation, in Gramsci's case, the proletariat seeking
to transform the bourgeois state, had to engage in a 'war of position', a process of
wide ranging social organisation and cultural influence. It is through this process
that the group creates, together with other groups and sectors of society, an historical bloc, the term borrowed from Georges Sorel that Gramsci uses to describe
the complex manner in which classes or their factions are related (Showstack
Sassoon, 1982, p. 14):

> ... every revolution has been preceded by an intense labour of criticism
> and by the diffusion of culture and the spread of ideas among masses of
> men [sic] who are at first resistant and think only of solving their own
> immediate economic and political problems for themselves who have no

ties of solidarity with others in the same condition. (Gramsci, 1977, p. 12; see original Italian quote in Gramsci, 1967, p. 19)

The primacy of cultural activity for the revolutionary process is therefore affirmed by Gramsci, an idea that reflects the influence of a number people, notably Angelo Tasca. As Clark (1977) has indicated, Gramsci wrote, in *Il Grido del Popolo*:

> Socialism is organization, and not only political and economic organization, but also, especially, organization of knowledge and of will, obtained through cultural activity (p. 53).

The Factory Councils and the Education of Adults

As a crucial area of 'Civil Society', adult education[4] was conceived of by Gramsci as having an important role to play in this 'war of position' both at the level of adult education within movements challenging the established state of affairs or at the level of individuals and enclaves operating in and against the state.[5] Gramsci, very much involved in adult education, as part of his work in the Italian Socialist and subsequently Communist parties, wrote of the existence of *altre vie* (other routes) when it comes to education and learning. Gramsci saw progressive and emancipatory elements within these *altre vie* that can complement the kind of Unitarian school he proposed, in Notebooks IV and XII, to advance the interests of the Italian working class. Gramsci's *Ordine Nuovo* group directed a lot of its energies, during the revolutionary climate which prevailed in Turin, prior to the Fascist take over, towards the Factory Council Movement that was, in effect, an adult education movement through which workers were 'educated' as producers rather than simply as 'wage earners' (Merrington, 1977, p. 158)—*salariati* (salaried employees) (Gramsci, 1967, p. 261)—and initiated into the process of industrial democracy.[6] For Gramsci, the Factory Councils were intended to provide the means whereby the proletariat could 'educate itself, gather experience and acquire a responsible awareness of the duties incumbent upon classes that hold the power of the state' (cited in Merrington, 1977, p. 159).

This was to constitute an important step for the working class in the direction of 'exercising leadership before winning Government power' (Gramsci, 1971, p. 57). The emphasis, in these writings, is on the acquisition of industrial democracy, the backbone of the workers' state.

There was to be 'collaboration between manual workers, skilled workers, administrative employees, engineers and technical directors' (Gramsci, 1977, p. 110). Through such collaboration, workers were to experience 'the unity of the industrial process' and see themselves 'as an inseparable part of the whole labour system which is concentrated in the object being manufactured' (ibid.; Italian original in Gramsci, 1967, p. 261). As such, they were to acquire complete mental control over the production process to 'replace management's power in the Factory' (Gramsci, in Mancini, 1973, p. 5). Furthermore, the knowledge acquired at the workplace would, according to Gramsci, lead to a greater understanding of the workings of society:

> At this point the worker has become a producer, for he [sic] has acquired an awareness of his role in the process of production at all levels, from the workshop to the nation to the world. (Gramsci, 1977, p. 111; Italian original in Gramsci, 1967, p. 261)

One assumes that the educational programme which the Factory Councils had to provide, in order to render workers capable of exerting such control, must mirror the spirit of democracy and collaboration it is intended to foster at the workplace and eventually in the envisaged democratic Workers' State (cf. Gramsci, 1977, p. 66). For the kind of environment generated by the Factory Councils was intended to prefigure that of the socialist state (once again, however, we must keep in mind Larrain's important caveat):

> The Socialist State already exists potentially in the institutions of social life characteristic of the exploited working class. To link these institutions, co-ordinating and ordering them into a highly centralized hierarchy of competences and powers, while respecting the necessary autonomy and articulation of each, is to create a genuine workers' democracy here and now ... . (Gramsci, 1977, p. 66; see Italian original in Gramsci, 1967, p. 206, 207)

The Factory Council Movement brought Turin, regarded by Gramsci as 'Italy's Petrograd', close to a revolution. The main reason for its ultimate failure was that its activity was not carried out in the context of the alliance called for by Gramsci through his later formulation of the concept of the 'historical bloc'. In retrospect, Gramsci noted that the insurgents, in Turin, were isolated (Adamson, 1980, p. 60). Yet the Factory council was not conceived of by Gramsci as the only agency responsible for the education of adults. In keeping with the idea of a 'war of position', the education of adults involved a cultural offensive on all fronts, across the entire complex of civil society (the term is used by Gramsci in a manner that is very different from the way it is popularly used nowadays).

Different Sites of Adult Learning

Gramsci's writings convey the idea that different sites of social practice can be transformed into sites of adult learning. As I have argued, his scattered writings reflect a lifelong effort to engage in counter-hegemonic activities in all spheres of social life. Gramsci comes across, in these writings, as an indefatigable organiser and educator who would leave no space unexplored to educate members of the 'subaltern' classes. The area of industrial production becomes an important site of learning. These workplace educational experiences are to be sustained, according to Gramsci, by cultural centres. The *Club di Vita Morale*, which he helped organise in 1917 and wherein workers read works and gave presentations to each other (De Robbio Anziano, 1987, p. 124), was one such centre. Another centre was the short-lived Institute of Proletarian Culture that drew inspiration from the Russian Proletkult (Gramsci, 1976, p. 216) and the group associated with the French journal

Clarté that included Romain Rolland (the author who formulated the well known phrase associated with Gramsci and the *Ordine Nuovo*: pessimism of the intellect, optimism of the will) and Henri Barbusse (Broccoli, 1972, p. 47).

Some of Gramsci's writings reveal a yearning, on his part, for the creation of a cultural association for workers, one that offers space where workers can debate all that is of interest to the working class movement. Gramsci wrote that such an institution 'must have class aims and limits. It must be a proletarian institution seeking definite goals' (Gramsci, 1985, p. 21; Italian original in Gramsci, 1967, p. 91). He also felt that such an association would cater to the need to integrate political and economic activity with an organ of cultural activity (Gramsci, 1985, p. 22). Gramsci might have been inspired, in this respect, by the writings of Anatoli Lunacarskij, who had an article on the issue translated into Italian and published in *Il Grido del Popolo*. And reference is made, in a piece in *L'Ordine Nuovo*, to the first experiences of a proletarian school. Gramsci glorifies this institute and its participants, extolling the latter's determination to learn, despite their tiredness after a day's work. And, according to Gramsci, what added to their merit was that they learnt not to simply advance personally, as with the bourgeois schools, but to help realise their dream of a better society (Gramsci, 1967, p. 290). The importance of such circles must have been recognised by Gramsci from the very beginning of his political work. Indeed there is evidence that the young Gramsci had, in 1916, delivered talks to workers' study circles in Turin on a variety of topics, including Marx, the Paris Commune, Romain Rolland and the French Revolution (Buttigieg, 1992, p. 68). His engagement as an adult educator therefore started at an early age during which time he was also greatly involved in journalism (ibid.).

Prison School

The ongoing commitment by Gramsci to explore opportunities for proletarian adult education is reflected in his efforts, despite obvious physical and external constraints, to help create a prison school (*scuola dei confinati*) at Ustica (De Robbio Anziano, 1987, p. 125) where he would both teach and learn. His long time friend Piero Sraffa, a professor of economics at Cagliari University and later Cambridge University, also provided help. Sraffa opened an account at a Milan bookstore for books to be forwarded to Gramsci. At this 'school', that Gramsci helped set up with Amadeo Bordiga and others, different courses relating to different levels of study were held (Lawner, 1973, p. 66). In a letter to Sraffa, dated 2 January 1927, Gramsci indicates the different grades into which the school was organised. It catered for people of different backgrounds some of whom were semi-illiterate, even though Gramsci pointed out that they were intellectually well developed. There were two courses in French (lower and superior) and a course in German (Gramsci, 1996, pp. 27, 28). While on the island of Ustica, an island on which he and other detainees were allowed to roam about, Gramsci studied German, Russian, economics and history, as he discloses in a letter to his sister in law, Tatiana Schucht, dated 9th December 1926 (Gramsci, 1996, p. 10). It is to be assumed, however, that Gramsci studied some of these subjects on his own, thanks also to the books procured on his behalf by Piero Sraffa.

Periodicals

This experience as well as the earlier experiences relating to Gramsci's pre-prison life as a 'full time revolutionary' indicates that, for Gramsci, transformative education can take place in a variety of sites of social practice. This strikes me as being well within the tradition of radical, non-formal adult education, particularly the tradition that incorporates the efforts of movements seeking structural change. One can infer from the pre-prison efforts, that the educational activities within the various sites were to be sustained by such media as cultural reviews that Gramsci, no doubt drawing on his own experience as a journalist, must have regarded as important instruments of informal adult education. The *Ordine Nuovo* was intended as a review of socialist culture and therefore as an important source of adult education. It constituted the means whereby cultural productions of the period were analysed from the standpoint of the 'subaltern' class whose interests the review purported to represent. Such a review must therefore have been intended as an important means of assisting the Turin workers in the important process of critically appropriating elements of the dominant culture. It also served as a means to develop the more emancipatory aspects of popular culture, with a view to creating a new culture reflecting an alternative *Weltanschauung*.

Adult Educator as Organic Intellectual

What type of adult educator did Gramsci have in mind? Does agency lie with a potential target-learning group? The agents who, in Gramsci's view, play a pivotal role in this 'war of position' are the organic intellectuals—cultural or educational workers who are experts in legitimation. They emerge 'in response to particular historical developments' (Ransome, 1992, p. 198), as opposed to traditional intellectuals whose 'organic' purpose is over as society enters a different stage of development (ibid.). Adult educators engaging in counter-hegemonic cultural activity are to be conceived of, according to the Gramscian conception, as intellectuals who are organic to the 'subaltern' groups aspiring to power. This implies that they should be politically committed to those they teach. Unless this occurs, there can be no effective learning. One of the reasons why Gramsci did not believe that the Italian 'popular universities' (adult education centres) operated in the interest of the proletariat was that the intellectuals involved were not committed to this class (Broccoli, 1972, p. 41). More care was taken, in these schools, to impress (*si bada più alla lustra*) than to teach effectively (Gramsci, 1967, p. 36) in a process described by Gramsci as that in which bagfuls of victuals (*sporte di vivere*) were distributed (Gramsci, 1967, p. 34). Gramsci argued that the working class should produce its own intellectuals or else assimilate traditional intellectuals, the process of assimilation being a crucial aspect of the 'war of position' itself. It is most likely that a social group's endeavours, in this regard, would be characterised by a combination of both processes.

Educational Needs of Industrial Working Class

As for the issue of whether there exists, in Gramsci, a social category with whom the responsibility for agency lies, one can argue that, despite his first hand knowledge of the peasant dominated South, it was to the industrial proletariat, located in Turin, that he looked for revolutionary potential. Although he attempted to deal, at some depth, with the Southern Question (cf. Gramsci, 1964, pp. 797–819; Gramsci, 1995; Verdicchio, 1995) and advocated an historical bloc characterised by a 'national-popular' alliance between the proletariat and the peasantry, he ascribed to the former the role of leadership or directorship (*direzione*) in the alliance:

> ... we favoured a very realistic and not at all 'magic' formula of the land for the peasants; but we wanted it to be realised inside the framework of the general revolutionary action of the two allied classes *under the leadership* of the industrial proletariat. (Gramsci, 1957, p. 30; Italian original in Gramsci, 1964, p. 799; Gramsci, 1997, p. 181; my emphasis)

Most of Gramsci's writings, which are relevant to adult education, focus on the educational needs of the industrial working class. The issue of adult literacy, an important concern for anyone dealing with adult education in the Southern Italian regions, where illiteracy was widespread, is given lip service in Gramsci's writings. There is a very short piece that explains the causes of peasant class resistance to compulsory education. It is one of the very few extant pieces by Gramsci on this topic, if not the only piece (Gramsci, 1964, pp. 235–236). In short, Gramsci's writings identify a specific adult education clientele. This can be explained by the fact that these writings are the product of his first hand experience as activist, organiser and adult educator, an experience that was confined to the city of Turin. He therefore wrote specifically about the area in which he was directly involved.

Pedagogy

There is also something to be said about the kind of pedagogy that ought to be encouraged. That Gramsci was concerned with mitigating hierarchical relations between those who 'educate' and 'direct' and those who learn can be seen from his writings concerning philosophy, language, culture, and hegemony relations. Echoing Marx's Third Thesis on Feuerbach ('the Educator must himself be educated'), he advocates a relationship that has to be 'active and reciprocal', one whereby 'every teacher is always a pupil and every pupil a teacher' (Gramsci, 1971, p. 350). The same applies to his views concerning educators. In his note on the Unitarian School, which led certain authors to argue that he advocated a conservative education (cf. Entwistle, 1979; Senese, 1991), or elements of such an education (De Robbio Anziano, 1987), for working class empowerment, Gramsci refers to the teacher who limits himself or herself to a straightforward transmission of facts as 'mediocre' (Gramsci, 1971, p. 36; Gramsci, 1975, p. 499). Such a teacher is closely associated with the 'old school' that, according to Gramsci, has its merits. He underlines these merits to move to one extreme in order to expose what he regarded as the shortcomings of the other, in this case, the Gentile Reforms. This school was, nevertheless, considered wayward enough by Gramsci to justify the struggle for its replacement (Gramsci, 1971, p. 36; Gramsci, 1975, p. 499). In fact, as Mario Aligero Manacorda (in Gramsci, 1972, p. xxix) states, the writing on the Unitarian School, highlighting the virtues of the old humanistic school, is an epitaph to this school. It laments the passing of this school that cannot continue to serve its purpose any longer since the social reality has changed. The problem for Gramsci, however, is that the new system that was being introduced for its replacement appeared to him to be a retrograde one, falling far short of his ideal of a fusion between the academic and the technical. The old school, which has to be replaced, has greater merit than the one proposed by Gentile possibly through the influence of his mentor, Benedetto Croce (see Borg & Mayo, 2002, p. 102).

In his epitaph for the outgoing school, Gramsci highlighted the merits of the conveyance of facts, an aspect of the old school, in reaction to what he perceived to have been the emerging practice of carrying out dialogue in a vacuum. The implication for adult educators seems to be that a certain degree of instruction needs to be imparted to render any dialogical education an informed one. The pedagogy is directive (it is intended towards a political goal), striking a balance between spontaneity and conscious direction—*spontaneità* and *direzione consapevole* (Gramsci, 1975, p. 328). Furthermore, the organic intellectual/adult educator is equipped with a body of knowledge and theoretical insight that, nevertheless, needs to be constantly tested and renewed through contact with the learners/masses. This explains Gramsci's advocacy of a dialectical relationship between adult educators/organic intellectuals and the learners/masses. The reciprocal educational relationship that he advocates and which was cited earlier exists throughout society as a whole and for every individual relative to other individuals. It exists between intellectual and non-intellectual sections of the population (Gramsci, 1971, p. 350).

Cultural Dimension of Workers' Education

What constitutes 'really useful knowledge' in this context? Quite often, we come across workers' education programmes that are restricted to production issues (e.g. labour studies), irrespective of whether they are narrow 'tool' or broader 'issue' courses. This comprises courses in negotiation theory, economics, labour studies and so forth. Seldom included are areas which cover a wider terrain, including areas that featured prominently in the repressed historical tradition of independent working class education and which provided the basis for the type of cultural studies developed in English adult education. Gramsci advocated a broader education encompassing all those areas of knowledge that constitute a terrain where values are conveyed and subjectivities are shaped. Gramsci focuses, in his writings, on both aspects of the conventional and problematic 'high' and 'low' culture divide.

Referring to the traditional school, in his writing on the Unitarian School, Gramsci argues that pupils learnt Greek and Latin for no immediate practical reasons but 'to know at first hand the civilization of Greece and Rome—a civilization that was a necessary pre-condition for our modern civilization'. He goes on to say:

> In other words, they learnt them to be themselves and know themselves consciously. (Gramsci, 1971, p. 37; Italian original in Gramsci, 1975, p. 1544)

His focus on both aspects of the 'high' and 'low' cultural divide is carried out as part of a constant search for a synthesis between the potentially emancipatory aspects of both. This is done with a view to providing the basis for a proletarian culture. It is perhaps for this reason that he expresses great concern, in the *Quaderni*, for the way in which areas of popular culture are incorporated by the dominant culture. For this reason, he expresses great interest in works like Dostoyevsky's novel which draws on the serial, and therefore popular, fiction to produce 'artistic' fiction, and, in so doing, it reveals the interplay between the 'popular' and the 'artistic' (Forgacs & Nowell Smith, 1985, p. 12).

Gramsci considered several elements of the 'canon' to be relevant to the needs of the working class. This could explain the enthusiasm he shows, in some of his reviews, for plays and writings by established figures which contain themes and moral actions that, he felt, resonate with the experiences of members of subordinated social groups. For instance, he seems to have seen in the figure of Ibsen's Nora Helmer, the protagonist in *A Doll's House* (cf. Gramsci, 1976: pp. 246, 247; Gramsci, 1985, p. 72), the basis for the 'new feminine personality' about which he writes in the notes on 'Americanism and Fordism' (cf. Gramsci, 1971, p. 296; Gramsci, 1975, p. 2149).

The inference that I draw from the foregoing is that such knowledge should feature in a programme of cultural preparation of workers developed on Gramscian lines. This knowledge should not, however, be treated unproblematically. The process involved is one of critical appropriation:

> Creating a new culture does not only mean one's own individual 'original' discoveries. It also, and most particularly, means the diffusion in a critical form of truths already discovered, their 'socialisation' as it were, and even making them the basis of vital action, an element of co-ordination and intellectual and moral order. (Gramsci, 1971, p. 325; Italian original in Gramsci, 1997, pp. 1377, 1378)

Language

The issue of mastering the dominant culture in order to transform it is also developed in other aspects of Gramsci's work. For instance, Gramsci advocates mastery of the dominant language for members of the 'subaltern' classes not to remain on the periphery of political life.[7] This does not mean that he endorsed the hegemony of this language (the Tuscan dialect so strongly favoured by Manzoni). It constituted, after all, a form of 'passive revolution' and did not connect with the various languages of subaltern groups that, as with all languages, reflect specific conceptions of the world. This has implications for adult literacy programmes. Gramsci believed in the importance of a national standard language but he favoured a process of linguistic hegemony characterised by the presence of a normative grammar that derived from the interactions of the spontaneous grammars found in the peninsula's different regions—a national popular standard language, if you will, which would be more democratic in that it would reflect the 'collective will' (see Ives, 2004, p. 100). And organic intellectuals had an important role to play in elaborating and creating connections between these spontaneous grammars, something which was not occurring in Gramsci's time, since those people with potential for intellectual leadership among the subaltern classes were co-opted partly through their being equipped with a normative grammar that was alien to the subordinated classes. This normative grammar, therefore, served to alienate potential organic intellectuals from these subaltern classes, rendering them traditional intellectuals instead—intellectuals whose activity deceptively appeared to be devoid of any social moorings when in actual fact this activity served to consolidate the hegemony of the dominant groups.[8] In the short piece, dealing with illiteracy, referred to earlier, he emphasises the need for peasants to learn a standard language to transcend their insular environment characterised by *campanilismo* (parochialism) (Gramsci, 1964, p. 236):

> If it is true that every language contains the elements of a conception of the world and of a culture, it could also be true that from anyone's language, one can assess the greater or lesser complexity of his [sic] conception of the world. Someone who only speaks dialect, or understands the standard language incompletely, necessarily has an intuition of the world which is more or less limited and provincial. (Gramsci, 1971, p. 325)

Moreover, he also felt that the proletariat would achieve greater unity through the ability to speak one common language, although he refutes the idea that Esperanto can constitute such a language. This unity would not be achieved if various regional groups, within the subaltern classes, confine themselves to merely speaking their own particular dialect.

Historical Dimension

For Gramsci, it is not only the dominant culture that has to be mastered in processes of adult education but also knowledge of history. As with the canon, which has its roots in the past, history too needs to be confronted, mastered and transformed. History should be a feature of working class adult education. He states:

> If it is true that universal history is a chain made up of efforts man [sic] has exerted to free himself [sic] from privilege, prejudice and idolatry, then it is hard to understand why the proletariat, which seeks to add

another link to the chain, should not know how and why and by whom it was preceded or what advantage it might derive from this knowledge ... (Gramsci, 1971, p. 41)

Philosophy of Praxis

There are, however, other issues, in so far as content is concerned, which are emphasised by Gramsci. The earlier discussion on workplace democracy highlights the importance that Gramsci attached to the workers' sharing of knowledge of the entire production process and of their learning economic and administrative skills. Being first and foremost a Marxist, Gramsci must have considered important a process of education through praxis. In fact, the 'philosophy of praxis' (Gramsci, 1975, p. 1437) was central to his work spanning across the *Quaderni*. It is Gramsci's overarching philosophy that he contrasts with 'common sense'. Gramsci saw ideas that reflect the dominant material relationships as residing in those areas he identifies with 'common sense' which contains elements of 'good sense' but which is, in effect, a distorted and fragmentary conception of the world. It is, according to Gramsci, a 'philosophy of non philosophers' (Gramsci, 1975, p. 1396). This is 'a conception of the world absorbed uncritically by the various social and cultural environments in which the moral individuality of the average man develops' (literal translation by Carmel Borg from Gramsci, 1975, p. 1396; see Borg & Mayo, 2002). Gramsci draws connections between popular religion, folklore (a specific body of beliefs, values and norms [Salamini, 1981] that is uncritical, contradictory and ambiguous in content) and common sense (Borg & Mayo, 2002, p. 91). The challenge, for Gramsci, is to supersede this common sense through a 'philosophy of praxis', the 'conscious expression' of the contradictions that lacerate society' (Larrain, 1979, p. 81). The 'philosophy of praxis' would undergo a process of elaboration similar to that experienced by Lutheranism and Calvinism before it develops into a 'superior culture' (Caruso, 1997, pp. 85, 86) or '*civiltà*'.

The 'philosophy of praxis' is that which enables this common sense to be transformed into 'good sense' and which warrants elaboration to provide the underpinning of an intellectual and moral reform. In contrast to the bifurcation advocated by Benedetto Croce (philosophy for intellectuals and religion for the people), the 'philosophy of praxis' is intended to be a philosophy that welds intellectuals and masses together in a historical bloc (Borg & Mayo, 2002, p. 89). It is intended to be an instrument for the forging of a strong relationship between theory and practice, consciousness and action (Hoare & Nowell Smith in Gramsci, 1971, p. XIII).

Education and Production

And the notion of praxis often appears in a manner that suggests an absolute fusion between education and the world of production. It is for this reason that Gramsci revealed a fascination for forms of art that stressed the relationship between human beings and industry. In fact, he reveals an albeit short-lived fascination for the Futurist movement (Gramsci, 1967: pp. 396, 397) for its having 'grasped sharply and clearly that our age, the age of big industry, of the large proletarian city and of intense and tumultuous life, was in need of new forms of art, philosophy, behaviour and Language' (Gramsci, 1985, p. 51). It is this preoccupation that led Gramsci to affirm, somewhat idealistically, the virtues of what Marx would have regarded as a 'polytechnical education', arguing for a strong relationship to be forged between education and production, a notion which Marx had specifically developed in the Geneva Resolution of 1866 (Livingstone, 1984, pp. 186, 187):

> Having become dominant, the working class wants manual labour and intellectual labour to be joined in the school and thus creates a new educational tradition (Gramsci, 1985, p. 43).

Migration and the question of Multi-ethnic Education

Some authors dealing with Gramsci's work, notably Verdicchio (1995) and Apitzsch (2002), have raised the issue of migration and multiculturalism with respect to his notes and other writings. There is much in Gramsci's work that can be of relevance to a process of adult education for multi-ethnic solidarity in an age of globalisation characterised by mobility of capital and labour (certainly not on an equal footing) across borders. The concept of 'national popular', so much emphasised by Gramsci, takes on a specific meaning in this context. What is 'national' is often tied to the culture of hegemonic ethnic groups and is related to the whole structure of hegemony. Concepts such as 'national identity', 'national culture' are thus challenged, in societies that are constantly becoming multiethnic, as part of the process of negotiating relations of hegemony within the countries concerned. A progressive adult education project on the lines indicated by Gramsci would contribute to this contestation, challenging, through the development of informed opinion, dominant constructions of the 'national' etc. Furthermore, as Verdicchio (1995, p. 11) so eloquently argues, with respect to his country of origin (he is an Italian scholar from Naples based in the USA), the 'Southern Question' ('*Quistione Meridionale*', as Gramsci calls it) extends beyond Italy through the presence elsewhere of the Southern Italian migrant diaspora. One can extend this consideration to the South at large to indicate how the 'question' of southern populations extends beyond this part of the world through the Southern diaspora. If one can take liberties with a statement by Verdicchio, one can say that the emigrant from the South is a 'de-contextualized expression of the contradictory process' of state formation in the country of origin. One of the challenges for critical adult education work with migrants, to emerge from this formulation, is that of enabling the migrants to read not only the world they now inhabit as immigrants but also the world they left. As Paulo Freire discovered, with respect to Brazil, the period of migration (exile in his case) presents an opportunity for a critical distancing from the world one once knew to 'relearn' it (a favourite Freire term with respect to Brazil) in a more critical vein (see the discussion in Freire & Faundez, 1989). The same would apply to critical educators, engaged in Northern countries, working with migrants from the world's southern regions. In this respect, there is relevance, for the current situation, in Gramsci's insistence that the industrial proletariat in the North of Italy, which included in large part, immigrants or the offspring of immigrants from the South, must bring the Southern Question to the forefront of the proletariat. In this respect, he maintains that the Turin communists had the undeniable merit of having brought the Southern Question to the attention of the workers' vanguard, identifying it as one of the key issues for the revolutionary proletariat's national politics. (Gramsci, 1997, pp. 181, 182) The Southern Question takes on a larger meaning and significance in this day and age. Furthermore, the national popular alliance of workers and peasants, which Gramsci called for with respect to Italy, takes on a larger more global North-South meaning in this age of mass migration from South to North. Adult education programmes of a truly internationally socialist kind, in northern contexts, must constantly foreground the issue of the South in the interest of generating North-South solidarity and confronting misplaced alliances (this includes the false alliance between 'labour' and 'management' against 'the competition') based on racist, labour market segmentation strategies. Such an anti-racist programme of adult education, allied to strong social action, can only be successful if rooted in political economy and an understanding of a history of colonialism. These are the sorts of elements that Gramsci sought to bring to his analysis of the Southern Question in Italy, with his emphasis on political economy and historical understanding of the Risorgimento and the process of 'internal colonialism' it brought about.

Conclusion: Adult Education for Counter-Hegemonic Action

To conclude, I would argue that Antonio Gramsci saw in the education and cultural formation of adults the key towards the creation of systematic and effective counter-hegemonic action. The attainment of an intellectual and moral reform entailed a lengthy process of education characterised by what Raymond Williams would call the 'long revolution'. Adult education in its many forms, formal, non-formal and informal, was to play an important role in this process. Organic intellectuals engaged in this lengthy process of working for social transformation were to explore a number of sites with the potential to serve as sites of transformative learning. Gramsci himself stood as a model in this regard with his unstinting efforts at engaging in projects and carving out spaces for adult learning both during his active years in the public domain and during moments of his incarceration. However it is not only to his various projects that adult educators need to turn to gain inspiration but also to the various theoretical insights deriving from his own revolutionary praxis, insights through which Antonio Gramsci has made a tremendous contribution to modern social and educational theory.

Notes

1. This chapter draws from Mayo, 1999.
2. In volume IV of his edited critical edition of the *Quaderni del Carcere*, Valentino Gerratana provides the list of texts by Marx and Engels that Gramsci cites in the Notebooks. These

include *Capital*, the *Theses on Feuerbach*, the *Contribution to the Critique of Hegel's Philosophy of Right (Introduction)*, *The Holy Family*, *The Eighteenth Brumaire of Louis Napoleon*, *Critique of the Gotha Programme*, besides numerous letters and articles (Gerratana in Gramsci, 1975, pp. 3062, 3063).

3. For a recent study on Croce see Rizi, 2003.
4. For a comprehensive overview of the way Gramsci's ideas have been taken up in adult education see Borg, Buttigieg and Mayo (2002).
5. For a recent empirical piece concerning the work of an adult education organization operating in and against the State see Mayo, 2005.
6. For an empirical study that derives inspiration from Gramsci's factory council work, see Livingstone (2002).
7. For an excellent text on language in Gramsci's writings, see Ives, 2004.
8. This section owes a lot to the rich discussion on the subject of 'Language and Hegemony in the Prison Notebooks' in Ives, 2004, Chapter 3.

References

Adamson, W. (1980) *Hegemony and Revolution* (Berkeley, CA, & London, University of California Press).

Allman, P. (1988) Gramsci, Freire and Illich: Their contributions to education for socialism, in: T. Lovett (ed.), *Radical Approaches to Adult Education. A reader* (London, Routledge).

Apitzsch, U. (2002) Gramsci and the Current Debate on Multicultural Education, in: C. Borg, J. Buttigieg, and P. Mayo (eds), *Gramsci and Education* (Lanham, MD, Rowman & Littlefield).

Borg, C. & Mayo, P. (2002) Gramsci and the Unitarian School. Paradoxes and Possibilities, in: C. Borg, J. Buttigieg, and P. Mayo (eds), *Gramsci and Education* (Lanham, MD, Rowman & Littlefield).

Borg, C., Buttigieg, J. & Mayo, P. (2002) Introduction. Gramsci and Education. A Holistic Approach, in: C. Borg, J. Buttigieg, and P. Mayo (eds), *Gramsci and Education* (Lanham, MD, Rowman & Littlefield).

Broccoli, A. (1972) *Antonio Gramsci e l'educazione come egemonia* (Firenze, La Nuova Italia).

Buttigieg, J. A. (2002) On Gramsci, *Daedalus*, Summer, pp. 67–70.

Clark, M. (1977) *Antonio Gramsci and the Revolution that Failed* (New Haven & London, Yale University Press).

Caruso, S. (1997) La riforma intellettuale e morale, in: Gramsci: *I Quaderni del Carcere. Una riflessione politica incompiuta*, ed. S. Mastellone (Turin, UTET Libreria).

De Robbio Anziano, I. (1987) *Antonio Gramsci e la Pedagogia del Impegno* (Naples, Ferraro).

Diskin, J. (1993) Gramsci in Rethinking Marxism, *International Gramsci Society Newsletter*, 2, pp. 18–20.

Entwistle, H. (1979) *Antonio Gramsci—Conservative Schooling for Radical Politics* (London, Routledge and Kegan Paul).

Festa, S. (1976) *Gramsci* (Assisi, Cittadella Editrice).

Fiori, G. (1970) *Antonio Gramsci: Life of a revolutionary* (London, New Left Books).

Forgacs, D. & Nowell Smith, G. (eds) (1985) *Antonio Gramsci, Selections from Cultural Writings.* (Cambridge, MA, Harvard University Press).

Freire, P. and Faundez, A. (1989) *Learning to Question. Pedagogy of liberation* (Geneva, World Council of Churches).

Gramsci, A. (1957) *The Modern Prince and Other Writings*, L. Marks (ed.) (New York, International Publishers).

Gramsci, A. (1964) *2000 Pagine di Gramsci*, Vol. 1, G. Ferrara & N. Gallo (eds) (Milan, Il Saggiatore).

Gramsci, A. (1967) *Scritti Politici 1* (Roma, Editori Riuniti).

Gramsci, A. (1971) *Selections from the Prison Notebooks*, Q. Hoare & G. Nowell Smith (eds) (New York, International Publishers).

Gramsci, A. (1972) *L'Alternativa Pedagogica*, M. A. Manacorda (ed.) (Firenze, La Nuova Italia).

Gramsci, A. (1975) *Quaderni del Carcere, Edizione Critica*, V. Gerratana (ed.) (Turin, Einaudi).

Gramsci, A. (1976) *Scritti 1915–1921*, S. Caprioglio (ed.) (Milan, Mozzi Editore).

Gramsci, A. (1977) *Antonio Gramsci, Selections from Political writings (1910–1920)*, Q. Hoare & J. Matthews (eds) (New York, International Publishers).

Gramsci, A. (1985) *Antonio Gramsci, Selections from Cultural Writings*, D. Forgacs & G. Nowell Smith (eds) (Cambridge, MA, Harvard University Press).

Gramsci, A. (1995) *The Southern Question*, P. Verdicchio (trans. and ed.) (Lafayette, IN, Bordighera Inc).

Gramsci, A. (1996) *Lettere dal Carcere* (two volumes), A. Santucci (ed.) (Palermo, Sellerio).

Gramsci, A. (1997) *Le Opere. La Prima Antologia di Tutti Gli Scritti*, A. Santucci (ed.) (Rome, Editori Riuniti).

Ives, P. (2004) *Language and Hegemony in Gramsci* (London, Pluto Press; Halifax N.S., Fernwood Publishing).

Larrain, J. (1979) *The Concept of Ideology* (London, Hutchinson).

Larrain, J. (1983) *Marxism and Ideology* (Atlantic Highlands, NJ, Humanities Press).

Lawner, L. (ed.) (1973) *Letters from Prison, Antonio Gramsci* (New York, The Noonday Press).

Livingstone, D. W. (1976) On Hegemony in Corporate Capitalist States: Materialist structures, ideological forms, class consciousness and hegemonic acts, *Sociological Inquiry*, 46:3, pp. 235–250.

Livingstone, D. W. (1984) *Class, Ideologies and Educational Futures* (Sussex, The Falmer Press).

Livingstone, D. W. (2002) Working Class Learning, Cultural Transformation, and Democratic Political Education: Gramsci's legacy, in: C. Borg, J. Buttigieg, and P. Mayo (eds), *Gramsci and Education* (Lanham, MD, Rowman & Littlefield).

Mancini, F. (1973) Worker Democracy and Political Party in Gramsci's Thinking. Occasional paper. (Bologna, School of Advanced International Studies, The Johns Hopkins University).

Marx, K. & Engels, F. (1970) *The German Ideology*, C. J. Arthur (ed.) (London, Lawrence and Wishart).

Mayo, P. (1999) *Gramsci, Freire and Adult Education. Possibilities for transformative education* (London, Zed Books).

Mayo, P. (2005) In and Against the State. Gramsci, war of position and adult education, *Journal of Critical Education Policy Studies*, 3:2, available at: http://www.jceps.com/index.php?pageID=article&articleID=49 (accessed 28 January 2006).

Merrington, J. (1977) Theory and Practice in Gramsci's Marxism, in G. S. Jones (ed.), *Western Marxism. A critical reader* (London, Verso).

Salamini, L. (1981) *The Sociology of Political Praxis—An Introduction to Gramsci's Theory* (London, Routledge & Kegan Paul).

Ransome, P. (1992) *Antonio Gramsci, A New Introduction* (London, Harvester/Wheatsheaf).

Rizi, F. F. (2003) *Benedetto Croce and Italian Fascism* (Toronto, University of Toronto Press).

Senese, G. B. (1991) Warnings on Resistance and the Language of Possibility: Gramsci and a pedagogy from the surreal, *Educational Theory*, 41:1, pp. 13–22.

Showstack Sassoon, A. (ed.) (1982) *Approaches to Gramsci* (London, Writers and Readers Publishing Cooperative Society).

Verdicchio, P. (1995) Introduction, in: A. Gramsci, *The Southern Question* (trans. P. Verdicchio) (West Lafayette, IN, Bordighera Inc.).

Williams, R. (1976) Base and Superstructure in Marxist Cultural Theory, in: R. Dale, G. Esland and M. Macdonald (eds), *Schooling and Capitalism* (London, Routledge and Kegan Paul).

3

The Revolutionary Party in Gramsci's Pre-Prison Educational and Political Theory and Practice

JOHN D. HOLST

> It is the proletarian vanguard, which is forming and educating its cadres, adding a further weapon—of theoretical consciousness and revolutionary doctrine—to the battery it is assembling to confront its enemies and the battles that await it. Without this weapon, the Party does not exist. And without the Party, there is no possibility of victory. (A. Gramsci, 1994/ 1925, p. 267)

It was during the summer of 1913 that Antonio Gramsci decided to apply for membership in the Italian Socialist Party, a membership that would be accepted by the end of the same year (Davidson, 1977, p. 63); he was 22 years old. This membership marked the beginning of Gramsci's nearly 24 years of militancy (active membership) in revolutionary parties that would only end with his death on April 27, 1937. Gramsci's militancy in the Italian Socialist Party (PSI) (1913–1921) and the Communist Party of Italy (PCI) (1921–1937) included prolific writing and editorial staff work for several Socialist (*Il Grido del Popolo, Avanti!, La Città Futura, L'Ordine Nuovo*) and Communist papers (*Lo Stato Operaio, L'Unità, L'Ordine Nuovo*); the establishment of party educational initiatives (Club of Moral Life, PSI; School of Culture, PSI; Institute of Proletarian Culture, PSI; correspondence school, PCI); local and national party leadership positions culminating in his position of general secretary of the Communist Party of Italy; representation of the PCI on the executive committee of the Communist International (including extended stays in the Soviet Union (1922–1923) and Vienna (1923–1924); and successful candidacy to the Italian parliament as a member of the PCI. From 1915, when Gramsci definitively ended his university studies, his life was wholly dedicated to party work.

While most of Gramsci's party work listed above, is well known to education scholars of Gramsci, and the educational aspects of his writings have been repeatedly analyzed, what remains a constant in education-based Gramsci studies is the nearly universal minimization (see Kachur, 2002 and Morgan, 2003 for exceptions) of this work for what it was, namely *party* work. For Gramsci, it would have been unthinkable to consider this work outside the framework of a revolutionary party. Yet, for contemporary educational scholars it seems unthinkable to consider Gramsci's work within the framework of a revolutionary party. In the vast majority of the educational scholarship on Gramsci, the fact that Gramsci did this work and would only have done this work inside the framework of a political party is either ignored, marginalized or treated as an historic curiosity of the nature of early 20th century political activism with little relevance for early 21st century political work. In this chapter I will emphasize the party nature of this work for two major reasons. First, I think it is very difficult to fully understand the nature of Gramsci's political and educational work without considering the fact that he felt a revolutionary party was essential. Second, and perhaps, more importantly, I believe that, at least in the context of the United States, the absence of a working class party is becoming increasingly evident. In light of this latter reason, I will conclude the chapter with what I consider to be lessons with continued relevance from Gramsci's theory and practice for the socio-political economic context faced by today's radical educators.

The goals of this chapter, then, are to outline Gramsci's interrelated conceptualization of the roles of the revolutionary party; the nature of education within and by the revolutionary party; and the aims of party education. For considerations of space, I will limit this analysis to Gramsci's pre-prison theory and practice, the period of his active militancy in the PSI and the PCI.

I will, however, in a section toward the end of the chapter, identify what I consider to be important points of continuity on education and the party between Gramsci's pre-prison work and his prison writings.

Key Elements of the Nature of Revolutionary Parties

Before entering into a discussion of specific roles Gramsci assigned to the party, it may be helpful to outline some of the key elements that Gramsci saw as defining the nature of a revolutionary party, the very elements that, in fact, made it revolutionary. First, a party is defined by class. For Gramsci (1994), the Socialist Party was 'the party of the working class ... bound by millions and millions of links to the Italian working population' (1920,[1] pp. 147–148). These bonds need to be strong enough so that the party becomes 'the expression of the interests of the proletarian class' (1977/1920, p. 167). In the final phase of his pre-prison years, Gramsci would enter into a sharp polemic with Amadeo Bordiga, precisely over the class nature of the Communist Party of Italy and its relationship to the working class. The minutes of the Central Committee's Political Commission in charge of preparing the documents for the party's 1926 Congress in Lyons report the following statement attributed to Gramsci (1978):

> We consider that in defining the party, it is necessary today to underline the fact that it is a 'part' of the working class, while the far left [Bordiga] ignores and undervalues this side of the definition of the party, giving fundamental importance instead to the idea that the party is an 'organ' of the working class. (p. 314)

The polemic with Bordiga would also reveal Gramsci's conviction that 'the proletariat must be guaranteed a leading function within the party itself' (p. 363). This would result in and from the party being organically of the working class and also would mean the party would need to rely on the capacities of the working class; capacities developed by the educational work of the party.

Second, Gramsci (1994) believed that a revolutionary party must 'immerse itself in the reality of the class struggle, as it is waged by the industrial and agricultural proletariat' (1920, p. 157). Therefore, the work of the party would be 'based on the necessities of their life and on the needs of their culture' (Gramsci, 2000/1919, p. 117). Although it was necessary for a revolutionary party to be solidly of and based in the working class and the peasantry and to work from their necessities of life and culture, this work must not merely follow along with wherever these struggles may spontaneously go. The party had a responsibility to provide leadership and guidance to these struggles and to perform these responsibilities pedagogically.

> This struggle must be waged in such a way as to show the great mass of the population that all the existential problems of the present historical period—the problems of bread, housing, light, clothes—can be resolved only when all economic power, and hence all political power, has passed into the hands of the working class. (1978/1921, p. 11)

This is the profoundly educational role of the party of which I will speak more below.

Third, a revolutionary party must be internationalist; it must understand that its regional and national struggles are a part of the movement of workers and peasants and all oppressed peoples around the world. The split from the Socialist Party and the formation of the Communist Party of Italy, was in no small part, a reflection of Gramsci's, along with others, conviction of the need to be the Italian party of the Third International of communist parties. The International was not, however, merely a coalition of parties, but represented the objectively revolutionary stage that the world was passing through of which the Russian Revolution was the greatest manifestation. This stage was marked by the formation of organizations (soviets/councils) of a new type. The soviets or councils, unlike revolutionary parties, were organs of political and economic power, the form that the dictatorship of the proletariat was taking in this period. Revolutionary parties, as we shall see below, had the roles of organizing, leading, educating and uniting the struggles of the popular classes, they were not organizations that would become the workers' state.

> To belong to the Communist International, therefore, is to link one's own institutions organically to the Russian and Hungarian proletarian states. The Communist International is not a bureaucratic headquarters of 'leaders' of the masses; it is a mass historical consciousness, objectified in a vast and complex general movement of the international proletariat. Hence it must consist of a network of proletarian organizations ... and these can be neither the socialist parties nor the craft federations.

> These institutions will carry on fulfilling their mission of educating and co-ordinating the various aspects of proletarian activity, but at this point they can no longer cope with the task of disciplining and leading the whole movement. (Gramsci, 1977/1919, pp. 80–82)

Gramsci's Conceptualization of the Roles of the Revolutionary Party

Phases of Gramsci's Pre-Prison Thinking on the Roles of the Party

During Gramsci's politically active, pre-prison years his thinking on the roles of the party can be divided into three phases based on his own experience and the broader situation of the revolutionary movement in Turin, in Italy and internationally. During Gramsci's early years in the Socialist Party up to the point at which reliable and extensive news of the historical significance of the Russian (Soviet) Revolution reaches Italian revolutionaries, there is very little originality in Gramsci's thinking and writing on the Party. During this phase, from roughly 1914 to the end of 1917, Gramsci (1994) identifies the Socialist Party, the Confederation of Labor and cultural or educational associations of the Party as the key organizations of revolution, yet he does not provide a fully elaborated theory of the relationship between these institutions.

> Given the nature of the environment in Turin ... , it is here that the first nucleus could emerge ... of a cultural organization with a distinct socialist and proletarian identity, which would become, along with the Party and the Confederazione del Lavoro, the third organ in the Italian working class's drive to assert its rights. (1917, p. 38)

If anything, in this early phase, Gramsci (1994) places heavy emphasis on the Party as the essential instrument of revolution. In his first published article, for example, he basically equates the party with an embryonic workers' state; while mentioning other 'organs,' he is vague as to what these might be.

> The Party is a State *in potential* ... which is seeking, through its daily struggle with this enemy, and through the development of its own internal dialectic, to create the organs it needs to overcome and absorb its opponent. (1914, p. 4)

With specific news of the Soviets in Russia and the growing movement among the industrial proletariat in Turin, Gramsci enters into a very active period of direct contact with militant workers in the Turin Factories and he begins to confront the role of the party as an instrument of revolution. It is in this second phase, from roughly 1918 to late 1920, when Gramsci develops his theory and program of the Factory Councils as the Italian manifestation of Soviets. As alluded to above, Gramsci (1994), like the Third International, regarded the emergence of Soviets or Councils as a world historical event, marking a new era in the history of humanity.

> We say that the present period is revolutionary because the working class is beginning to exert all its strength and will to found its own State. This is why we say that the birth of the Factory Councils is a major historical event—the beginning of a new era in the history of the human race. (1994/1920, p. 165)

While in the earlier phase, Gramsci wrote of the Party as a state *in potential*, in this second phase, Gramsci (1977) clearly identifies the Factory (and peasant) Councils and their organization and coordination on regional, national and international levels as the organs of popular state power.

> The proletarian dictatorship can only be embodied in a type of organization that is specific to the activity of producers, not wage-earners, the slaves of capital. The factory Council is the nucleus of this organization ... . The Council is a class, a social institution ... . Hence the Council realizes in practice the unity of the working class ... . The Factory Council is the model of the proletarian State. (1977/1919, p. 100)

In this second phase, Gramsci identifies the Councils, the trade unions and the Party as the three key organizations of revolution.

> This, then, is the network of institutions in which the revolutionary process is unfolding: the Councils, the trade unions, the Socialist Party. The Councils, historical products of society, brought into being by the need to master the apparatus of production; products born of the newly achieved self-awareness of the producers. The trade unions and the Party, voluntary associations, driving forces of the revolutionary process, the 'agents' and 'administrators' of the revolution. (1977, p. 146)

Gramsci (1994) is emphatic at this point that the Party is not a state *in potential* but an instrument that educates, coordinates, leads and guides the popular movement toward the realization of the dictatorship of the proletariat through the full formation and coordination of urban and rural Councils.

> The Socialist party and the trade unions ... will not be immediately identifiable with the proletarian State ... . The Party must continue in its role as the organ of communist education, the furnace of faith, the depository of doctrine, the supreme power harmonizing the organized and disciplined forces of the worker and peasant classes, and leading them towards their goal (1994/1919, p. 97)

Moreover, Gramsci (1977) identifies the error of equating the Party apparatus with the form of the revolutionary process as a major cause of the defeat of the German revolutionary upsurge of the period.

> The proletariat's organs of struggle are the 'agents' of this colossal mass movement, and the Socialist Party is undoubtedly the primary 'agent' in this process of destruction and neo-formation—but it is not and cannot be seen as the form of the process, a form malleable and plastic to the leaders' will. German Social-Democracy ... effected the paradox of violently forcing the process of the German proletarian revolution into the form of its own organization, believing it was thereby dominating history ... . It shackled and domesticated the revolution. (1977/1919, p. 143)

With the September 1920 defeat of the factory occupations following on the heels of the defeat of the April general strike in Turin, Gramsci's writings increasingly place blame for these defeats on the reformism within the PSI, the PSI's failure to provide revolutionary leadership within the working-class and peasant organizations, and the PSI's failure to theoretically understand, and, therefore transmit, the historic significance of the period of which the Factory Councils were the highest expression.

In what we can call this, the third phase of Gramsci's theorization of the role of the party, Gramsci, along with others, steps up the fight for the formation of an Italian communist party aligned with the Third International. Based on what he had identified as the errors and shortcomings of the PSI, a major concern for Gramsci in the Communist Party of Italy will be cadre formation. With the strategies of the Councils and later cells and worker and peasant committees—that rely heavily on the capacity of working-class and peasant militants at the base—Gramsci argues that the party must have a strong educational program for theoretical and ideological development of its members in order to prevent the repetition of the types of defeats the revolutionary movement suffered in the 1919–1920 period. So, while in what I am identifying as the third phase of Gramsci's thinking on the party he does not give up on the idea of organs of state power beyond the party, he does emphasize a stronger leadership role for the party in pushing forward the revolutionary process through its members organically based in the myriad of working-class and peasant organizations.

The Organizing and Leadership Role of the Party

For Gramsci the political party had a responsibility to play a key role in building the organizations that arose from the spontaneous struggles of the working class and peasantry. This organizational role, however, also had a guiding and leadership element to it; party members were not to merely tag along with any and all ideas that sprang up from the spontaneity of the day-to-day struggles of the popular classes. Party members, as activists in the organizations of workers and peasants were to 'transform the rebellious impulses sparked off by the conditions that capitalism has created for the working class into a revolutionary consciousness and creativity' (Gramsci, 2000/1920, p. 96). As the 'political organization of the conscious avant-garde of the proletariat,' the party 'has the historical task of organizing the class of impoverished workers and peasants into a ruling class' (Gramsci, 1977/1920, p. 154). In other words, the party, if it is truly a revolutionary party, is made up of the most conscious and prepared elements of the popular classes, and, therefore, is not only prepared to lead but carries a responsibility to lead. This leadership and organizing role and the very party members who carry it out, however, have to be rooted in the day-to-day realities of the popular classes. The party does not stand apart from the popular classes; it is an actual reflection of the best elements of them. Gramsci (1977) described this delicate act of leading and organizing from within when explaining the success of the original *L'Ordine Nuovo* program of the Factory Councils.

> The workers loved *L'Ordine Nuovo* ... [b]ecause in its articles they rediscovered a part, the best part, of themselves. Because they felt its articles were pervaded by that same spirit of inner searching that they experienced ... . Because its articles were not cold, intellectual structures, but sprang from our discussions with the best workers; they ... were virtually a 'taking note' of actual events, seen as moments of a process of inner liberation and self-expression on the part of the working class. (1920, pp. 293–294)

In this period of the Factory Council movement Gramsci, (1977) argued that the immediate organizing tasks of the Socialist Party were:

> ... to promote the development of proletarian factory institutions wherever they exist and to set them up where they have not yet emerged. To co-ordinate them locally and nationally. To make contact with similar institutions in France and England. And finally ... to generate teeming communist forces who ... will defend the [then existing Soviet] Republics in the first instance and, in subsequent stages of the general process of development of revolutionary consciousness and power, will bring into being the International of Communist Republics. (1977/1919, p. 82)

Gramsci (1978) would carry these ideas through to the Communist Party of Italy's 1926 Lyons Theses.

> The party leads the class by penetrating into all the organizations in which the working masses are assembled; and by carrying out, in and through these, a systematic mobilization of energies in line with the programme of the class struggle. (p. 368)

The Unifying Role of the Party

A fundamental aspect of the organizing and leadership role of the party is to build unity among all the social sectors/classes facing exploitation under capitalism. The primary classes in this unity are the industrial proletariat and the peasantry, but the party must work to build unity even beyond these two classes.

> The Socialist Party ought to embody the vigilant revolutionary consciousness of the entire exploited class. Its task is to draw the attention of all the masses to itself, to ensure that its directives become their directives and to win their permanent trust, so that it may become their guide and intellect. (Gramsci, 1994/1920, p. 157)

Gramsci (1994), like Marxists of the time, believed that it was the industrial proletariat that had demands for which the resolution would entail a revolutionary solution to the crisis of capitalism. Therefore, the unifying role of the party must consist in a unity around the demands and leadership of the industrial proletariat in the revolutionary process.

> By becoming the trusted 'democratic' party of all the oppressed classes, by keeping in contact with all sections of the working people, the Communist Party can lead all sections of the populace to acknowledge the communist proletariat as the ruling class which must take over State power from the capitalist class. (1994/1920, p. 171)

It is important to point out that Gramsci's original conceptualization of hegemony is tied to the unifying role of the party under discussion here and that this conceptualization is fully elaborated in his pre-prison writings. This may come as a surprise since so much of the scholarship on Gramsci's ideas of hegemony focus on his writings in the *Prison Notebooks* and tend to emphasize ideological imposition of ruling classes on oppressed classes. Yet, when we consider the fact that he adopted the term hegemony from the publications of the Third International available to him before his imprisonment (Bellamy, as cited in Gramsci, 1994, p. xxvii), it is not surprising then to see Gramsci articulating a concept of hegemony, and more specifically proletarian hegemony, as a part of the unifying role of the revolutionary party. So, for example, in 1925 Gramsci (1978) says there are two fundamental problems that arise in an analysis of the current situation:

> What real political activity our party should continue to carry out, in order to bring about a coalition of all the anti-capitalist forces led by the (revolutionary) proletariat in the given situation ... . In other words, we must examine what the essential problems of Italian life are; and which solution to them will encourage and bring about the revolutionary alliance of the proletariat with the peasants, and accomplish the hegemony of the proletariat. (p. 305)

In his final writing before arrest, his notes on the Southern Question, Gramsci (1978) refers to the work of the Turin section of the Socialist Party in the period of the Factory Councils (1919–1920) as precisely working toward unity and the hegemony of the proletariat.

> The Turin communists posed concretely the question of the 'hegemony of the proletariat': i.e. of the social basis of the proletarian dictatorship and of the workers' State. The proletariat can become the leading [*dirigente*] and the dominant class to the extent that it succeeds in creating a system of class alliances which allows it to mobilize the majority of the working population against capitalism and the bourgeois State. (1978/1926, p. 443)

The Parliamentarian Role of the Party

Gramsci, unlike others in the SPI and CPI, argued that it was important for the party to engage in electoral and parliamentarian politics. Gramsci had three very specific reasons for arguing this role. His first two reasons were stances held within the Marxist tradition dating back to at least Engels. Marxists generally have argued that engagement in the electoral process is both a forum for propaganda or educational work on issues of the day and a way through vote tallies to gauge a party's support and its enemies' support among various classes and regions of a nation. The third reason, particular to periods of revolutionary upsurge, was that party members elected to parliament could act to paralyze the parliamentary process itself. It should be understood that Gramsci's revolutionary stance took him to a complete rejection of bourgeois forms of democracy in all its manifestation, including parliaments and electoral politics. For Gramsci (1977), the parliament, as an instrument of the bourgeois state must be exposed as an instrument of the brutal rule of the bourgeoisie, and done away with through revolution.

> Using its own means and systems, the revolutionary vanguard needs to bring into being the material and moral conditions that will prevent the propertied class from peacefully governing the broad masses; conditions that will force it, through the intransigence of the socialist [parliamentary] deputies under Party discipline and control, to terrorize the broad masses, strike them blindly and so make them rise up in arms. Such a goal can only be pursued today through parliamentary action, understood in the sense of action which immobilizes Parliament, strips the democratic mask away from the ambivalent face of the bourgeois dictatorship and reveals it in all its horrible and repugnant ugliness. (1977/1919, pp. 127–128)

Moreover, Gramsci saw the paralyzing of the parliamentary apparatus in the political sphere combined with the paralyzing of the extraction of surplus value in the economic sphere by the growing power of workers' organizations as a two-pronged assault on the major forms and spheres of bourgeois power.

> The Italian class of producers ... has succeeded in marshalling a concentration of forces which has put an end to the utility of parliament as the basis of State power and as the constitutional form of political government. The class of the exploited in Italy has thus struck a crippling blow at the political apparatus of capitalist supremacy ... . The corporative movement ... has ... paralyzed the capitalist labor market ... . The capitalist order of production has been rocked to its foundations by these achievements ... . The economic foundations of capitalist organization, which reaches its apex in the bureaucratic-parliamentary State, have been destroyed, through the sabotage of the primary source of capitalist power: the freedom to extract surplus value. (1977/1919, pp. 130–131)

The Educational Role of the Party

I will now turn to a discussion of what I have already referred to in passing as the educational role of the party and continue in subsequent sections to outline in more detail the nature of this education and the aims of this education.

As is widely known, Gramsci (1994) placed a great amount of importance on the role of education in the struggle for socialism and the educational role of the party in that struggle. 'The concrete task of building the future cannot be undertaken without a collective, collaborative effort of explanation, persuasion and mutual education' (1919, p. 96). What we would now call nonformal education was, in fact, his first and most sustained party work. As Williams (1975) details, Gramsci 'was an instant success at small-group teaching at the FGS [Socialist Youth Federation] centre. The night streets were loud with argument as he and his class talked their way home' (p. 49). Moreover, the whole pre-prison 'literary legacy' Gramsci left us, is actually a collection of his propaganda/educational work with the Socialist and Communist press. For Gramsci there were three primary forms of education that the party needed to perform. First, the party needed nonformal educational institutions examples of which I listed above in the introduction. These institutions' role was the ideological formation of cadre.

This formation would allow them to be better prepared to carry out the party's roles of leading and guiding the day-to-day struggles of the working class and peasantry.

> The correspondence course must become the first phase of a movement to create small party schools, designed to create organizers and propagandists who are Bolsheviks and not maximalists: who in other words have brains as well as lungs and a throat ... . The older and more skilled elements should be the instructors in these schools ... . Certainly, it is not with these pedagogic methods that the great historical problem of the spiritual emancipation of the working class can be resolved. But it is not some utopian resolution of this problem which we are aiming to achieve ... . Our task is to improve our cadres; to make them capable of confronting the forthcoming struggles. (Gramsci, 1978/1924, p. 227)

The second educational role of the party was a variation on Foley's (1999) 'learning in struggle' that, due to its more directive nature, we could call 'education in struggle'. In other words, it was incumbent upon party cadre to be immersed in the organizations and struggles of the popular classes and to take advantage of every opportunity to act pedagogically in raising people's awareness of the larger socio-political economic issues and forces at play and the paths that lead to the successful resolution of the struggles with which the classes were engaged.

> The office of the Communist Party ... is that of acting on the great masses as a psychological catalyst, to lead them into realizing in reality—consciously, through an act of will—the new relations that the new conditions have made possible. (Gramsci, 1994/1920, p. 177)

The third educational role of the party is more of a combination of the first two in that Gramsci saw it as a responsibility of the party to create materials—we can include the press in this context—that members at the base could use in their day-to-day work in the organizations and struggles of the popular classes. So, for example, in a 1924 letter to leadership in the PCI, Gramsci (1978) says,

> ... an agitation and propaganda committee should collect all such local and national material as is necessary and useful for the party's agitational and propaganda activity. It should study local situations, propose forms of agitation, and compose leaflets and programs to orient the work of the local bodies. (p. 201)

Lastly, Gramsci (1985) was also acutely aware of the informal education that took place among the popular classes that could be out of the immediate reach of the party.

> The proletariat is less complicated than might appear. They have spontaneously formed an intellectual and cultural hierarchy, and reciprocal education is at work where the activity of the writers and propagandists cannot penetrate. In workers' circles and leagues, in conversations outside the factory, the word of socialist criticism is dissected, propagated, made ductile and malleable for every mind and every culture. In a complex and varied environment like that of a major industrial city the organs of capillary transmission of opinion,

which the will of the leaders would never succeed in creating and setting up, arise spontaneously. (1985/1918, pp. 33–34)

This informal education could, however, also come as a result of the organizational work of the party in taking a leading role in the formation of such working class-led institutions as the Factory Councils. Gramsci, in fact, realized that since these organizations were of and led by the working class (including party members), they would also be the engines of the most profound and rapid education of the workers. In analyzing the significance of what came to be called Red Sunday during the height of the factory occupations in September of 1920, Gramsci (1994) commented that 'one day like this has to be worth ten years ... of normal propaganda, of absorbing revolutionary notions and ideas at the normal rate' (p. 198).

The Nature of Party Education

Since the nature of party education is related to the nature of the party itself and since each role of the party has educational aspects, Gramsci's concept of the nature of party education may already be evident. It should suffice, therefore, to briefly summarize three aspects of the nature of party education.

The Class Nature of Party Education

Like the party, the educational work of the party is defined by class. Gramsci (1994) understood this fact from very early on in his membership in the PSI. 'The kind of Cultural Association which the socialists should promote must be one whose scope and aims are defined by class. It must be an institution of the proletariat, directed to precise ends' (1917, p. 36).

Education Linked to the Needs of the Popular Classes in Struggle

The idea that the educational work of the party should be based on 'precise ends,' and ends directly related to the actual struggles of workers and peasants is carried through the entirety of Gramsci's pre-prison period and encompasses nonformal education and what I am calling education in struggle. In fact, Gramsci's well-known criticism of the non-party educational initiatives of the Popular Universities had to do with their lack of any real connection to the struggles of the popular classes. This criticism, however, Gramsci (1994) extended to the failed nonformal educational initiatives of the working class parties themselves. He argued that the 'fundamental reason for these failures is the absence of any link between the "schools" ... and an actual, objective movement' (1925, p. 266). For Gramsci (1994), the nature of this nonformal education cannot be abstract, divorced from the precise needs and goals of the struggles taking place.

> Neither 'objective study' nor 'disinterested culture' can have any place in our ranks ... . We are a militant organization, and, in our ranks, the aim of studying is to enhance and refine the capacities for struggle of both individuals

and the organization as a whole ... . Education and culture are, for us, no more than a theoretical consciousness of our immediate and long-term ends and the manner in which we can best succeed in translating them into practice. (1994/1925, p. 266)

Gramsci also understood that education based on the needs of the popular classes in motion had an unsurpassed richness to it. This became acutely evident during the height of the Factory Council movement.

> [With the factory councils] the communists organized in the Party and the local committees would be presented with a vast arena for concrete pro-paganda ... . A system of worker democracy ... (integrated with equivalent peasant organizations) ... would be a magnificent education in politics and administration, and it would involve the masses, down to the last man, schooling them in determination and perseverance ... . Through workshop meetings and ceaseless work of propaganda and persuasion on the part of the most politically aware elements, it would be possible to bring about a radical transformation in worker psychology. The masses would become better prepared and equipped for the exercise of power. An awareness would develop of the duties and rights of comrades and workers—an awareness which would be all the more concerted and effective because it would have been generated from living, historical experience. (pp. 98–99)

The Collective Nature of Party Education

Collectivity for Gramsci must be both in the nature of party education and a result of it. In an early 1918 article on his work in the Socialist Club of Moral Life he describes the specific methodology he employed in leading discussions on readings and the results of this methodology.

> In this way, a discussion opens up, which ideally continues until *all* those present have been enabled to understand and absorb the most important results of this collective work ... . We want to create a reciprocal bond of trust: an intellectual and moral communion, uniting us all. (1994, p. 52)

More broadly, Gramsci (1994) believed that collectivity marked and resulted from communist practice which he described as a 'collective, friendly debate, which modifies people's consciousness, uniting them and filling them with an overwhelming enthusiasm for action' (1919, p. 99).

The Aims of Party Education

As we have seen, Gramsci believed that party education was not an abstract exercise; it had to be oriented to specific aims. These aims, due to the dialectical nature of Gramsci's theory and practice are, related to both the nature of education and the nature of the party. In this section, I will outline what I see as the four most important aims Gramsci assigned to party education.

Linking Individuals with Collectives

Gramsci (1977) believed that the party 'must educate individuals to forge permanent and organic links of solidarity with each other (1918, p. 57). This included the idea that individuals must come to the "conviction that the only feasible road to individual and social well-being is via political and economic organization" ' (pp. 57–58). Moreover, with the formation of the Third International, Gramsci (1994) extended this idea to encompass an internationalist perspective by insisting upon a 'comprehensive educational program designed to make the Italian working people aware of the truth that the proletarian revolution is a world phenomenon and that each individual event must be considered and judged within a world context' (1920, p. 159).

Leadership Development and the Exercise of Power

Since Gramsci assigned a leadership role for the party in the spontaneous struggles of the popular classes, it follows that he believed an aim of party education must be the development of leadership capacity among its members. In historical terms, Gramsci (1994) saw the emergence of the Communist Parties in the wake of the Russian Revolution as marking the period in which the working class was in ascendance as a class.

> The Communist Party is the instrument and the historical form of the process of inner liberation through which the worker is transformed from *executor* to *initiator*; from *mass* to *leader* and *guide*, from pure brawn to a brain and a will. (1994/1920, p. 191)

More concretely, the party had to perform specific educational tasks in order for the working class to realize its historical potential.

> Workers enter the Communist Party not only in their capacity as workers … . They enter it as *Communist* workers—as political activists, that is, as theorists of socialism, not simply as generic rebels. And, in the Party, through its discussions, thorough its readings and through the Party schools, they develop continually and become leaders. (1994/1925 p. 271)

The historic potential of working class leadership was not confined to merely leading working class organizations. Gramsci believed that humanity was entering into one of those rare periods in its history when a new class was ascending with the potential to fundamentally transform society. When Gramsci (1994) spoke of leadership, then, he also referred to leadership of whole societies, and, therefore, an aim of party education had to be training the working class to be a ruling class of a new type, in a state of a new type.

> Human society is undergoing an extremely rapid process of decomposition, corresponding to the process of the dissolution of the bourgeois State … . It becomes necessary to form a rock-solid socialist State … . We must re-educate the proletariat … . This means training the proletariat in the practice of dictatorship, in self-government. (1994/1919, p. 105)

Guiding the Popular Classes along the Line of March of the Revolutionary Process

As a Marxist, Gramsci understood that revolutions were not coups or the spouting of militant rhetoric but, rather, historical processes with qualitative economic, social, cultural and ultimately political transformations of societies. This historical process as defined by Marx and Engels (1848/1948, p. 22), is translated into English as the 'line of march' of the revolution. Two interrelated aims of party education follow from this understanding of revolution. First, the party as a whole must be able to understand and anticipate the line of march of the revolution and, then, educate its members in understanding the line of march. Second, party educational work in the broader movements should orient these movements along the line of march.

> We must strive to promote the organic creation of a communist party that will not be a collection of dogmatists or would-be-Machiavellis, but a party of revolutionary communist action, a party with a precise awareness of the historical mission of the proletariat and capable of guiding the proletariat towards the accomplishment of this mission. (Gramsci, 1994/1920, p. 172)

Building the Political Independence of the Working Class

If the historic mission of the working class was the revolutionary transformation of capitalist society, this could only be accomplished if the working class broke with bourgeois hegemony and asserted its independence as a class capable of assuming the leadership of a new society. Party education within the popular movements had the aim of breaking 'the bond of apparent legality which still unites the majority of the population within the form of bourgeois institutions' (Gramsci, 1977/1919, p. 138). Gramsci (1978) saw the formation of the PCI as a great step in this direction for the working class.

> With the creation of the Communist Party, the working class has broken all its traditions and asserted its political maturity. The working class no longer wishes to collaborate with other classes in the development or transformation of the bureaucratic parliamentary State. It wishes to work positively for its own autonomous development as a class. (1978/1921, p. 33)

Continuity of Ideas in the *Prison Notebooks*

Gramsci was arrested on November 8, 1926. Due to the conditions of his imprisonment, he is cut-off from direct political work and from exercising any leadership in the Italian Communist Party. His prison writings, therefore, lose the sense of immediacy and organic link with the revolutionary movement that so characterize his pre-prison writings. This situation leads Hoare and Smith (1971) to argue that 'Gramsci's writings in prison ... . have an organic continuity with the political universe within which Gramsci had operated prior to his arrest; they manifest a radical disjuncture from the political universe which existed by the time that they were written' (p. lxviii). We can, therefore, identify themes related to the party and education that Gramsci carries forward into the *Prison Notebooks*. In referring to the continuity of themes and issues in Gramsci's journalistic work and the note-books, Buttigieg (1992) says his 'early writings ... constitute, as it were, the pre-history of the prison notebooks' (p. 17).

In the *Prison Notebooks* Gramsci (1971) continues to argue that parties are prin-cipally class organizations. 'Classes produce parties, and parties form ... the leaders of civil and political society ... . There cannot be any formation of leaders without the theoretical, doctrinal activity of parties' (p. 227). Moreover, he continues to argue that it is through party organization that the class leadership can be organically embedded in the movement of the popular classes, and, thereby, play its educational role in the formation of the class as a collective, as a 'class-for-itself'.

> With the extension of mass parties and their organic coalescence with the intimate (economic-productive) life of the masses themselves, the process whereby popular feeling is standardized ceases to be mechanical and casual ... and becomes conscious and critical. Knowledge and a judgment of the importance of this feeling on the part of the leaders is no longer the product of hunches ... . Rather it is acquired by the collective organism through 'active and conscious co-participation', through 'compassionality', through experience of immediate particulars, through a system which one could call 'living philology'. In this way a close link is formed between great mass, party and leading group, and the whole complex, thus articulated can move together as 'collective-man'. (p. 429)

In reflecting upon his work in Turin around the Factory Councils, we see the continuation of Gramsci's earlier ideas on the importance and limitations of the spontaneous movement of the popular classes and the importance and limitations of leadership and how the limitations of both are overcome when, between the two, there is a real, living, dialectical and pedagogical relationship. In addition, these reflections also reveal how Gramsci continued to view the winning of state power as the aim of the party's educational and leadership development work.

> The leadership was not 'abstract'; it ... . applied itself to real men, formed in specific historical relations, with specific feelings, outlooks, fragmentary conceptions of the world, etc., which were the result of 'spontaneous' combinations of a given situation of material production with the 'fortuitous' agglomeration within it of disparate social elements. This element of 'spontaneity' was not neglected and even less despised. It was *educated*, directed, purged of extraneous contaminations; the aim was to bring it into line with modern theory—but in a living and historically effective manner ... . It gave the masses a 'theoretical' consciousness of being creators of *historical* and institutional *values*, of being founders of a State. This unity between 'spontaneity' and 'conscious leadership' or 'discipline' is precisely the real political action of the subaltern classes. (p. 198)

Conclusion

It is one thing for academics to try to accurately reflect the meaning Gramsci attached to specific terminology or to try to reconstruct a Gramscian pedagogy. It is all together different, however, to consider what remains of relevance of a political praxis rooted in Italy between the two World Wars of last century for contemporary radical adult education practice. As a way of conclusion, I would like to outline what I consider to be some of the most important lessons we can draw from Gramsci's pre-prison writings for a radical adult education practice today. I will limit my considerations to the specific context of the United States of America.

Political Independence of the Working Class

I should clarify that by working class, I am not referring to an early 20th Century, industrial-based definition of the working class. While it is beyond the scope of this chapter, readers are referred to the work of Zweig (2000) in considering the contemporary make up of the working class in the United States, which constitutes over 60% of the nation's population. The working class must achieve political independence. In the U.S., this will need to be manifested in the formation of a multiracial, multiregional working class political party. This party will initially not be of an openly revolutionary character as in Gramsci's period, but will need to be a party that clearly identifies a working class in the U.S. as the majority class with distinct interests from the class in power. For the working class to become in Gramsci's (2000) words, 'distinct and individuated' (1918, p. 38), it will need to proceed from a complete break from the Democratic Party. In addition, a party of this nature will need to articulate the demands of the so-called new social movements from a working class perspective. In other words, it will need to reflect the interests and demands of the working class as it actually is: majority female and disproportionately formed by people of color.

Understanding the Line of March

It is essential that a party be able to understand and anticipate the line of march of socio-political economic change and also be able to teach this capacity for understanding and anticipating the line of march. As Gramsci (2000) explained, 'political genius can be recognized precisely by this capacity to master the greatest possible number of concrete conditions necessary and sufficient to determine a process of development' (1919, p. 86). This is a fundamental aspect of leadership at the individual and organizational level, without which a person or organization must merely tag along with rather than guide political action.

Understanding Revolutions as Historical Processes

Related to the idea of the line of march, is Gramsci's (1994) understanding of revolution itself.

> The proletarian revolution is not the arbitrary act of an organization that declares itself to be revolutionary, or of a system of organizations that declare themselves to be revolutionary. The proletarian revolution is an extremely long-term historical process that manifests itself in the emergence and development of certain production forces ... within a certain historical context ... . At a certain point in this process, the new productive forces are no longer able to develop or organize themselves in an autonomous fashion within the official framework of the human community of the time. It is in this phase that the revolutionary act occurs. This consists in a violent effort to smash apart this existing framework and to destroy the entire apparatus of economic and political power within which the revolutionary productive forces had been trapped ... and to construct a new kind of State within whose framework the newly liberated productive forces can develop and expand. (p. 163)

Given this analysis of the revolutionary process, I believe it is essential for radical adult educators today to consider whether the new microchip-based technologies represent productive forces that are attacking the social relations of production based on the industrial-epoch in qualitatively destructive ways and, therefore, marking the beginnings of an era with the potential for revolutionary change. On a global scale, and the United States is in no way an exception to this process, we are witnessing a growing polarization of wealth and poverty as more and more people are faced with less and less stable work or no work at all. There is a growing sector of the working class that is finding itself increasingly on the margins of the labor market, or basically permanently locked out of this labor market. Are we, therefore, witnessing the growth of a potentially revolutionary sector of society outside the 'official framework' (labor exchanged for wages) of the industrial era? Is this growing sector of the homeless, permanently unemployed and marginally employed a potentially revolutionary class? A class for which, as Gramsci (2000) said, 'communism [distribution based on need and not ability to pay] is a vital necessity' (p. 116)?

Understanding One's Place in History

The polarization and accompanying institutional crises brought on by major socio-political economic change impacts the apparatuses of the left as well. Any analysis of the line of march must attempt to understand the nature of the particular epoch one is working in, the prospects for change, the nature of that change and the likely agents of that change. In today's climate, I believe it is essential that radical adult educators confront the fact that the traditional organizations of social change such as trade unions are in serious crisis. Is this another indicator of epochal change? In the United States, working people, as the labor movement is increasingly moribund, are seeking new forms of organization outside of the trade unions, in workers' centers, poor people's movements, and non-collective bargaining-based organizations such as the Coalition of Immokalee Workers. In Latin America, the landless, the homeless and the unemployed, are organizing outside the traditional left organizations as well. We can learn from Gramsci's willingness to see the emergence of the internal commissions in the factories as embryonic forms of organizations that had revolutionary potential. Are the new forms of organization emerging among the working class and marginalized sectors of society today potentially revolutionary or at least pointing to fundamental socio-political economic changes? While the particular conjuncture of Gramsci's (1977) praxis is no longer our own, his method of analysis is still very relevant.

> The period of history we are passing through is a revolutionary period because the traditional institutions for the government of human masses, institutions which were linked to old modes of production and exchange, have lost any significance and useful function they might have had ... . But it is not only bourgeois class institutions which have collapsed and fallen apart: working-class institutions too, which emerged while capitalism was developing and were formed as the response of the working class to this development, have entered a period of crisis and can no longer successfully control the masses. (1920, p. 175)

Working with and from the People

We need theory to understand the questions I pose above regarding the socio-political economic epoch through which we are moving and the prospects for change in this period. As much as we need theory, however, radical adult education must also be based in the spontaneous struggles of working-class people around their real needs and interests. The best indicator of the line of march, as Gramsci (1977) argued, are people themselves.

> The masses of workers and peasants are the only genuine and authentic expression of the historical development of capital. By the spontaneous and uncontrollable movements which spread throughout their ranks and by relative shifts in the position of strata ... , the masses indicate the precise direction of historical development, reveal changes in attitudes and forms, and proclaim the decomposition and imminent collapse of the capitalist organization of society ... . If one becomes estranged from the inner life of the working class, then one becomes estranged from the historical process that is unfolding implacably, in defiance of any individual will or traditional institution. (1977/1920, pp. 173–174)

For Gramsci, radical praxis of an authentically educational nature does not consist of preaching a dogma, but rather, working in a dialogical, pedagogical, and directive way with the real needs of those most negatively impacted by unfolding socio-political economic changes; those for whom a new social order is a vital necessity.

Note

1. In addition to citing the year of publication of the source, I will place the year of original publication of quotations in the parenthetical reference at the end of each reference.

References

Buttigieg, J. A. (1992) Introduction, in: A. Gramsci, *Prison notebooks, Vol. 1*, J. A. Buttigieg, ed.; J. A. Buttigieg & A. Callari, trans. (New York, Columbia University Press).

Davidson, A. (1977) *Antonio Gramsci* (London, Merlin).

Foley, G. (1999) *Learning in Social Action* (London, Zed Books).

Gramsci, A. (1971) *Selections from the Prison Notebooks*, Q. Hoare & G. Nowell-Smith, eds & trans. (New York, International Publishers).

Gramsci, A. (1977) *Selections from Political Writings, 1910–1920*, Q. Hoare, ed.; J. Mathews, trans. (London, Lawrence and Wishart).

Gramsci, A. (1978) *Selections from Political Writings, 1921–1926*, Q. Hoare, ed. and trans. (Minneapolis, MN, University of Minnesota Press).

Gramsci, A. (1985) *Selections from Cultural Writings*, D. Forgacs and G. Nowell-Smith, eds; W. Boelhower, trans. (Cambridge, MA, Harvard University Press).

Gramsci, A. (1994) *Pre-Prison Writings*, R. Bellamy, ed.; V. Cox, trans. (New York, Cambridge University Press).

Gramsci, A. (2000) *The Antonio Gramsci Reader*, D. Forgacs, ed. (New York, New York University Press).

Hoare, Q. & Smith, G. N. (1971) Introduction, in: A. Gramsci, *Selections from the Prison Notebooks*, Q. Hoare & G. N. Smith, eds & trans. (New York, International).

Kachur, J. L. (2002) The Postmodern Prince: Gramsci and anonymous intellectual practice, in: C. Borg, J. Buttigieg & P. Mayo (eds), *Gramsci and Education* (Lanham, MD, Rowman & Littlefield), pp. 307–330.

Marx, K. & Engels, F. (1948) *The Manifesto of the Communist Party*, S. Moore, trans. (New York, International) (Original work published 1848).

Morgan, W. J. (2003) *Communists on Education and Culture, 1848–1948* (New York, Palgrave).

Williams, G. A. (1975) *Proletarian Order* (London, Pluto Press).

Zweig, M. (2000) *The Working Class Majority: America's best kept secret* (Ithaca, NY, Cornell University Press).

4
Introducing Giovanni Gentile, the 'Philosopher of Fascism'

Thomas Clayton

It is incredible that so few Gramsci scholars writing in English have explored the rich literature on the *Riforma Gentile*—the educational reform set in motion in 1923 by Giovanni Gentile, Mussolini's first Minister of Public Instruction. Not a single reference to Gentile's own writings or to contemporaneous research on Italian education appears in David Forgacs' and Geoffrey Nowell-Smith's commentary in *Selections from Cultural Writings* (Gramsci, 1985), for example, or in Forgac's notes in *The Antonio Gramsci Reader* (Gramsci, 2000). In *Selections from the Prison Notebooks* (Gramsci, 1971) and *Further Selections from the Prison Notebooks* (Gramsci, 1995), editors Quintin Hoare, Nowell-Smith, and Derek Boothman cite none of Gentile's educational work, though they do mention others of his publications. In his notes to *The Modern Prince and Other Writings* (Gramsci, 1957), Louis Marks refers to no original material for his biography of Gentile, while concluding inaccurately that he 'supported fascism from the start' (p. 190). Indeed, of all Gramsci's work translated into English, only the second volume of the *Prison Notebooks* edited by Joseph Buttigieg mentions even a single primary source on the *Riforma Gentile* (Gramsci, 1996).

The same pattern continues among education scholars interested in Gramsci. No original material on the Gentile educational reform appears to have been examined by Diana Coben (1998), for instance, or by the authors collected in *Gramsci and Education*, despite the editors' concern that Gramsci has been appropriated by commentators who ignore the 'specific historical context' in which he wrote, notably the 'controversy surrounding the educational reforms put in place by the Fascist ideologue and minister of education, Giovanni Gentile' (Borg *et al.*, 2002, p. 9). Nor do Gramsci scholars concerned with the language policy implications of the 1923 educational reform engage Gentile or his contemporaries: not Leonardo Salamini (1981) in *The Sociology of Political Praxis*, or Steven Mansfield (1984) in 'Introduction to Gramsci's "Notes on Language,"' or Niels Helsloot (1989) in 'Linguists of All Countries'; while Peter Ives (2004) refers to no original material on Gentile in *Gramsci's Politics of Language*, in an earlier version of his first chapter he does reference an important secondary source, Henry Harris' (1960*b*) *The Social Philosophy of Giovanni Gentile* (Ives, 1998).

In fact, the only Gramsci-education scholar to have done his homework on Gentile is the very one repeatedly savaged by Henry Giroux (1980, 2002)—who, incidentally, gives no indication of having read Gentile or about Gentile—for his alleged misunderstanding of Gramsci's educational positions: Harold Entwistle. In preparing his remarkable (and controversial) study *Antonio Gramsci: Conservative Schooling for Radical Politics*, Entwistle (1979) drew on a wide range of contemporaneous material about the *Riforma Gentile*. To begin, he read Gentile's *The Reform of Education*, the 1922 English translation of *La Riforma dell'Educazione* originally published in 1920. Entwistle then explored a balanced group of scholars who had personally studied education in fascist Italy: from Ernesto Codignola (1930), a partisan professor who had helped Gentile implement the reform; to Herbert Schneider and Shepard Clough (1929), American academics who conducted impressive research in Italy for their marvelous and dispassionate *Making Fascists*; to Lamberto Borghi (1951[1]), an Italian scholar whose earlier English-language contribution on fascist education (Borghi, 1944) has been judged 'violently hostile' and 'cruelly unfair' to Gentile (Harris, 1960a, pp. 34–35).[2]

Outside Gramsci studies, there has lately been a resurgence of interest in—almost a rehabilitation of—the 'philosopher of fascism', as Gentile is often known. In the United States, several new books assume a decidedly positive attitude toward their subject, notably Myra Moss' (2004) *Mussolini's Fascist Philosopher: Giovanni Gentile Reconsidered*, A. James Gregor's (2001) *Giovanni Gentile: Philosopher of Fascism*, and Gregor's new translations of *Origins and Doctrine of Fascism*, *What is Fascism?*, and *The Reform of Education* (Gentile, 2002). In Italy, academic attention (for example Turi, 1995; see Di Scala, 1998) has coupled with political-popular action. In 1994, the left wing of the Rome city government—the *Giunta di Sinistra*—convened a 'somewhat improvised but well-attended' conference on Gentile on the 50th anniversary of his death (Turi, 1998, p. 918). Also in that year, Italy issued a postage stamp commemorating the philosopher; in what Gabriele Turi (1998) terms 'one of history's ironies', the stamp is dated 28 October 1994, the anniversary of the 'March on Rome' that first brought the fascists to power in Italy (p. 918).

Within Gramsci studies broadly and Gramsci-education studies more specifically, however, the man Gramsci himself once described as 'the Italian philosopher who has made the greatest contribution in the field of thought in recent years' remains fundamentally unexplored and unknown (Gramsci, 1918; cited in Femia, 1981, p. 265). My goal for this chapter is to begin filling this void. In the largest part of this chapter, I explore Gentile's academic life, his philosophical agenda, and his political career. Having thus established a basis for understanding the *Riforma Gentile*, I then survey the substantial contemporaneous and contemporary English-language material about it. I cannot completely fill the void about Gentile in a short chapter, of course, and so I engage this literature only lightly and briefly in conclusion, for the primary purpose of illustrating the danger of eschewing it.

Gentile's Academic Life

Giovanni Gentile was born in Castelvetrano, in western Sicily, on 30 May 1875. Spencer Di Scala (1998) characterizes his family—mother and father Theresa Curti and Giovanni—as 'modest' (p. 211). It seems likely that he grew up speaking Sicilian, which would have been the dominant medium in small-town Sicily in the 19th century. Though considered a 'dialect' or 'variety' of standard Italian, Sicilian is linguistically distinct enough to constitute a separate language (Gordon, 2005). In an address delivered to elementary school teachers in 1919, Gentile (1922a) reports acquiring 'language ... from the dear lips of my mother' and from 'conversations [with] those who ... were with me in my native town and exchanged with me their thoughts and their sentiments' (p. 24). Though he is using 'language' metaphorically here, as one example of something all Italians 'shared in common', in fact in this description of naturalistic language acquisition Gentile is almost certainly referring to that variety particular to his own speech community (Gentile, 2002, *RE*,[3] p. 81). In any event, we know that he spoke Sicilian (A. James Gregor, personal communication, 13 December 2004).[4]

Gentile probably learned standard Italian in schools, where the national language served as the medium of instruction according to the policies of the Casati Law of 1859; learning Italian as a second language, particularly if he did so as an older child, might well explain why he 'always spoke [standard] Tuscan Italian with an accent' (A. James Gregor, personal communication, 13 December 2004). Gentile attended elementary school in the village of Campobello di Mazara; he completed his primary education at a *ginnasio* in Castelvetrano. He then studied at the *Liceo Classico Ximenes*, a secondary school in Trapani, the capital of his home province. Completing high school, Gentile received a scholarship to the *Scuola Normale Superiore* in Pisa, where he studied philosophy with Donato Jaja, who had been a pupil of Bertrando Spaventa, Italy's most influential disciple of Hegel in the 19th century. Under Jaja's tutelage, Gentile 'became imbued with the ambition to ... restore the idealist tradition ... in philosophy' in Italy; I discuss Gentile's idealism more specifically in the following section (Harris, 1960a, p. 1). Gentile graduated with his *laurea* from Pisa in 1897.

After teaching in high schools in Campobasso and Naples and completing a further degree at the University of Florence (the *libera docenza*), in 1903 Gentile assumed a position at the University of Naples, where he taught his first course on 'The Rebirth of Idealism'. In the same year, Gentile cofounded the journal *La Critica* with Benedetto Croce, and the two began a sometimes-stormy collaboration intended to 'shake Italy out of the doze of naturalism and positivism back to idealistic philosophy' (Croce, 1922, p. vii). In *La Critica*, Gentile focused among other things on pedagogy, thus continuing a project he had begun with several essays published between 1895 and 1901 (for discussion, see Moss, 2004, pp. 26–28). In contributions including *L'Insegnamento della Filosofia nei Licei* (*The Teaching of Philosophy in High Schools*, 1900) and 'Il Concetto Scientifico della Pedagogia' ('The Scientific Concept of Pedagogy', 1901), Gentile defended the teaching of philosophy in high schools relative to a ministry order that it be cancelled, and he began to sketch a broader philosophy of education, namely that 'education was to serve as a means whereby Italian culture and spirit were to be morally renewed' (Moss, 2004, p. 27).

In 1906, Gentile took a position at the University of Palermo. While there, he announced his philosophy of 'actual idealism' in a short essay, 'L'Atto del Pensare come Atto Puro' ('The Act of Thinking as Pure Act', 1912). He expanded his ideas into a 'systematic theoretical statement of his position' in *Teoria Generale dello Spirito come Atto Puro* (1916), which H. Wildon Carr translated into English as *The Theory of Mind as Pure Act* (1922b) (Harris, 1960a, p. 3). Gentile continued his educational explorations at Palermo, gaining national prominence as an advocate of religious instruction in schools by writing articles such as 'Scuola Laica' ('The Lay School', 1907; for discussion see, Harris, 1960b, pp. 66–76). His experiences teaching pedagogy at the university inspired his two-volume 'masterwork in the idealistic philosophy of education', *Sommario di Pedagogia come Scienza Filosofica* (1913–1914) (Holmes, 1937, p. xii). Merritt Thompson translated this work into English as *Dynamic Idealism as a Philosophy of Education*, though he could not find a publisher for it (see Thompson, 1959).[5] Fortunately for English readers, Thompson (1934) includes a 90-page abridgement of the *Sommario* as an appendix to an earlier study of Gentile; several translated excerpts also appear in Codignola's (1930) essay on education in Italy (see in particular pp. 370–376).

When Donato Jaja died in 1914, Gentile assumed his former professor's chair at Pisa, and in 1917 he moved to the University of Rome as a chair in the history of philosophy. In the latter year, he published another major application of his actual idealism, *Sistema di Logica come Teoria del Conoscere* (*System of Logic as Theory of Knowledge*, 1917), parts of which appear in English translation in Roger Holmes' (1937) *The Idealism of Giovanni Gentile*. During and immediately following the First World War, Gentile wrote and spoke extensively about education. His disagreements with a reform proposed by Minister of Public Instruction Agostino Berenini in 1918 led to a variety of specific proposals, which were quickly collected and published as a pamphlet, *Il Problema Scholastico del Dopoguerra* (*The Scholastic Problem of the Postwar Period*, 1919b) (for discussion, see Harris, 1960b, pp. 155–159). Also in 1919, Gentile delivered a series of lectures to elementary-school teachers in Trieste, shortly after this city in what is now Friuli-Venezia Giulia was ceded to Italy by Austria-Hungary.[6] These lectures were published the following year as *La Riforma dell'Educazione: Discorsi ai Maestri di Trieste* (Gentile, 1920b). Dino Bigongiari translated this book as *The Reform of Education* (Gentile, 1922a), and Croce (1922) wrote a laudatory preface for it.

By the time *La Riforma dell'Educazione* appeared in 1920, Gentile had begun a transition that would lead him from the 'charmed circle of the academic world' to a political career (Harris, 1960b, p. 131). It is important to note that, at this point, he had already developed a mature intellectual vision in the form of his unique philosophical position, actual idealism. In fact, with the exception of *La Filosofia dell'Arte*, which was published in 1931 (translated as *The Philosophy of Art* in 1972), Gentile had 'largely completed his theoretical work by the time Mussolini came to power' in 1922 (Turi, 1998, p. 914). Further, he had been writing and thinking about education for 25 years, and his proposals for educational reform were well-known in Italy— indeed, 'some scholars were describing him as the most influential teacher in Europe', even the 'world' (Carr, 1922, p. xix; Moss, 2004, p. 18). In the following section, I review Gentile's philosophy before returning to his political career.

Gentile's Philosophy and Agenda

Gentile's philosophical contributions have been examined in English by a surprising number of scholars, considering how relatively few of his works have been translated.[7] For contemporaneous discussions of Gentile's idealism, the reader may wish to compare Angelo Crespi's (1926) hostile chapter in *Contemporary Thought of Italy* (pp. 149–211) with Holmes' (1937, *op. cit.*) sympathetic analysis. There are useful discussions of Gentile's philosophy in Thompson's (1934) *The Educational Philosophy of Giovanni Gentile* (Chapter Three in particular) and Lorenzo Minio-Paluello's (1946) *Education in Fascist Italy* (Part Two, Chapter Two). In 1960, Harris (1960b, *op. cit.*) published his exceptional study of Gentile's thought relative to political change in Italy. More recently, Gregor's (2001, *op. cit.*) and Moss' (2004, *op. cit.*) volumes have appeared; the former balances philosophy, context, and parsimony impressively, and I draw on it frequently in the paragraphs that follow. For other discussions, see the extraordinary review of English language research on Gentile in Harris' (1960a) introduction to his translation of *Genesis and Structure of Society* (Gentile, 1960); no such review has been undertaken for texts published since 1960.

Croce's (1922) comment in his introduction to *The Reform of Education* provides one point of access to Gentile's philosophy: As young men, the two philosophers dedicated themselves to 'shak[ing] Italy out of the doze of naturalism and positivism' (p. vii). Positivism, the prevailing philosophy in Europe in the 19th century, can be defined as the science of articulating the 'positive empirical laws that govern ... all things and their development' (Gregor, 2001, p. 7). As the 'scientism' and 'mechanistic materialism' of positivism grew to dominate Italian thought by the turn of the 20th century, so too did other ways of understanding the world fade, to the extent that social phenomenon came to be seen as nothing more than 'epiphenomenal products of deeper processes taking place in the material foundation of collective life' (Gregor, 2001, p. 8). In Italy, the hegemony of the positivist worldview inspired, among other things, a fatalistic attitude toward the underdevelopment that had led many millions to emigrate to the United States and other countries. Prime Minister Francesco Nitti personified this philosophy in the period immediately following the First World War, repeatedly claiming 'that economic impoverishment and social turmoil had been forced on the Italian people through the necessity of events' (Moss, 2004, p. 17).

Gentile challenged one application of positivism in a very early essay. In 'Una Critica del Materialism Storico' ('A Critique of Historical Materialism', 1897), Gentile 'reflected on the inadequacy of materialistic determinism'—that is, Marxism—'as an explanatory device in any explication of social processes' (Gregor, 2001, p. 10). Gentile's larger project might be described as a voluntarist response to positivism, or, to use a contemporary phrase, an attempt to reclaim human agency. Invoking Hegel and Spaventa, Gentile argued that people are not mere flotsam tossed about on a sea of external forces. Indeed, he continued much as Berkeley had responded to Locke, what may appear to be the 'external, objective world' is in fact 'either invented or constructed by thought, and can be nothing other than thought' (Gentile, 1920a, cited in Gregor, 2001, p. 20; also see Gentile, 1922b, Chapter 1). In its furthest expression, Gentile's actual idealism—that reality is the actualization of thought—attained a unity far exceeding Berkeley, who understood God as outside human consciousness, or Croce (1922), whose thought allowed for unresolved 'distinction and dialectics' (p. x). Accordingly, what some call Gentile's 'absolute' idealism held that all things were to be 'embraced, penetrated and resolved into the "act of thinking"' (Gregor, 2001, p. 20).

At first glance, Gentile's philosophy appears in danger of collapsing into solipsism, a state of being in which 'each of us ... would be a "windowless monad", creating and inhabiting his own subjective world' through the pure, individual act of thinking (Gregor, 2001, p. 23). In fact, however, Gentile did not endorse this relentless relativism, but advocated a common, nationalist project: the realization of the Risorgimento, that movement toward national unification that had begun in Italy in the early 19th century. For Gentile, the spirit that had inspired Italians to create the new nation in 1861—the 'conviction that life is not what it is, but what it ought to be; and only that life is worthy of being lived which is as it ought to be, with all its duties and difficulties, requiring always efforts of the will, abnegation, and hearts disposed to suffer in order to make possible the good'—had, by the 1870s, been 'overwhelmed and obscured' (Gentile, 2002, *ODF*, pp. 6, 11). Gentile's voluntarist philosophy aimed, fundamentally, at the renovation of this spirit and the subsequent 'regeneration of the Italian people' and nation (Caserta, 1974, p. 20).

The logical problem for Gentile lay in the contradiction between the individual and the national. How can the act of *individual* thinking advance a *national* project? He resolved this contradiction in perhaps the most accessible language in his lectures to schoolteachers in Trieste in 1919. Harris (1960b) characterizes this attempt as a 'rather crude dichotomy', though it might better be termed a dialectic in the Hegelian tradition (p. 2). Gentile (2002, *RE*) opened with the thesis: 'Each makes of himself a center and from that center he constructs, thinking and doing, his own world', a 'world of values, of desired goods that embellish his life, or evils that he rejects and abhors, all of which have their origins in his will'. These worlds at first seem to be completely separate. Indeed, Gentile argued, after the lecture 'each of us will go our own way without losing anything of himself, conserving his own proper individuality'. This conservation of individuality also extends along the historical dimension, for though our 'elders lived on earth before us' today we 'live and develop our personality without them' (p. 78).

But this is 'only one side', Gentile (2002, *RE*) continued (p. 78). There is also something 'so different that the one appears to be the negation of the other', something that 'unites human beings rather than dividing them' (pp. 78, 81). After suggesting language as one such unifying activity, Gentile fully embraced his antithesis. In seeming contradiction to individual will, there exists also the 'majestic will that is the will of Italy'; this 'will of the State reveals itself ... in law', both public and moral (pp. 83, 82). Of course, Gentile set up the dialectic only so that he could resolve it, notably by acknowledging the 'intimacy' by which individual and state wills are 'joined and fused' (p. 83). Gentile illustrated his synthesis by reference to himself. 'My will is not only my own; it is a universal will', he explained. 'It is a form of universality embodied in a political community in which single individuals associate and unite themselves in a higher individuality historically distinct from other political entities'. Ultimately, my 'true volition is the will of the State acting as a particular will' (p. 84). In the final analysis, 'I will what the law wishes' (p. 82).

It is certainly possible to read a tendency toward authoritarianism in Gentile's synthetic fusion—some might say subordination—of the individual to the state. Indeed, scholars continue to debate the relationship between Gentile's 'organic, antiliberal concept of the state and society' and the rise of fascism in Italy (Turi, 1998, p. 920). Regardless, Gentile himself did not see individuals as constrained by the joining of their own and state will, but rather as freed through their recognition of it. Our 'freedom is realized only in a system', he wrote, 'by means of which my will is will and not simply weak fancy, when it is at the same time the will of everybody else' (Gentile, 1913–1914; cited in Codignola, 1930, p. 375). Importantly, the 'willed collective moral choices' made by Italians would resolve the 'urgent problems that afflicted retrograde Italy at the turn of the century' (Gregor, 2001, p. 29). In Gentile's (2002, *ODF*) own words, Italians imbued with a new voluntarist spirit would 'create a unified soul', 'construct ... the new Italy', and fulfill the promise of the Risorgimento (pp. 14, 18–19).

Gentile's Political Career

Though Gentile served on the city of Pisa's Committee for Civil Preparation and Mobilization during the early years of the First World War, his political engagement began in earnest only after the October 1917 defeat at Caporetto, where more than 300,000 Italian soldiers suffered casualties. Against a rising hysteria about the Italian rout and retreat to the Piave River, Gentile preached 'national solidarity and discipline' in a flood of editorials in newspapers, principally *Resto del Carlino* in Bologna and *il Nuovo Giornale* in Florence; many of these contributions were collected and published in 1919 as *Guerra e Fede* (*War and Faith*, 1919a) (Harris, 1960b, p. 134). Against a tendency to blame the antiwar faction in the national government for the catastrophe, Gentile suggested instead that the problem lay in a failure of the national spirit or morale. More specifically, in an article titled 'La Colpa Comune' ('The Common Responsibility', 1918) he argued that 'if the schools had created a genuine sense of patriotism before the war, the military disaster would never have happened' (Harris, 1960b, p. 135).

Ernesto Codignola brought Gentile's idea to the first postwar conference of the Federation of Secondary School Teachers, held in Pisa in 1919; at the conference, he 'pronounced ... against the majority of the secondary-school teachers that they had been responsible for the Italian failures in the war' (Minio-Paluello, 1946, p. 66). Following the predictably hostile response, Codignola founded a new educational organization, the *Fascio di Educazione Nazionale*, which Gentile joined (see Codignola, 1935, pp. 259–262, for text from his proposal for the new teachers' organization). The *Fascio di Educazione Nazionale* was, as Minio-Paluello (1946) points out, 'absolutely independent' of the *Fasci di Combattimento* organized by Benito Mussolini in 1919 (p. 66). In fact, the term 'fasci' had been used in Italy since the latter decades of the 19th century by a variety of 'more or less homogenous [groups] held together ... by ideal and disciplinary chains'; from the Latin word referring to the bundle of rods surrounding a protruding axe and carried ahead of Roman magistrates as a symbol of authority, *fascis*, by the beginning of the First World War the term had come to be used in Italy by disparate 'internationalist-socialist and revolutionary groups' (Moss, 2004, p. 17).

Gentile had no interaction with Mussolini before 1922. As the reader will recall, Mussolini had been a leader in the Italian socialist party and the editor of the party's journal, *Avanti!*, before being expelled in 1914 over his advocacy for intervention in the First World War. Though he was involved in a *fascio* of 'young men ... eager for Italian participation in the war' in Milan in 1915, it was not until after military duty in the war that he founded the *Fasci di Combattimento*, on 23 March 1919 (Schneider, 1928, p. 13). The many similar fascist organizations throughout Italy—sometimes referred to as *squadre d'azione* to signify their action orientation—gradually came together under Mussolini's leadership during the period extending through the 6 November 1921 formation of the *Partito Nazionale Fascista*. In broad terms, the fascists felt that the government had not responded adequately to at least two events: the rise of communism (reaching its zenith with the occupation of factories in 1920), and the frustration of Italian territorial claims at the end of the war, particularly to Fiume in Dalmatia (for histories of the rise of fascism, see Finer, 1935; Nolte, 1966; Schneider, 1928; Villari, 1926).

Even the most sympathetic observers acknowledge that the fascists' methods after 1919 were 'not al[ways] praiseworthy' (Villari, 1926, p. 46). Indeed, the 'half-military and half-anarchical' action squads waged a 'war on Bolshevism', beginning with the destruction of the offices and printing plant of *Avanti!* in Milan on 15 April 1919 (Minio-Paluello, 1946, p. 64; Schneider, 1928, p. 63). This act 'was like a signal for similar enterprises all over the country', Schneider (1928) comments: 'Strikes were broken up, parades were turned into street battles, labor offices were sacked and burned, guns, clubs and castor oil were used freely' (p. 64). It was during this period that the 'bands of young men ... patrol[ling] the streets and roads on punitive expeditions' began to wear the black shirts with which they would come to be associated (Villari, 1926, p. 41). Luigi Villari (1926) offers an apology for the fascists that resonates with another, which I discuss below: 'The only real forces operating for law and order were the Fascist *squadre*', he begins. While their 'action was violent and illegal', they were merely 'doing what the Government should have done, [but] dared not do' (pp. 41, 42).

The period of violence scholars refer to as 'squadrism' ended with the 28 October 1922 'March on Rome', in which 50,000 fascists descended on the capital city. The '*coup d'état* was by no means ... as violent as is commonly believed'; in fact, there was 'no fighting and no opposition' (Schneider, 1928, pp. 80, 82). Following brief negotiations in which the fascist leader exploited his strong position, the king invited Mussolini to form a new government. On 31 October 1922, Gentile agreed to serve as the Minister of Public Instruction in this coalition government made up of Fascists, Liberals, Nationalists, Popular Party members, and Social Democrats. While neither a member of the fascist party nor a supporter of Mussolini during his ascendancy, Gentile's admiration for the fascist project—he celebrated the March on Rome, for instance, as an important step in 'a progression from a passive acceptance of events to an active attempt to create a new reality' (Moss, 2004, p. 19)—may have inspired him to accept the appointment. More pragmatically, Gentile welcomed the chance 'to put into effect the proposals' in education he had been advocating for decades (Harris, 1960b, p. 160).

Scholars disagree about Mussolini's thinking in appointing Gentile to head the education ministry. Harris (1960b) argues that the fascist leader 'had no educational program and no real interest in the subject', was 'at a loss' for an educational leader, and may have been influenced toward Gentile 'by a coincidence of nomenclature'— that is, by the similarity in name between their respective organizations, the *Fasci di Combattimento* and the *Fascio di Educazione Nazionale* (pp. 161, 160). According to Gregor (2001), however, 'Mussolini's invitation ... was anything but casual' (p. 33). In fact, by 1921 Mussolini had realized that fascism 'required "a body of doctrine" if it were not to self-destruct'; previously, he had 'declared repeatedly that Fascism was a movement, not a doctrine' (Gregor, 2001, p. 34, citing a letter from Mussolini to Michele Bianchi; Minio-Paluello, 1946, p. 64). With Gentile, Gregor (2001) argues, Mussolini consciously sought someone capable of 'incorporat[ing into] a coherent doctrin[e] the views of all the elements [of fascism] that had fallen behind its gui-dons' (p. 34). To put it more simply, Mussolini brought Gentile into his government not only as the education minister, but also as a philosopher—the 'philosopher of fascism'.

While it should by now be clear that Gentile did not support fascism from the start, as Marks mistakenly claims in his translation of *The Modern Prince* (Gramsci, 1957), it would not be overstating the case to say that he enthusiastically embraced the regime and his role in it after 1922. After joining the *Partito Nazionale Fascista* on 31 May 1923 in a letter that aligned the fascist movement with the Risorgimento (for the text of the letter, see Harris, 1960b, pp. 167–168), Gentile set to work laying the philoso-phy of actual idealism over fascist history. Minio-Paluello (1946) describes this effort, which Gentile conducted in articles, books, and speeches over the course of the next 10 years, as 'giving Fascism and intelligent soul' (p. 67). Gentile's project perhaps commenced in an address entitled 'Il Fascismo e la Sicilia' ('Fascism and Sicily'), which he delivered in Palermo during the 1924 election campaign, on 31 March; Schneider (1928) translated segments of this speech in an appendix to *Making the Fascist State* (see pp. 345–347). The address was collected with other of Gentile's comments on fascism in the book *Che Cosa è il Fascismo: Discorsi e Polemiche* (1925a; for the text of the Palermo speech, see pp. 38–60 of the *Opere Complete* edition); Gregor translated significant portions of *Che Cosa è il Fascismo* as *What is Fascism?* (Gentile, 2002, *WF*; see pp. 59–65 for portions of the Palermo speech, which Gregor renames 'Fascism and Its Opponents').

'[L]iberty is to be sure the supreme end and rule of every human life', Gentile argued in Palermo, 'but in so far as individual and social education bring about its realization, actualizing this common will in the individual, it manifests itself as law and hence as state' (cited in Schneider, 1928, p. 347). Pushing quickly beyond his familiar synthesis, he then offered an apology for fascist violence that 'unluckily became his most famous utterance' (Harris, 1960a, p. 4). At times, he suggested, the state may have to resort to force to secure the liberty of individuals; to put this in terms that recall Gentile's own definition of liberty or freedom, the state may at times be justified in forcing individuals to recognize the fusion of their own and state will. Indeed, the 'maximum of liberty always coincides with the maximum force of the State' (Gentile, 2002, *WF*, p. 64). All force exercised to this end 'is a moral force', Gentile concluded, 'for it is always an expression of will; and whatever be the argument used—preaching or black-jacking—its efficacy can be none other than its ability finally to receive the inner support of a man and to persuade him to agree to it' (cited in Schneider, 1928, p. 347).

Gentile's sophistic 'attempt to make Fascist violence an expression of the new philosophical freedom' generated considerable controversy in 1924, earning him the moniker 'philosopher of the truncheon' (Harris, 1960b, p. 177; Gentile, 2002, *WF*, p. 64). Gentile tried to deflect criticism with a footnote inserted in the published version of the speech; it is perhaps not surprising that most contemporary scholars fail to acknowledge this effort to soften the totalitarianism he endorsed in person (see, for example, Buttigieg's note in his translation of Gramsci [1996, p. 685, note 3]; though also see Boothman's comment in Gramsci [1995, p. 581, note 95]). He did not intend to valorize or justify private force, Gentile (2002, *WF*) belatedly explained, but rather force deriving from the national will during a period of revolution when 'the State was in crisis and its force was gradually transferred from its fictive, if legal, organs to its real, if illegal, organs' (p. 64). Gentile made a similar apology in his most extensive philosophical discussion of fascism, *Origini e Dottrina del Fascismo* (*Origins and Doctrine of Fascism*, 1929), which Gregor recently translated (Gentile, 2002, *ODF*). 'The action squads' of the 1919–1922 period, he argued, 'were the military force of a virtual State ... in the process of realizing itself' (p. 19).

Gentile left the Ministry of Public Instruction on 1 July 1924, after only 20 months in office.[8] Though out of the cabinet, Gentile continued to serve the fascist regime, in myriad ways. He sat as a member of the Grand Council of Fascism for most of the 1920s. He chaired the Commission on Constitutional Reform first convened in August 1924; this committee played a central role in the process of 'Mussolinization' that followed the 3 January 1925 'declar[ation of] war on any and all opposition to fascist governance' (Nolte, 1966, p. 218; Moss, 2004, p. 20).[9] His 'Il Manifesto degli Intellettuali Italiani Fascisti agli Intellettuali di Tutte le Nazioni' ('Manifesto of Italian Fascist Intellectuals to Intellectuals of All Nations', 1925b), signed by participants at the first Congress of Fascist Intellectuals in Bologna in March 1925, amounted to 'an idealized account of the history of the Fascist movement and of its relation to the Risorgimento' (Harris, 1960b, p. 183). Croce, who was forever hardened to Gentile after this document was published, wrote a rebuttal, signed by liberal intellectuals, that described fascism as 'an incoherent and bizarre mixture of appeals to authority and demagogy' (cited in Moss, 2004, p. 21).

Continuing his career as fascism's 'intellectual-in-residence', Gentile founded the National Institute of Fascist Culture in 1925 and served as its president until 1937 (Koon, 1985, p. 33). Among other duties in this post, he edited the institute's official journal; cofounded with Croce in 1922 as *Nuova Politica Liberale* (*New Liberal Politics*), this journal was renamed *L'Educazione Politica* (*Political Education*) in 1923, *Educazione Fascista* (*Fascist Education*) in 1927, and *Civiltà Fascista* (*Fascist Civilization*) in 1934. Gentile also edited the *Enciclopedia Italiana*—the 'principle cultural monument of the Fascist period'—from 1925 to 1944 (Harris, 1960a, p. 5). In 1932, the article 'Dottrina del Fascismo' ('Doctrine of Fascism') appeared in the encyclopedia, under Mussolini's signature. In fact, Gentile wrote the first part of this entry (for more and less extensive translations and discussions, see Finer, 1935, pp. 164–229; Minio-Paluello, 1946, pp. 123–126). It might be possible to read the completion of Gentile's political-philosophical project, and of Mussolini's apparent expectations of him, in this article. In fascism, Gentile and Mussolini argued with one voice, 'man is seen in his immanent relation to a superior law; and this law is an objective Will, transcending individuals and lifting them to the stage in which they realize that they are members of a "spiritual" society' (cited in Minio-Paluello, 1946, p. 124).

Though he did not support fascism from its beginning, Gentile remained loyal to the regime and its leader to the end. After Mussolini's dismissal by the king on 25 July 1943, Gentile retreated with him to the Repubblica di Salò, the fascist enclave in northern Italy that survived until the end of the Second World War; there, he served as president of the *Accademia d'Italia*, the fascist reincarnation of the venerable *Accademia dei Lincei*. Mussolini would of course be killed by his compatriots, on 28 April 1945. Gentile died earlier. Returning from the prefecture in Florence to his villa on the outskirts of the city, Gentile was waylaid and assassinated by communist partisans on 15 April 1944.

The *Riforma Gentile*

Having introduced Gentile's academic life, his philosophical project, and his political career, it should now be possible to understand and appreciate the educational reform he implemented as Minister of Public Instruction. In this penultimate section, therefore, I review the English-language material on the *Riforma Gentile* that may be useful for scholars interested in pursuing such inquiry—and, more specifically, for scholars interested in complementing Gramsci's notes on education in fascist Italy with diverse contemporaneous and contemporary discussions of the same subject.

Gentile's reform captured the imagination of the world in the 1920s, and as a result there is a wealth of information about it available to English language readers. Contemporaneous comments on the reform can be found in popular magazines like *The Nation* and the *Quarterly Review* (Edman, 1922; Villari, 1929), for instance, as well as in scholarly journals such as the *Church Quarterly Review*, *The Historical Outlook*, the *International Journal of Ethics*, and *The Journal of Education and School World* (respectively, Duckworth, 1927; Duggan, 1929; Evans, 1933; Rebora, 1924). While some of these articles constitute serious attempts to understand Gentile's educational reform relative to his philosophy (notably Valmai Evans' [1933] 'Education in the Philosophy of Giovanni Gentile'), discussions such as Director of the Institute of International Education Stephen Duggan's (1929) 'The Fascist Conception of Education' might better be described as anecdotal. Excitement about educational change in Italy in the 1920s reached even into the literary realm; a 1925 visit to Italy inspired William Butler Yeats to read *The Reform of Education* and, ultimately, to write the poem 'Among School Children' (for a discussion, see Harper, 1997).

Beyond those producing short articles about the *Riforma Gentile*, a succession of scholars from the United States and the United Kingdom—often Italian émigrés or their descendants—studied the reform as it evolved and published dissertations and monographs about it. In this category appear Howard Marraro's *Nationalism in Italian Education* (1927) and *The New Education in Italy* (1936; for a briefer review, see Marraro, 1933), Minio-Paluello's (1946) *Education in Fascist Italy* (largely completed before the end of the Second World War), Thompson's (1934) *The Educational Philosophy of Giovanni Gentile*, and Harold Goad's and Michele Catalano's (1939) *Education in Italy*. Other scholars devote chapters to education in books with broader scopes, among them Peter Riccio (1929) in *On the Threshold of Fascism* (Chapter 5) and Schneider and Clough (1929) in *Making Fascists* (Chapter 5); Italian diplomat Luigi Villari (1926) discusses education in Chapter 9 of *The Fascist Experiment*. Marraro distinguishes himself in this group, in my opinion, for though he is perhaps overly sympathetic with the early fascist regime, he also appends translations of important original policy documents to both his 1927 and 1936 volumes.

Marraro and Riccio completed their research while at Columbia University, which became a center in the United States for studies of fascist education. Isaac Kandel of Columbia's Teachers College did much to disseminate information about the Gentile reform—and about what scholars term the subsequent 'retouching' of it—through the *Educational Yearbook*, which he founded in 1924 and edited until it ceased publication in 1944. Except for the final entry, written in 1944 when the Second World War had made communication with Italy impossible and he solicited an article from an expatriate living in New York (Borghi, 1944), Kandel relied exclusively on Italian educators intimately associated or familiar with fascist education, notably (and sequentially) Ugo Spirito (1925), Codignola (1930, 1931, 1933, 1935, 1937, 1939), and Iclea Picco (1940); A. Malvezzi De'Medici (1932) contributed an entry on education in Italy's African colonies. Kandel himself included sections on Italy in his ground-breaking *Essays in Comparative Education* (1930) and *Comparative Education* (1933). Kandel (1947) also compared education in fascist states, including Italy, for a study solicited by the US Congress; in his chapter on 'Education and Thought Control', Kandel treats Gentile fairly, concluding that 'there was not much in Gentile's reform that was Fascist' (p. 28).

Another center for studies of Italian education formed in London, though not at a single institution. The Royal Institute of International Affairs, known today by its address, Chatham House, solicited several monographs focusing exclusively or partially on educational change in Italy. Minio-Paluello's (1946, *op. cit.*) commissioned study for the Royal Institute might well be the definitive statement on the subject, as Harris (1960a) suggests; though it does not include the original material appended by Marraro (1927, 1936), it does contain analysis of the final stage of the fascist educational experiment. Daniel Binchy's (1941) *Church and State in Fascist Italy*, also published for the Royal Institute, discusses both secular and Catholic education under the fascist regime (Chapters 16 and 17). During the same period, entries on Italian education appeared in *The Year Book of Education*, published after 1935 by the University of London Institute of Education, though these were neither as frequent nor as extensive as those collected by Kandel for the *Educational Yearbook* at Teachers College in New York. As did Kandel, editors of *The Year Book of Education* solicited contributions from Italian educators, notably Marino Lazzari (1932), Salvatore Vallitutti (1937), Elio Pallazzo (1939), and Guido De Ruggiero (1948).[10]

Scholarly interest in education in fascist Italy slowed after World War II, but it has never stopped. Studies have been published relatively recently, for instance, on Gentile's educational philosophy (Caserta, 1974) and religion in fascist schools (Wolff,

1980). Clive Foss' (1997) examination of the textbooks that began to be produced in 1930 includes beautiful color reproductions of illustrations and cover material. Roberta Pergher's (2003) analysis of education and the 'Italianization' of South Tyrol, one of the territories Italy gained after World War I, complements the contemporaneous account by Robert Dunlop (1929). Tracy Koon (1985) has produced the most substantial analysis of fascist education in Italy in recent years; *Believe, Fight, Obey*—the title echoes a motto of the fascist state[11]—examines the political socialization of youth, focusing on educational programming after Gentile's tenure at the Ministry of Public Instruction. Moving briefly beyond English, readers of other languages may wish to review Michel Ostenc's (1980) *L'Education en Italie Pendant le Fascism* or Jürgen Charnitzky's (1994; see Albisetti, 1996) *Die Schulpolitik des Faschistischen Regimes in Italien (1922–1943)*, both of which have been translated into Italian (Ostenc, 1981; Charnitzky, 1996). Charnitzky includes an impressive list of references in Italian, German, French, and English. Harris (1960*a*) cites some English language reference material not mentioned here (pp. 57–61).

Reading Gramsci and his commentators against the extensive literature on the *Riforma Gentile* is a surprising—and somewhat disturbing—exercise: It would be generous to say that Gentile is treated simplistically in the Gramsci literature, though it would be more accurate to describe him as maligned and misrepresented in it. As a way of briefly introducing the rich literature on Gentile's education reform and at the same time bringing this chapter to a close, in the paragraphs that follow I review a few instances where scholars reading Gramsci but eschewing other relevant sources have, quite simply, got it wrong. To put it more positively, I conclude by underscoring certain areas where Gramsci-education scholars may benefit from broadening the scope of their inquiry.

- *On the influence of Croce.* The educational reforms Gentile enacted after 1923 were neither 'based on the proposals of ... Croce', nor had they been 'worked out by Croce' (Boothman in Gramsci, 1995, p. xxxi; Hoare & Nowell-Smith in Gramsci, 1971, p. 24; for other suggestions of a Crocean foundation to the *Riforma Gentile*, see Borg & Mayo, 2002, p. 102; Forgacs in Gramsci, 2000, p. 416, note 3; Mansfield, 1984, p. 123). Indeed, it is unambiguously clear that when Croce headed the education ministry in 1920 it was he who 'attempted to put into practice certain reforms in line with Gentile's ideas'—ideas the latter had been writing and speaking about since 1895 (Thompson, 1934, p. 5; though see Minio-Paluello, 1946, p. 68, on Croce's indirect influence).
- *On the Ministry of Education.* Several commentators imply that Gentile changed the name of the Ministry of Public Instruction to the Ministry of National Education (Boothman in Gramsci, 1995, p. xxx; Forgacs in Gramsci, 2000, p. 416, note 3). In fact, this happened in 1929, long after Gentile had left office, and it coincided with the beginning of the 'fascistization' of Italian schools, a period in which the regime 'eliminated the best aspects of the Gentile reform and exaggerated its authoritarian bent' (Koon, 1985, pp. 34, 86). The third and final period of the fascist educational experiment commenced in 1939 with Giuseppe Bottai's School Charter; unlike Gentile, Minister of National Education Bottai had indeed been a fascist from the start.

- *On 'instruction' and 'education'.* By focusing on the distinction Gentile raised between 'instruction' and 'education' (discussed by Gramsci in 'In Search of the Educational Principle', 1971, pp. 35–36), scholars miss two important points (Boothman in Gramsci, 1995, pp. xxx–xxxi; Buttigieg in Gramsci, 1996, p. 581, note 2; Hoare & Nowell-Smith in Gramsci, 1971, p. 24). First, Gentile's pedagogical reform responded to the same positivist obsession with 'encyclopaedic knowledge' that Gramsci himself had criticized in an article published in *Il Grido del Popolo* in 1916 (Gramsci, 2000, p. 56). Second, unlike Croce, Gentile would never leave a distinction unresolved. Predictably, then, he did not advocate the abandonment of instruction, but rather its 'liberat[ion] from the deadly oppression of mechanism' (Gentile, 1922*a*, p. 167). Invoking his now-familiar method, Gentile suggested a synthesis that became the new pedagogical principle in Italian schools. 'Instruction is ... educative', he wrote, as long as it 'demonstrat[es] the immanence of the whole in the particle' (Thompson, 1934, p. 166, citing his abridgement of Gentile's [1913–1914] *Sommario di Pedagogia*; for the original text, see the first volume of the *Opere Complete* edition, p. 239).
- *On the 'ball of thread'.* Readers knowledgeable about Gentile will be mystified equally by Gramsci's (1991) description of the student's brain as a 'ball of thread which the [Gentile reform era] teacher helps to unwind' (p. 211) and by Boothman's (in Gramsci, 1995, p. xxx) genetic interpretation of this statement. A better metaphor for Gentile's teaching-learning process would be 'communion', for he conceived of pedagogy as an act of spiritual joining: the 'blessed work of love that has parents united with children, the masters with the unlettered, and human beings with each other, ... so that all may rise together from one height, to another still higher, more elevated' (Gentile, 2002, *RE*, p. 86). Minio-Paluello (1946) correctly reads the dialectic that resolves in Gentilian pedagogy: 'Teacher and pupil are not two different persons; [at the moment of] teaching-and-learning [,] all duality disappears' (p. 71).
- *On vocational schools.* Gramsci (1971) notes the 'steady growth of specialised vocational schools' after 1923, and he probes the implications for democracy of this component of Gentile's reform: It 'gives the impression of being democratic', he argues, while in fact reproducing social inequity (pp. 27, 40). What Gramsci does not mention, and what commentators writing about this note (and Gramsci's related advocacy for common or humanistic schools) do not explore, is how Gentile engineered the tracking of secondary students into one kind of school or another (Borg & Mayo, 2002, pp. 93–94; Buttigieg in Gramsci, 1996, p. 571, note 1; Buttigieg, 2002, pp. 130–132; Coben, 1998, pp. 38–41; among others). In fact, students gained admission to various secondary schools based on their performance on examinations evaluated by an independent board (on the examinations, see Marraro, 1936, pp. 103–106; for the structure and content of the exams, see the same text, pp. 338–375). While Gramsci's (1971) concern about the advantages enjoyed in schools by children of 'traditional intellectual famil[ies]' remains valid, it may be worth examining how this new matriculation structure actually affected access to and democratization of the classical *ginnasio-liceo* schools (p. 42).
- *On religion in schools.* Gramsci demonstrates a great depth of knowledge about religious instruction in schools, as well as the Hegelian argument that undergirded this aspect of the Gentile reform; he followed developments surrounding the introduction of religious teaching carefully while in prison and apparently had several books and

pamphlets on the subject, some written by Gentile (Gramsci, 1991, pp. 283, 546, note 2; 1994, p. 243; 1995, pp. 409, 436; 1996, pp. 188–189, 220–225, 229, 328–329). Despite Gramsci's own clarity, however, contemporary commentators sometimes mislead readers on Gentile's actual position. In failing to mention that Gentile adamantly opposed the Concordat that extended religious education into secondary schools in 1929, for instance, Buttigieg (in Gramsci, 1996, pp. 578, note 6) implies the former minister's universal approval for compulsory Catholic education classes in Italian schools.

- *On grammar and standard Italian.* In 'Grammar and Technique', Gramsci (1985, pp. 185–187) raised concerns about language policy and teaching in reform-era schools. All scholars who explore this theme agree with Forgacs and Nowell-Smith: 'No provision was made for the normative teaching of Italian' (in Gramsci, 1985, p. 166; also see Forgacs in Gramsci, 2000, p. 417, note 12; Helsloot, 1989, p. 554; Ives, 2004, p. 43; Mansfield, 1984, p. 123; Salamini, 1981, p. 192). Scholars' typical conclusion— that the reform language policy 'confined [students] to the ghettoes of their dialects'— implies strongly that Gentile jettisoned standard Italian in favor of local varieties as instructional media (Forgacs in Gramsci, 2000, p. 417, note 12). Nothing could be further from the truth. In fact, Gentile enthusiastically supported the teaching and learning of standard Italian, as even the most cursory glance through reform curricula (such as those reproduced throughout Marraro [1936]) illustrates. What he did not countenance was the use of *grammars*—or dictionaries, or handbooks, or other 'instruments of culture that are only too often converted into engines of torture'—that would invite positivist instruction and disrupt the educative communion that extended beyond students and teachers to include the texts they engaged (Gentile, 1922a, p. 157).

Historicizing Gramsci, Respecting Gentile

A number of scholars have recently cautioned against the casual application of Gramsci's ideas to contemporary debates. Within Gramsci-education studies, for instance, Giroux (2002) argues that 'Gramsci's work [cannot] simply be appropriated outside of his own history and the challenges it posed' (p. 56). 'It is important ... to avoid the temptation and resist the tendency to remove Gramsci's ideas [from] their specific historical context and apply them simplistically and unproblematically to the present situation', continues Buttigieg (2002, p. 122). We must 'return Gramsci to his historical context', Adam Morton (2003) concludes relative to discussions in political theory, 'before discerning any contemporary relevance' in his writings (p. 137).

Scholars expect that the Gramsci historicization project will end with a rebuttal to books like *The Schools We Need*, in which Eric Hirsch (1996) harnesses Gramsci's ideas to a 'political[ly] liberal and ... educational[ly] conservative' agenda in *fin-de-siècle* America (p. 6). I am more concerned with the beginning of the project. As we have seen in this chapter, there exists a huge body of literature on Giovanni Gentile and his educational reform, though Gramsci-education scholars writing in English have neither read it nor incorporated it in their analyses. By engaging this literature, scholars will be better able to understand Gramsci's contemporaneous educational critique, and they will be better prepared to evaluate the contemporary appropriations of his ideas. Not incidentally, Gramsci-education scholars who read Gentile and about Gentile will gain an appreciation for the philosopher's complexity. With this complexity foregrounding subsequent inquiry, we will cease dismissing Gentile as a fascist caricature and begin granting him appropriate respect. As Turi (1998) puts it, we will see that 'it is proper to depict Gentile as a man in all the lights and shadows of his character and to describe the diverse, and often positive, results of his intellectual teachings', while remaining ever mindful of the 'conservative traits' that defined 'his relation with politics' (p. 933).

Notes

1. Entwistle gives 1960 as the date of this publication, though I can find no reference to a 1960 edition of the book.
2. Gramsci scholars writing in Italian have attended better to Gentile; see in particular Mario Manacorda's (1970) *Il Principio Educativo in Gramsci* and Angelo Broccoli's (1972) *Antonio Gramsci e l'Educazione come Egemonia*.
3. The Reform of Education; see the annotation to Gentile (2002) in the reference section.
4. Gregor studied at Columbia University with Paul Oskar Kristeller, who had known Gentile well. Gentile arranged an assistant professorship of German for Kristeller upon the latter's arrival in Italy as a refugee from Nazi Germany in the early 1930s. Later, when Italian citizenship became impossible for Kristeller with the passage of racial laws in 1938, Gentile underwrote his emigration to the United States (Gregor, 2001; Turi, 1998).
5. My extensive search for this document has been unsuccessful.
6. According to the terms of the 1915 London Pact, Italy agreed to attack its long-term ally Austria-Hungary in exchange for political support for irredentist claims on Dalmatia, Istria (where Trieste is located), and South Tyrol.
7. See the reference section for a discussion of Gentile's body of work. There, I include citations of all of Gentile's major works that have been translated into English; Harris (1960a, pp. 53–54) notes a few additional shorter translations.
8. Turi (1998) argues that Gentile 'submitted his resignation ... not to protest the assassination of the Socialist deputy Giacomo Matteotti [on 10 June 1924] but rather to avoid weakening the Mussolini government by his continued presence in the cabinet following his sponsorship of an unpopular reform' (p. 929). Marraro (1936) disagrees: 'Though his critics attributed his resignation to the widespread opposition to his reforms, it was definitely and positively asserted by high government officials that the reasons for his resignation were independent of the school reform' (p. 295).
9. It was relative to this suppression of dissent, of course, that Gramsci and other members of the communist party were imprisoned. Gentile (1925a) included his report from the Commission in *Che Cosa è il Fascismo* (see pp. 165–208 of the *Opere Complete* edition; see Gentile, 2002, *WF*, pp. 68–75, for a translated excerpt from the report).
10. Guido de Ruggiero served as Minister of Public Instruction in post-fascist Italy, in 1944.
11. Finer (1935) notes a fourth injunction to Italians during the fascist regime: 'Believe! Obey! Work! Fight!' (p. 163).

References

Works by Gentile

The Fondazione Giovanni Gentile per gli Studi Filosofici at the University of Rome issued, and Sansoni / Le Lettere of Florence published, Gentile's *Opere Complete* (*Complete Works*) in 55 volumes between 1955 and 2001. For the original publications that comprise the *Opere*

Complete, see Vito Bellezza's (1950) comprehensive *Bibliografia Degli Scritti di Giovanni Gentile*, or Harris' (1960b, pp. 335–361) abbreviated bibliographical index (which uses Bellezza's numbering system). Following, I give both the original and reprinted citations for publications referred to in this chapter.

Gentile, G. (1929) *Origini e dottrina del fascismo* (Rome, Libreria del Littorio). Reprinted in *Politica e cultura, Vol. 1* (*Opere Complete, 45*), pp. 369–457.

Gentile, G. (1897) Una critica del materialismo storico. *Studi Storici*, 6, pp. 379–423. Reprinted in *La filosofia di Marx: Studi critici* (*Opere Complete, 28*), pp. 11–58.

Gentile, G. (1900) *L'insegnamento della filosofia nei licei: Saggio pedagogico* (Palermo, Sandron). Reprinted as *Difesa della filosofia* (*Opere Complete, 38*).

Gentile, G. (1901) Il concetto scientifico della pedagogia. *Rendiconti della Accademia dei Lincei*, 9, pp. 637–671. Reprinted in *Educazione e scuola laica* (*Opere Complete, 39*), pp. 1–38.

Gentile, G. (1907, 15 September–15 October) Scuola laica. *Nuovi Doveri*, pp. 178–190. Reprinted in *Educazione e scuola laica* (*Opere Complete, 39*), pp. 73–132.

Gentile, G. (1912) L'atto del pensare come atto puro. *Annuario della Biblioteca Filosofica di Palermo*, 1, pp. 27–42. Reprinted in *La riforma della dialettica hegeliana* (*Opere Complete, 27*), pp. 183–195.

Gentile, G. (1913–1914) *Sommario di pedagogia come scienza filosofica* (Vols. 1–2) (Bari, Laterza). Reprinted as *Opere Complete, 1–2*.

Gentile, G. (1916) *Teoria generale dello spirito come atto puro* (Pisa, Mariotti). Reprinted as *Opere Complete, 3*.

Gentile, G. (1917) *Sistema di logica come teoria del conoscere* (Pisa, Spoerri). Reprinted as *Opere Complete, 5–6*.

Gentile, G. (1918, 25 January) La colpa comune, *Resto del Carlino*. Reprinted in *Guerra e fede* (*Opere Complete, 43*), pp. 60–63.

Gentile, G. (1919a) *Guerra e fede: Frammenti politici* (Naples, Ricciardi). Reprinted as *Opere Complete, 43*.

Gentile, G. (1919b) *Il problema scholastico del dopoguerra* (Naples, Ricciardi). All of Gentile's contributions to this pamphlet were reprinted in an appendix to *La nuova scuola media* (*Opere Complete, 40*), pp. 271–328, though entries by other contributors (including Ernesto Codignola) were not.

Gentile, G. (1920a) *Discorsi di religione* (Florence, Vallecchi). Reprinted as *Opere Complete, 37*.

Gentile, G. (1920b) *La riforma dell'educazione: Discorsi ai maestri di Trieste* (Bari, Laterza). Reprinted as *Opere Complete, 7*.

Gentile, G. (1922a) *The reform of education*, Dino Bigongiari, trans. (New York, Harcourt, Brace).

Gentile, G. (1922b) *The theory of mind as pure act*, H. Wildon Carr, trans. (London, Macmillan).

Gentile, G. (1925a) *Che cosa è il fascismo: Discorsi e polemiche* (Florence, Vallecchi) Reprinted in *Politica e cultura, Vol. 1* (*Opere Complete, 45*), pp. 3–224.

Gentile, G. (1925b) Manifesto degli intellettuali Italiani fascisti agli intellettuali di tutte le nazioni. *L'Educazione Politica*, 3, pp. 137–140. Reprinted in *Politica e cultura, Vol. 2* (*Opere Complete, 46*), pp. 5–13.

Gentile, G. (1931) *La filosofia dell'arte* (Milan, Treves). Reprinted as *Opere Complete, 8*.

Gentile, G. (1960) *Genesis and structure of society*, H. S. Harris, ed. & trans. (Urbana, IL, University of Illinois Press).

Gentile, G. (1972) *The philosophy of art*, G. Gullace, ed. & trans. (Ithaca, NY, Cornell University Press).

Gentile, G. (2002) *Origins and doctrine of fascism, with selections from other works*, A. J. Gregor, ed. & trans. (New Brunswick, NJ, Transaction). Other selections include *What is Fascism?* and *The Reform of Education*; in this chapter, I identify specific translations as ODF, WF, and RE.

Other Sources

Albisetti, J. (1996) Review of *Die schulpolitik des faschistischen regimes in Italien (1922–1943)*, by Jürgen Charnitzky, *American Historical Review*, 101, p. 206.

Bellezza, V. (1950) *Bibliografia degli scritti di Giovanni Gentile* (Florence, Sansoni).

Binchy, D. (1941) *Church and State in Fascist Italy* (London, Oxford University Press for the Royal Institute for International Affairs).

Borg, C. & Mayo, P. (2002) Gramsci and the Unitarian School: Paradoxes and possibilities, in: C. Borg, J. Buttigieg & P. Mayo (eds), *Gramsci and education* (Lanham, MD, Rowman and Littlefield), pp. 87–108.

Borg, C., Buttigieg, J. & Mayo, P. (2002) Gramsci and Education: A holistic approach, in: Carmel Borg, J. Buttigieg & Peter Mayo (eds), *Gramsci and education* (Lanham, MD, Rowman and Littlefield), pp. 1–23.

Borghi, L. (1944) Post-war Educational Reconstruction in the United Nations: Italy, in: I. L. Kandel (ed.), *Educational Yearbook, 1944* (New York, Bureau of Publications, Teachers College, Columbia University), pp. 173–216.

Borghi, L. (1951) *Educazione e autorità nell'Italia moderna* (Florence, La Nuova Italia).

Broccoli, A. (1972) *Antonio Gramsci e l'educazione come egemonia* (Florence, La Nuova Italia).

Buttigieg, J. (2002) Education, the Role of Intellectuals, and Democracy: A Gramscian reflection, in: C. Borg, J. Buttigieg & P. Mayo (eds), *Gramsci and education* (Lanham, MD, Rowman and Littlefield), pp. 121–132.

Carr, H. W. (1922) Translator's Introduction, in: G. Gentile, *The Theory of Mind as Pure Act*, H. W. Carr, trans. (London, Macmillan), pp. xi–xix.

Caserta, E. (1974) Gentile's Educational Theory: A revaluation, *Italian Quarterly*, 18:70, pp. 20–36.

Charnitzky, J. (1994) *Die schulpolitik des faschistischen regimes in Italien (1922–1943)*. (Tübingen, Max Niemeyer).

Charnitzky, J. (1996) *Fascismo e scuola: La politica scolastica del regime (1922–1943)*, L. S. Bürge, trans. (Florence, La Nuova Italia).

Coben, D. (1998) *Radical heroes: Gramsci, Freire and the politics of adult education* (New York, Garland).

Codignola, E. (1930) The Philosophy Underlying the National System of Education in Italy, J. de Simone, trans., in: I. L. Kandel (ed.), *Educational Yearbook, 1929* (New York, Bureau of Publications, Teachers College, Columbia University), pp. 317–425.

Codignola, E. (1931) The Expansion of Secondary Education: Italy, A. Gisolfi, trans., in: I. L. Kandel (ed.), *Educational Yearbook, 1930* (New York, Bureau of Publications, Teachers College, Columbia University), pp. 343–386.

Codignola, E. (1933) The Relation of the State to Religious Education and Public and Private Schools: Italy, M. Scacciaferro, trans., in: I. L. Kandel (ed.), *Educational Yearbook, 1932* (New York, Bureau of Publications, Teachers College, Columbia University), pp. 295–314.

Codignola, E. (1935) Teachers' Associations: Italy, in: I. L. Kandel (ed.), *Educational Yearbook, 1935* (New York, Bureau of Publications, Teachers College, Columbia University), pp. 351–367.

Codignola, E. (1937) Italy, in: I. L. Kandel (ed.), *Educational Yearbook, 1937* (New York, Bureau of Publications, Teachers College, Columbia University), pp. 319–335.

Codignola, E. (1939) The Meaning of a Liberal Education in the Twentieth Century: Italy, in: I. L. Kandel (ed.), *Educational Yearbook, 1939* (New York, Bureau of Publications, Teachers College, Columbia University), pp. 221–235.

Crespi, A. (1926) *Contemporary Thought of Italy* (New York, Alfred A. Knopf).

Croce, B. (1922) Introduction, in: G. Gentile, *The Reform of Education*, D. Bigongiari, trans. (New York, Harcourt, Brace), pp. vii–xi.

De Ruggiero, G. (1948) Italy: Education under Fascism, *The Year Book of Education, 1948* (London, Evans Brothers and the University of London Institute of Education), pp. 566–577.

De'Medici, A. M. (1932) Native Education in the Italian Colonies, in: I. L. Kandel (ed.), *Educational Yearbook, 1931* (New York, Bureau of Publications, Teachers College, Columbia University), pp. 645–677.

Di Scala, S. (1998) Review of *Giovanni Gentile: Una biografia*, by Gabriele Turi, *Journal of Modern History*, 70, pp. 210–211.

Duckworth, F. R. G. (1927) Gentile and the Teaching of Literature and Language, *Church Quarterly Review*, 103:206, pp. 201–215.

Duggan, S. (1929) The Fascist Conception of Education, *The Historical Outlook*, 20, pp. 224–225.

Dunlop, R. (1929) The Italianisation of South Tyrol, *Quarterly Review*, 252, pp. 199–220.

Edman, I. (1922) An Italian Idealist [Review of *The Reform of Education*, by Giovanni Gentile], *The Nation*, 115, pp. 636, 638.

Entwistle, H. (1979) *Antonio Gramsci: Conservative schooling for radical politics* (London, Routledge and Kegan Paul).

Evans, V. B. (1933) Education in the Philosophy of Giovanni Gentile, *International Journal of Ethics*, 43, pp. 210–217.

Femia, J. (1981) *Gramsci's Political Thought: Hegemony, consciousness, and the revolutionary process* (Oxford, Clarendon Press).

Finer, H. (1935) *Mussolini's Italy* (London, Victor Gollancz).

Foss, C. (1997) Teaching Fascism: Schoolbooks of Mussolini's Italy, *Harvard Library Bulletin*, 8:1, pp. 5–30.

Giroux, H. (1980) Review of *Antonio Gramsci: Conservative schooling for radical politics*, by Harold Entwistle, *British Journal of Sociology of Education*, 1, pp. 307–315.

Giroux, H. (2002) Rethinking Cultural Politics and Radical Pedagogy in the Work of Antonio Gramsci, in: C. Borg, J. Buttigieg & P. Mayo (eds), *Gramsci and Education* (Lanham, MD, Rowman and Littlefield), pp. 41–65.

Goad, H. & Michele C. (1939) *Education in Italy* (Rome, Laboremus).

Gordon, R. (2005) *Ethnologue: Languages of the world* (15th edn.) (Dallas, TX, SIL International).

Gramsci, A. (1918, 19 January) Il socialismo e la filosofia attuale, *Il Grido del Popolo*.

Gramsci, A. (1957) *The Modern Prince and Other Writings*, L, Marks, ed. & trans. (New York, International).

Gramsci, A. (1971) *Selections from the Prison Notebooks*, Q. Hoare & G. Nowell-Smith, eds & trans. (New York, International).

Gramsci, A. (1985) *Selections from Cultural Writings*, D. Forgacs & G. Nowell-Smith, eds; W. Boelhower, trans. (Cambridge, MA, Harvard University Press).

Gramsci, Antonio (1991) *Prison Notebooks: Vol. 1*, J. Buttigieg, ed. & trans. (New York, Columbia University Press).

Gramsci, Antonio (1994) *Letters from Prison, Vol. 2*, F. Rosengarten, ed.; R. Rosenthal, trans. (New York, Columbia University Press).

Gramsci, Antonio (1995) *Further Selections from the Prison Notebooks*, D. Boothman, ed. & trans. (Minneapolis, University of Minnesota Press).

Gramsci, Antonio (1996) *Prison Notebooks: Vol. 2*, J. Buttigieg, ed. & trans. (New York, Columbia University Press).

Gramsci, Antonio (2000) *The Antonio Gramsci Reader: Selected writings, 1916–1935*, D. Forgacs, ed.; Q. Hoare, G. Nowell-Smith, J. Mathews & W. Boelhower, trans. (New York, New York University Press).

Gregor, A. J. (2001) *Giovanni Gentile: Philosopher of fascism* (New Brunswick, NJ, Transaction).

Harper, M. (1997) The Authoritative Image: 'Among school children' and Italian educational reform, *Studies in the Literary Imagination*, 30:2, pp. 105–118.

Harris, H. S. (1960a) Introduction, in: Giovanni Gentile, *Genesis and Structure of Society*, H. S. Harris, ed. & trans. (Urbana, IL, University of Illinois Press), pp. 1–63.

Harris, H. S. (1960b) *The social philosophy of Giovanni Gentile* (Urbana, IL, University of Illinois Press).

Helsloot, N. (1989) Linguists of All Countries ... !: On Gramsci's premise of coherence, *Journal of Pragmatics*, 13, pp. 547–566.

Hirsch, E. D. (1996) *The Schools We Need and Why We Don't Have Them* (New York, Doubleday).

Holmes, R. (1937) *The Idealism of Giovanni Gentile* (New York, Macmillan).

Ives, P. (1998) A Grammatical Introduction to Gramsci's Political Theory, *Rethinking Marxism*, 10:1, pp. 34–51.

Ives, P. (2004) *Gramsci's Politics of Language: Engaging the Bakhtin circle and the Frankfurt school* (Toronto, University of Toronto Press).

Kandel, I. L. (1930) *Essays in Comparative Education*. (New York, Bureau of Publications, Teachers College, Columbia University).

Kandel, I. L. (1933) *Comparative Education* (Boston, Houghton Mifflin).

Kandel, I. L. (1947) Education and Thought Control, in: *Fascism in Action: A documented study and analysis of fascism in Europe* (Washington, DC, Legislative Reference Service, Library of Congress), pp. 23–36.

Koon, T. (1985) *Believe, Fight, Obey: Political socialization of youth in fascist Italy, 1922–1943* (Chapel Hill, NC, University of North Carolina Press).

Lazzari, M. (1932) Education in Italy, *The Year Book of Education, 1932* (London, Evans Brothers), pp. 858–877.

Manacorda, M. (1970) *Il Principio Educativo in Gramsci: Americanismo e conformismo* (Rome, Armando Armando).

Mansfield, S. (1984) Introduction to Gramsci's 'Notes on Language', *TELOS*, 59, pp. 119–126.

Marraro, H. (1927) *Nationalism in Italian Education* (New York, Italian Digest and News Service).

Marraro, H. (1933) *Handbook for American Students in Italy* (New York, Institute for International Education and the Italian Historical Society).

Marraro, H. (1936) *The New Education in Italy* (New York, S.F. Vanni).

Minio-Paluello, L. (1946) *Education in Fascist Italy* (London, Oxford University Press for the Royal Institute for International Affairs).

Morton, A. (2003) Historicizing Gramsci: Situating ideas in and beyond their context, *Review of International Political Economy*, 10, pp. 118–146.

Moss, M. E. (2004) *Mussolini's Fascist Philosopher: Giovanni Gentile reconsidered* (New York, Peter Lang).

Nolte, E. (1966) *Three Faces of Fascism: Action française, Italian fascism, national socialism*, L. Vennewitz, trans. (New York, Holt, Rinehart and Winston).

Ostenc, M. (1980) *L'éducation en Italie pendant le fascism* (Paris, Publications de la Sorbonne).

Ostenc, M. (1981) *La scuola Italiana durante il fascismo*, L. Libutti, trans. (Bari, Laterza).

Pallazzo, E. (1939) The Humanitarian Society, Milan, *The Year Book of Education, 1939* (London, Evans Brothers and the University of London Institute of Education), pp. 578–581.

Pergher, R. (2003, August) *Teaching 'Italianness': The Italianization efforts of the fascist regime in South Tyrol under the auspices of female teachers*. (Lund, Paper presented at the European Feminist Research Conference).

Picco, I. (1940) Problems of Adult Education: Italy, in: I. L. Kandel (ed.), *Educational Yearbook, 1940* (New York, Bureau of Publications, Teachers College, Columbia University), pp. 203–226.

Rebora, P. (1924) Educational Advancement Abroad: Education reforms in Italy, *The Journal of Education and School World (London)*, 56, pp. 609–612.

Riccio, P. (1929) *On the Threshold of Fascism* (New York, Casa Italiana, Columbia University).

Salamini, L. (1981) *The Sociology of Political Praxis: An introduction to Gramsci's theory* (London, Routledge and Kegan Paul).

Schneider, H. & Clough, S. (1929) *Making Fascists* (Chicago, University of Chicago Press).

Schneider, H. (1928) *Making the Fascist State* (New York, Oxford University Press).

Spirito, U. (1925) Educational Developments in 1924: Italy, H. Marraro, trans., in: I. L. Kandel (ed.), *Educational Yearbook, 1924* (New York, Bureau of Publications, Teachers College, Columbia University), pp. 329–352.

Thompson, M. (1934) *The Educational Philosophy of Giovanni Gentile* (Los Angeles, University of Southern California Press).

Thompson, M. (1959) A Neglected Educator, *The Educational Forum*, 24, pp. 49–57.

Turi, G. (1995) *Giovanni Gentile: Una biografia* (Florence, Giunti).

Turi, G. (1998) Giovanni Gentile: Oblivion, remembrance, and criticism, L. Cochrane, trans., *Journal of Modern History*, 70, pp. 913–933.

Vallitutti, S. (1937) Elementary Education in Italy, *The year book of education, 1937* (London, Evans Brothers and the University of London Institute of Education), pp. 790–801.

Villari, L. (1926) *The Fascist Experiment* (London, Faber and Gwyer).

Villari, L. (1929) New Developments in the Relations between the Papacy and the State, *Quarterly Review*, 252, pp. 15–31.

Wolff, R. (1980) Catholicism, Fascism and Italian Education from the Riforma Gentile to the Carta della Scuola 1922–1939, *History of Education Quarterly*, 20, pp. 3–26.

5

Global English, Hegemony and Education: Lessons from Gramsci

PETER IVES

> Every time that the question of language surfaces, in one way or another, it means that a series of other problems are coming to the fore: the formation and enlargement of the governing class, the need to establish more intimate and secure relationships between the governing groups and the national-popular mass, in other words to reorganize the cultural hegemony.
>
> Antonio Gramsci 1935 (1985, p. 183, Q29§3)[1]

> 'What is grammar?' ... in all the countries of the world, millions upon millions of textbooks on the subject are devoured by specimens of the human race, without those unfortunates having a precise awareness of the object they are devouring.
>
> Antonio Gramsci, Letter of 12 December 1927 (1994 vol. 1, p. 160)

These sentiments of Antonio Gramsci are even more relevant today than when they were written more than 70 years ago. David Graddol estimates that by 2010–2015, two billion people, a third of the entire human population, will be learning English (Graddol, 2006, p. 14). Add this to the billion or so people who already have some competence in English and, according to these calculations, half the world's population will have a degree of facility in the English language as compared to a mere 250 million in 1952 (Crystal, 1997, p. 25).[2] Such figures tell us little about the proficiency reached or especially the impact of this learning on the lives of these billions of students of English. As is too often the case, the most publicized information on the spread of English throughout the world tends to isolate the phenomenon from changes in power and economic relationships, de-politicizing it and treating it as an inevitable or quasi-natural trend over which humans have little or no control. Abram De Swaan, to give one example from the political science literature, argues that despite the history 'of British colonialism initially [and] of American military and economic hegemony later [to the predominance of English] ... the spread of English is the mostly unintended outcome of expectations held and decisions made accordingly by hundreds of millions of people across the globe' (De Swann, 2001, pp. 141–2).[3] Alistair Pennycook notes of many similar approaches, 'The spread of English is taken to be natural, neutral and beneficial' (1995, p. 54; see also Crystal, 1997, pp. 8–22). Even Philippe Van Parijs, who is very concerned with the injustices created by its spread, argues that overall English as a lingua franca is beneficial for Europe and the world, 'If we want all sorts of workers', women's, young people's, old people's, sick people's, poor people's associations to organise on the ever higher scale required for effective action, we must equip them with the means of talking to one another without the need for interpreting boxes and the highly skilled and paid professionals who go in them' (Van Parijs, 2004, p. 118). He argues that justice requires various means of redistributing the costs of English teaching to everyone who benefits from the existence of a common lingua franca, especially monolingual English speakers.

Of course, there are many who disagree, arguing that the spread of English itself is inextricable from imperialism and domination whether economic, cultural or political. There is a large body of literature critical of the spread of English across the globe. Far from improving lives by offering greater communication, such studies, as Pennycook summarizes, '... show that English threatens other languages, acts as a gatekeeper to positions of wealth and prestige both within and between nations, and is the language through which much of the unequal distribution of wealth, resources, and knowledge operates' (1995, p. 55). The concept of 'hegemony', implicitly or explicitly influenced by Gramsci, is often mobilized within such critical approaches precisely to counter the arguments put forth by the advocates of 'global English'.[4] 'Hegemony' is used to illustrate that whether or not individuals, institutions or states 'choose' (seemingly freely) to learn, teach or facilitate English, the spread of English is part and parcel of unequal power relationships (e.g. Ashcroft *et al.*, 1989; Eriksen, 1992; Kachru, 1997, p. 230; Macedo *et al.*, 2003; Rassool, 1998, pp. 90–1; Tollefson, 2000, p. 16). Some scholars expressly discuss Gramsci's writings in the context of the global hegemony of English (e.g. May, 2001, pp. 12, 92, 215; Holborow, 1999; Parakrama, 1995, pp. 60–5; Phillipson, 1992, pp. 65–76; Romaine, 1997, p. ix; Shannon, 1995; Tsuda, 1997, pp. 22–23). In her wide-ranging comparative study of linguistic globalization, Selma Sonntag even suggests quite astutely that 'it is particularly in the realm of language use that the full implication of [Gramsci's] hegemony for structure and agency are most apparent' (Sonntag, 2003, p. 6).[5]

Yet, to my knowledge, these debates around 'global English' and related ones around minority language rights have never been related to Gramsci's discussions of language, education, a national language in Italy, or his specific integration of language politics within his better known cultural and political theory.[6] At first blush, one may even question the use of Gramsci's writings for a critical analysis of 'global English' considering that, as will be discussed below, he was very much in favour of the spread of a 'standard' national language for all of Italy.[7] Many of his reasons were similar to those of Van Parijs and other proponents of English as a global lingua franca. Gramsci castigated both the Italian liberal and fascist governments for their failures in spreading a truly common language. However, by putting these arguments within their appropriate contexts, this chapter will show how and why Gramsci's writings on language and hegemony can and should be used to help frame more critical inquiries into the global spread of English.

My major point is that from a Gramscian perspective, the spread of English is a problem to the extent that its role within particular hegemonic blocs prevents subaltern social group consciousness from developing and creating critical and counter-hegemonic responses.[8] His analysis of language politics in Italy in the 1920s and 1930s can help us address Sonntag's question, 'Can global English be a counter-hegemonic medium facilitating democratic deliberation in an emerging transnational civil society or will it remain the linguistic feature of a global marketplace, where youth worldwide uncritically adopt the insidious commercial values that it embodies?' (Sonntag, 2003, p. 30).[9] Gramsci's analysis shows what he thinks is required for a global language to be progressive and enhancing of democracy. In his terminology to be explained below, the normative grammar of any 'common language' will be an impediment to progressive social change if it is imposed from a language of different social groups and their experiences. For English, or any language, to foster truly democratic inclusion it must be the creation of an interaction among the multiple 'spontaneous grammars' of the speakers of the common language. This perspective brings questions about resistance and counter-hegemonic possibilities to the fore. While implementing such a framework for an empirical analysis of 'global English' is beyond the scope of this chapter, I will provide an example of the type of analysis this should entail by looking at Gramsci's own writings on the language politics of his Italy. This will reveal that scholars of language politics attracted to Gramsci's concept of 'hegemony' are sensing a perspective that has distinct advantages to other approaches.

One obvious point of comparison is the work of Pierre Bourdieu who perhaps provides a more comprehensive description of the power dynamics inherent in linguistic interactions (Bourdieu, 1991; Bourdieu and Passeron, 1990). Gramsci shares many similarities with Bourdieu; however, where Bourdieu relies on the notions of 'symbolic domination', Gramsci's description of hegemony has been attractive to those who want to emphasize the consensual basis of language shift to English. In his insightful comparison of Gramsci and Bourdieu's positions on language politics, Kerim Friedman argues that, '... Gramsci's theory of *hegemony* is grounded in the political process of establishing consent, rather than [Bourdieu's focus on] the institutional process of reproducing it' (Friedman, 2005, pp. 239–40). Drawing on the work of Kathryn Woolard, Niloofar Haeri and F. Niyi Akinnaso, Friedman illustrates the importance of Gramsci's framework for understanding how languages gain their legitimacy and by extension the possibilities of 'alternative language markets', to use Bourdieu's terms, or the legitimation of what I would call more progressive hegemonies or counter-hegemonies (Friedman, 2005, pp. 253–9). Especially since the legitimacy of English in many areas is still very much in question, Gramsci's attention to the process whereby some languages become hegemonic is crucial.

Theories of linguistic imperialism or the hegemony of English have come under attack for being one-sided in that they take 'for granted that the colonizing nation possesses the power to impose its will on a "subject" population ... . It is tacitly overlooked that the oppressed might themselves determine or influence the bounds of policy' (Brutt-Griffler, 2002, pp. 62–3). An adequate understanding of Gramsci's notion of hegemony does not fall prey to such problems. Indeed, while Gramsci's criticisms of liberal, bourgeois and fascist hegemonies have been the most influential, his ultimate (albeit failed) goal was to create a progressive hegemony for the Italian Communist Party. Any analysis inspired by Gramsci must take this aim of facilitating progressive change and the agency of the oppressed as fundamental.

'Hegemony' is a useful concept in the context of language education precisely because it gives the lie to the common-sense position that individuals freely choose what languages they wish to learn and thus, the shift to English is 'the people's choice'. While there may be some useful research conducted on the complex reasons why individuals, families, community groups, regional territories, and states foster the teaching of English or any other language, such approaches are in danger of apologizing for and helping reinforce a regressive 'hegemony of English'.[10] As Gramsci describes, language use is intimately tied to education, culture, ideology and politics. It cannot be divorced from questions of subordination and domination but also contains possibilities for resistance and struggle in what Gramsci calls the 'war of position' in preparation for social change and a 'war of maneuver' (see Ives, 2004b, pp. 107–10; Sonntag, 2003, pp. 6, 31).

It would be overly ambitious for one chapter to attempt a full-blown Gramscian approach to 'global English' and the role of education in it. However, by addressing the considerable lacuna in Gramscian scholarship around language, education and politics, I hope to lay some of the groundwork needed for a Gramscian intervention in debates around globalization, language education, democracy and power.

Gramsci's Concern with Language

Given the neglect of Gramsci's writings on language within Gramsci scholarship, it is no surprise that language scholars drawn to Gramsci may not be aware of his own concern with language. Gramsci is often portrayed as having 'jettisoned' or 'abandoned' his studies in historical linguistics at the University of Turin when he chose to devote himself to political journalism around 1915 (e.g. Buci-Glucksmann, 1980, p. 9; McLaren *et al.*, 2002, p. 152). Many general introductions and overviews only briefly mention his interest in language (e.g. Femia 1981, p. 44; Adamson, 1980, pp. 124, 150–1, 230 and no mention in Simon, 1991). It is, of course, true that in 1915 he joined the staff of *Il Grido del Popolo*. In December 1916, he accepted the full time position as editor of the local news of the Turin edition of *Avanti!* enabling him to support himself. He never finished his degree at the University of Turin. However, to suggest that he abandoned his studies of language by leaving university seriously underestimates the extent to which, as Dante Germino notes, 'Gramsci saw very early ... that in a vital sense language *is* politics, for it affects the way people think about power' (Germino, 1990, p. 27).

Scholars have aptly illustrated that Gramsci's conception of 'education' cannot be reduced to 'schooling' but rather 'amounts to nothing less than the fundamental operations of hegemony' (Borg *et al.*, 2002, p. 8; and Monasta, 2002). To suggest that Gramsci's interest in language and linguistics was confined to his early years in university is to employ an overly narrow notion of 'education' as well as to ignore his persistent concern with the politics of language as an integral aspect of hegemony. Indeed, if Gramsci had given up his studies of linguistics, how could we understand his final prison notebook on grammar in which he picks up on many themes that had occupied him and his professor, Matteo Bartoli, in 1912 and 1913?

For Gramsci, language politics and the molecular operations of power within linguistic differences were intimately bound with his life experiences as a Sardinian who moved to mainland Italy to pursue university education. Gramsci was born just thirty years after Italy was politically unified, at a time when *la questione meridionale* [the Southern Question] could not be separated from *la questione della lingua* [the language question]. It is estimated that in 1861 between two and a half (De Mauro, 1986, p. 43) and twelve percent of the population of the newly proclaimed Kingdom of Italy (Moss, 2000, p. 200), spoke anything that could be considered 'standard' Italian. The veritable absence of a 'standard' national Italian language was seen as an obstacle to Italy becoming a successful, modern nation-state. Some context will highlight how Gramsci's advocacy of a 'national' Italian language is not contradictory to his criticisms of the specific methods by which Italian was 'standardized' and imposed.

Gramsci's 1918 Rejection of Manzoni's Strategy for a National Language

In 1868, Alessandro Manzoni, author of the classic novel, *The Betrothed*, was appointed to head a government commission on the spread of a 'standard' language throughout Italy. Steeped in the Romanticist advocacy of spoken, living languages over written ones, Manzoni proposed the language of the Florentine bourgeoisie as 'standard' Italian.[11] Together with the government funding of dictionaries and grammars, the plan was to recruit school teachers from the Tuscan region, have Tuscans instruct teachers from other regions, and sponsor student travel to Tuscany (see Moss, 2000; and Maiden, 1995, pp. 6–10). As with the creation of most European 'standard' national languages, the education system was one of the most important instruments of language policy in addition to mandatory military service, an enlarged state bureaucracy and better road and communications systems. The context surrounding the spread of English internationally is obviously very different, but as Phillipson has shown, the British and US state machineries have been active in establishing the global hegemony of English (Phillipson, 1992, pp. 137–72).

Gramsci was very critical of Manzoni's approach. His initial criticisms are evident in an article from 1918 against the proposal that the Italian Socialist Party adopt Esperanto. Gramsci chastised both proponents of Esperanto and Manzoni for attempting to '*create*' a common Italian language through the imposition of an '*artificial*' language (or what would be experienced as such) on speakers in a futile attempt to replace their previous language.[12] Gramsci argues that:

> ... not even a national language can be created artificially, by order of the state; that the Italian language was being formed by itself and would be formed only in so far as the shared life of the nation gave rise to numerous stable contacts between the various parts of the nation; that the spread of a particular language is due to the productive activity of the writings, trade and commerce of the people who speak that particular language. (Gramsci, 1985, p. 28)

Gramsci cites the renowned linguist, Graziadio Isaia Ascoli, who had argued that the linguistic 'substratum' of the speakers' previous languages would continue to exert pressures on the newly imposed language and, thus, its imposition would be partial and continually challenged.[13]

Gramsci is not only critical of the practicalities of Manzoni's solution, but problematizes the very desire or need for a common or single lingua franca. It is worth quoting a long passage from this article because it could be applied to many arguments in favour of global English:

> The advocates of a single language are worried by the fact that while the world contains a number of people who would like to communicate directly with one another, there is an endless number of different languages which restrict the ability to communicate. This is a *cosmopolitan,* not an international anxiety, that of the bourgeois who travels for business or pleasure, of nomads more than of stable productive citizens. They would like artificially to create *consequences* which as yet lack the necessary *conditions* ... (Gramsci, 1985, p. 27)

Thus, as early as 1918, Gramsci interrogates the most prominent economic and class reasons that underlie the desire for a 'global' language. Here he is critical of such a 'cosmopolitan' perspective because it presupposes class and cultural inequalities. This, of course, mirrors the dynamic that he develops more extensively in his Prison Notebooks with his concepts of a 'passive revolution'—a 'revolution' without a revolution—whereby superficial alterations are made to avoid the economic, social and political crises that are coming to the fore. But such 'passive revolutions' do not address the profound reasons for such crises (see Gramsci, 1971, pp. 104–20; and Ives, 2004b, pp. 102–10 for its relation to linguistic metaphors).

Yet, Gramsci's argument in 1918 *seems* to rely on a rejection of state intervention in language planning. Together with the perhaps questionable valorization of 'productive citizens' (over 'non-productive' ones) and the neglect of subaltern people who immigrate and need to communicate, here Gramsci *appears* to be reducing successful language spread to economic development and integrated markets. It is *as if* in 1918 Gramsci accepts that 'language spread'—as described in my introduction concerning 'global English'—is 'natural' or at least determined by the economy (Gramsci, 1985, pp. 28–29). Here I will not rehearse the more complex possible interpretations of his position in this ambiguous article[14] because he clearly moves beyond it in his prison writings where he stresses the always interconnected relations between civil society (where he seems here to suggest 'language is formed by itself') and the state (e.g. Buttigieg, 1995). He also integrates such concerns with his ideas on language, 'common sense', 'good sense', ideology and philosophy (see Coben, 2002; Ives, 2004b, pp. 72–81). His prison writings include discussions of education and immigration not apparent in this short article from 1918. By focusing on Gramsci's period in prison, we can see how he made these connections and their potential uses for current analyses of 'global English'.

Advocacy of a National Popular Common Language in the *Prison Notebooks*

By 1935 in his 29th Prison Notebook, the last one he began, he clearly argued that the State could and should play an active role in language planning. In other words, the spread of a 'common language' is not politically natural or neutral:

> Since the process of formation, spread and development of a unified national
> language occurs through a whole complex of molecular processes, it helps
> to be aware of the entire process as a whole *in order to be able to intervene
> actively in it with the best possible results* [emphasis added]. One need not
> consider this intervention as 'decisive' and imagine that the ends proposed
> will all be reached in detail, i.e. that one will obtain a *specific* unified language.
> (Gramsci, 1985, p. 183, Q29§3)

What remains consistent with his 1918 position is the attack on how and why the
Italian State chose to intervene in language-use because it was a top-down imposition
of a 'static', predetermined language (which is what he means by 'decisive' and
'specific') against the existing languages (see Ives, 2004a, pp. 40–51). Gramsci insists
that the selection and propagation of any language (or what he calls the 'normative
grammar' of a language) is a 'political act' intimately related to 'national-cultural
politics'. Moreover, it was part of more general poorly constructed attempts at cultural
regressive hegemony (Gramsci, 1985, p. 182, Q29§2). Thus, Gramsci clearly rejects
the very idea that any 'common language' whether Italian or English could be 'neutral'
or purely determined by economic necessities.[15]

He develops and makes more consistent his earlier critique of Manzoni and this time
relates it clearly to the Notebooks' themes of hegemony, culture and the national-
popular collective will (see Ives, 2004b, pp. 110–14). In this more fully articulated
analysis, 'the education system' is listed as the first of eight 'sources of diffusion of
linguistic innovations', followed by '2) newspapers; 3) artistic writers and popular
writers; 4) the theatre and sound films; 5) radio; 6) public meetings of all kinds,
including religious ones; 7) the relations of 'conversation' between the more educated
and less educated strata of the population ... [and] 8) the local dialects, understood
in various senses ...' (Gramsci, 1985, p. 183, Q29§3).

Just as Gramsci develops rather than totally retracts his 1918 critique of Manzoni,
he also extends his criticisms of Esperanto using it as a moniker for tendencies within
positivist philosophy and science for reduction, narrow mindedness and a lack of
critical historicism (Gramsci, 1995, p. 304, Q11§45, see Ives, 2004b, pp. 59–60). But
here despite his criticisms of how and why standard Italian language was propagated,
Gramsci clearly supports the active involvement in creating a 'national' language:

> ... it is rational to collaborate practically and willingly to welcome everything
> that may serve to create a common national language, the non-existence
> of which creates friction particularly in the popular masses among whom
> local particularisms and phenomena of a narrow and provincial mentality
> are more tenacious than is believed. (Gramsci, 1985, p. 182, Q29§2)

Again, a superficial reading of these passages may suggest that Gramsci favours the
spread of a 'common language' as long as it is not 'imposed' but rather 'freely chosen'
by the language learners and that it would decrease tensions among subaltern groups.
However, such an interpretation would fly in the face of Gramsci's very notion of
hegemony as a critique of the 'freely chosen' nature of the acceptance of the dominant classes' worldview (and language) to the neglect of the organization of that

consent which is never totally free from coercion (e.g. Gramsci, 1971, p. 263, Q6§88). In this way, Gramsci challenges the overly simple and static question of whether the spread of English is beneficial or not. He accepts that a 'common language' can have very important benefits for certain individuals and social groups but also for the society as a whole in terms of increased possibilities of communication and solidarity, however, this acceptance does not mitigate his concern with the political inequalities often associated with these 'benefits'. Instead, for Gramsci, the crucial point is how this 'common language' is created or selected, and how it is spread.

A more detailed analysis will reveal that Gramsci's position is actually quite close to that of Ngũgĩ Wa Thiong'o, one of the fiercest critics of the role of imperial languages within colonialism and neo-colonialism. He writes, 'A common language of communication within a country, a common language of communication for the world: that is the ideal, and we have to struggle for it. But that language, whichever it would be, should not be planted in the graveyard of other languages within one country or in the world' (1993, p. 39).[16] As I will illustrate, Gramsci provides a rich explanation for how the real atrocity of such a graveyard of other languages occurs when it creates or reinforces cultural, political and economic inequalities. Gramsci does not let such criticism foreclose the growth of common languages that can foster democratic participation and decrease subordination.

I will first show the dangers that Gramsci saw in the absence of a common Italian language in order to see where Gramsci concurs in a limited way with some conservative critics of minority rights and advocates of global English. This will highlight Gramsci's insights into how language can be used to divide and 'ghettoize' people of specific social groups. Gramsci is especially concerned with how lack of access to dominant languages can exclude subaltern social groups from power, wealth and influence.

Gramsci's Critique of the Fascist Education Act

As has been emphasized, much of Gramsci's prison writings on education, including language education, must be understood in the context of his strong reaction against the Fascist Education Act of 1923, the *riforme Gentile*, of the newly appointed Minister of Education, Giovanni Gentile (Borg and Mayo, 2002, p. 93; Buttigieg, 2002, p. 129). Gentile took the opportunity provided by Mussolini to implement a plan of educational reform that he had developed starting as early as 1907 (Harris, 1960) under the influence of Benedetto Croce (Hoare & Nowell Smith, 1971, p. 24).

Of the many criticisms Gramsci made of Gentile's reform, he is most vociferous about the Act's exclusion of the teaching of 'grammar'. Gentile follows Croce's position that 'grammar' is distinct from both logic and aesthetics and is really a technical issue (see Ives, 2004a, pp. 37–40). For Croce, the teaching of grammar is akin to 'mere' instruction rather than a more broadly considered holistic education. Gramsci rejects this understanding of 'grammar' on philosophical and political grounds (Ives, 2004a, pp. 40–51). He is particularly scathing about how this definition of grammar is used to exclude working-class and other subaltern children from national culture and politics:

Is grammar only the technical aspect of language? At all events, are the idealists (especially the Gentilians) justified in their arguments about the uselessness of grammar and its exclusion from the schools? If one speaks (expresses oneself with words) in a manner which is historically determined by nations and linguistic areas, can one dispense with teaching this 'historically determined manner'? Granted that traditional normative grammar was inadequate, is this a good reason for teaching no grammar at all, for not being in the least concerned with speeding up the process of learning the particular way of speaking in a certain linguistic area, or rather leaving 'the language to be learnt through living it', or some other expression of this sort used by Gentile or his followers? All in all, this is a 'liberalism' of the most bizarre and eccentric stripe. (Gramsci, 1985, pp. 185–6, Q29§6)

Gramsci's point here mirrors in the realm of language instruction, what he describes elsewhere concerning education more generally. As Borg and Mayo describe, 'Gentile's Reform meant that working-class children are denied access to a skill which [Gramsci] must have considered fundamental for them to be able to convert common sense to good sense' (2002, p. 95).

Gramsci argues that:

If grammar is excluded from education ... it cannot thereby be excluded from 'real life' ... . In practice the national-popular mass is excluded from learning the educated language, since the highest level of the ruling class, which traditionally speaks standard Italian, passes it from generation to generation, through a slow process that begins with the first stutterings of the child under the guidance of its parents, and continues through conversation (with its 'this is how one says it', 'it must be said like this, etc.) for the rest of one's life. In reality, one is 'always studying grammar (by imitating the model one admires, etc.). (Gramsci, 1985, pp. 186–7, Q29§6)

Here Gramsci incorporates arguments similar to many conservative critics of minority language rights. For example, in Randolph Quirk's discussion that questions, but ultimately clings to, the notion of 'standard' languages, he notes, 'Certainly, ordinary folk with their ordinary common sense have gone on knowing that there are standards in language and they have gone on crying out to be taught them ... . Disdain for élitism is a comfortable exercise for those who are themselves securely among the élite' (Quirk, 1985, p. 6). Similarly, Janina Brutt-Griffler criticizes Robert Phillipson arguing that in British Africa, 'Far from forming part of "enlightened education" ... local language education [and the lack of English language education] ... had the very opposite purpose, viz., to cut off the disadvantaged socioeconomic classes from virtually all enlightenment ...' (2002, p. 78). In the quite different context of a critique of Will Kymlicka's approach to minority rights, Thomas Pogge argues that 'the fundamental duty of a just public education system is to promote the best interests of each and every child and to do so equally. This duty must trump any desire to increase or decrease the prominence of this or that language or culture in the US' (Pogge 2003, p. 118). In these various examples, education of the dominant language and its 'standards' are being supported for the presumed benefit of those most disadvantaged.

Gramsci's criticisms of Gentile's reform hinge on a similar concern. It may be detrimental and disempowering especially for 'subaltern' or 'disadvantaged' children to be denied skills in the dominant language. Indeed, Gramsci's context makes this much more stark given the fascist attempt to keep working-class and peasant children from being able to participate or interact with the national Italian elites.

However, Gramsci takes a much broader perspective than Quirk, Brutt-Griffler, Pogge and other conservative critics of minority language rights. Gramsci investigates the underlying reasons why 'ordinary folk cry out' to be taught the standards that can enable them to enter into the hegemonic power structures so as individuals they can survive and perhaps achieve a modicum of security or power and success. He goes much further than Pogge in understanding that there are structural and historical reasons that explain specific tensions between the interests of individual children and the languages and cultures from which they emerge. One example of this will be illustrated below in Gramsci's discussion of 'spontaneous grammar'. Gramsci is not content, as Quirk and Pogge are, to leave the questions of why *this* standard is prestigious or the social and historical reasons for and continuing effects of the marginalization of the non-dominant language (see Pogge, 2003, pp. 105–8).[17] Gramsci undermines Brutt-Griffler's argument that 'the desire for English is not some form of Western ideological hegemony playing itself out in the actions of the colonial oppressed of Africa and Asia. Rather, it was a rational response and a conscious strategy to resist colonial rule built on the exploitation of labor' (2002, p. 73). Gramsci's perspective shows that ideological hegemony cannot be so easily divorced from rational, conscious responses to colonization. The rationality of the conscious strategy to learn English is defined precisely by the ideological and institutional hegemony that structures the experience of colonialism. By refusing to address the political issues of hegemony, Brutt-Griffler cannot entertain the question of whether such strategies can produce structural changes capable of transforming conditions of colonial and so-called post-colonialism or neo-colonialism. She cannot determine when they might just allow individuals to adapt to the given circumstances by learning English when those scarce resources could be more effectively put towards learning other languages or towards other purposes. The conservative critics of so-called non-standard languages or minority language rights have thus reduced their analysis to such a narrow individualistic outlook as to curtail any significant redress to current subordination apart from individual assimilation.

The dynamic I am describing here closely mirrors the debates over whether or not Gramsci is proposing 'conservative' schooling for 'radical' politics, as Harold Entwistle argues. Entwistle's study highlights Gramsci's concern that to wrestle with and change the hegemonic power, organic intellectuals from dominated classes must be able to crack the code, have knowledge of, and speak the language of the dominant classes (Entwistle, 1979).

However, Entwistle and other conservative education critics' reading of Gramsci have been thoroughly and convincingly rebuffed (Buttigieg, 2002; Borg & Mayo, 2002; Giroux, 2002; Morrow & Torres, 2002). As we have seen in Gramsci's discussions of language education, he is well aware that subaltern groups cannot effectively struggle against dominant classes without knowledge of the tools and resources of education that are otherwise withheld from oppressed social groups. This is why elements of his writings on education can be (mis)read as 'conservative'. As Borg and Mayo show with a detailed analysis of Gramsci's proposed educational system and his critique of Gentile's reform, 'What Gramsci seems to be advocating is a process of education which equips children with the necessary acumen to be able to participate in an informed dialogue' (Borg and Mayo, 2002, p. 100). This provides a crucial point when addressing 'global English'; where does the teaching and usage of English equip people, average people, not just elites, to actively participate in meaningful and effective dialogue? And where does it in affect detract from such activity? As Pennycook writes, 'The issue, then, is not simply English for access to certain jobs and so forth, but rather the master's tools in order to dismantle the master's house' (Pennycook, 1998, p. 84). Under what circumstances does learning English enable such dismantling, and under what circumstances does it further entrench psychological, cultural, economic and political subordination? Gramsci is developing an educational model and theory of language to enable students to move from the 'common sense' of their family and subaltern social environments dominated by a more powerful social group and culture, to a 'good sense' and then a critical and political position of the 'philosophy of praxis' that can help overturn those conditions of subjugation (see Coben, 2002).

Gramsci expressed this point perhaps most influentially in his radical reading of Machiavelli's *The Prince*. Against Croce's interpretation of Machiavelli as the founder of a neutral science of politics 'serving reactionaries and democrats alike', Gramsci insisted that Machiavelli was writing for 'those who are not in the know'. 'Anyone born into the traditional governing stratum acquires almost automatically the characteristics of a political realist, as a result of the entire educational complex which he absorbs from his family milieu ...' Instead, Gramsci argued, Machiavelli was writing for the revolutionary class, 'it was they whom [Machiavelli] intended to educate politically' (Gramsci, 1971, p. 135, Q13§20; see also Fontana, 1993).

This grave concern of Gramsci's with language and education in maintaining oppression and inequalities in power among social groups explains his desire for a truly national common language the 'non-existence of which creates friction particularly among the popular masses ...' as quoted above. Gramsci's conclusion to his critique of Gentile's exclusion of grammar from the curriculum makes absolutely explicit that he is not simply favouring local languages and mother tongues for some 'essentialist' or romantic attachment to 'authentic' languages (see Pennycook, 1998). 'There [in Gentile's position] is all the reactionary thought of the old liberal view, a "laissez faire, laissez passer" which is not justified, as it was in Rousseau (and Gentile is more like Rousseau than he thinks) by opposition to the paralysis of Jesuit education, but which has become an abstract, "ahistorical" ideology' (Gramsci, 1985, p. 187, Q29§6). These criticisms accord perfectly with Gramsci's general rejection of Gentile's reform as 'destined not merely to perpetuate social differences but to crystallise them ...' (Gramsci, 1971, p. 40, Q12§2).

This critique of the Fascist Education Act and his advocacy of a common language for Italy, could lead one to believe that Gramsci would be in favour of not only the spread of English world wide but even the inclusion of it in education systems around the globe. Just as Gramsci castigated the Fascists for withdrawing adequate language and grammar instruction for subaltern social groups in Italy in the 1920s, advocates of 'global English' argue that not devoting significant resources to teaching English across the globe is debilitating, favouring those who have access to English learning contexts. But this would be a one-sided understanding of Gramsci's position on the politics of common languages. To understand the other side of his position more clearly, we have to turn to his writings on language and education as aspects of one's worldview and the possibilities of developing critical consciousness.

Language Imposition and Childhood Education

By looking at Gramsci's critique of Gentile's Fascist Education Reform, we have seen why Gramsci would be critical of the lack of a national common language in which an entire population including subaltern groups could be educated. Without such a language, dominant social groups can solidify their hold on elite positions within society by using their language to exclude the vast majority from the type of knowledge and skills required to grapple with questions of national politics and power. While Gramsci's focus of the 'nation' and the 'nation-state' as the community in need of a 'common language' may raise questions concerning 'cultural-linguistic pluralism inside the boundaries of the state' (Nimni, 1991, p. 113), understanding Gramsci's specific historical reasons for making this argument in the context of Italy better enables us to utilize his insights, as noted above, into political aspects of denying subaltern groups access to 'common languages'.[18]

This leads us to perhaps one of the central questions in debates on 'global English', how do we distinguish the imposition of a language from the truly 'free choice' to learn one? We must first ask why Gramsci is critical of the imposition of a language. We have seen that in his early critique of Esperanto and Manzoni in 1918, he focused on the practical problems of imposing a 'common language' if it was not the result of more thorough economic, social and political change throughout Italy. We have also noted that by his prison period, he expanded this critique and connected it to broader concerns with common sense, spontaneous philosophy and cultural hegemony.

Reinforcing this point is Gramsci's insistence that language learning is a central feature of the intellectual formation of children. He clearly sees linguistic ability as related to personal identity and self-worth, ability to think critically and creatively and is much more than just acquiring an instrument of communication. On 26 March, 1927, Gramsci sent a letter to his sister, Teresina, concerning her son, Franco:

> I hope that you will let [Franco] speak Sardinian and will not make any trouble for him on that score. It was a mistake, in my opinion, not to allow Edmea [Gramsci's niece] to speak freely in Sardinian as a little girl. It harmed her intellectual development and put her imagination in a straitjacket ... the Italian that you will teach them will be a poor, mutilated language made up of only the few sentences and words of your conversations with him, purely childish; he will not have any contact with the general environment

and will end up learning two jargons and no language: an Italian jargon for official conversation with you and a Sardinian jargon learned piecemeal to speak with the other children and the people he meets in the street or piazza. I beg you, from my heart, not to make this mistake and to allow your children to absorb all the Sardinian spirit they wish and to develop spontaneously in the natural environment in which they were born ... . (Gramsci, 1994, p. 89)[19]

While Gramsci favours children speaking their local or vernacular languages, he encourages them to learn other languages and is fully aware of the prestige and cultural politics involved in these questions of which languages children learn to speak. In a letter to his other son, Giuliano, Gramsci reflects on his own childhood noting that his classmates had great difficulty with speaking Italian, giving him a position of superiority over them (Gramsci, 1994 vol. 2, p. 356). He writes that sometimes better knowledge of Italian makes a student, 'seem to be more intelligent and quick, whereas sometimes this is not so, ...'(Gramsci, 1994 vol. 1, p. 240).

These letters complement Gramsci's discussion of how 'Language also means culture and philosophy (if only at the level of common sense) (Gramsci, 1971, p. 349, Q10§44) ... and how 'spontaneous philosophy' is contained in '1. language itself, which is a totality of determined notions and concepts ... 2. "common sense" and "good sense"; 3. popular religion ...' and that 'in "language", there is contained a specific conception of the world' (Gramsci, 1971, p. 323, Q11§12). To give up one's language, by necessity or apparent choice, is to lose a culture and a sense of oneself and one's history, as the defenders of minority languages argue.[20] For Gramsci, this creates insurmountable obstacles to the process of creating an inventory of the fragmentary elements of 'common sense' so that one can use critical reasoning and work them into 'good sense' and the philosophy of praxis.

Common Language without Imposing Language

How then do we understand Gramsci's criticisms of Manzoni, his concerns with children learning their local languages and, in short, his resistance to the hegemony of the national language (or his notion that language is an important element of the dominant hegemony), with his advocacy of a national, common language? The answer to this question contains responses to many of the criticisms that have been lodged against the advocacy of minority languages and linguistic rights in the context of the increasing spread of English.[21] It is precisely this dynamic which attracts scholars like Sonntag and Phillipson to Gramsci's notion of hegemony. It contains the structural critique of the internalization of domination with a focus on its cultural characteristics, and the potential for agency in creating resistance. I hope to illustrate this point well enough through a summary of my more extensive argument that Gramsci's discussion of different types of 'grammar' displays some of the central dynamics of 'hegemony' (Ives, 2004a, pp. 37–50; Ives, 2004b, pp. 89–100).

After rejecting Benedetto Croce's narrow definition of 'grammar' noted above (Gramsci, 1985, pp. 179–80, Q29§1), Gramsci asks 'How many forms of grammar can there be?'. He answers that there are two basic forms, those that are 'spontaneous' or 'im-manent' (what he also calls 'historical grammar') and operate more or less unconsciously, 'by which one speaks "according to grammar" without knowing it' (Gramsci, 1985, p. 180, Q29§2). And there is 'normative grammar' which is the conscious normative structure of rules that dictate how a language should be used. This is often, but not always, written, and one of the primary resources for teaching language. Gramsci expands this traditional notion of 'normative grammar' by defining it as being made up of 'reciprocal monitoring, reciprocal teaching and reciprocal "censorship" expressed in such questions as "What did you say?", "What do you mean?", "Make yourself clearer", etc. and in mimicry and teasing. This whole complex of actions and reac-tions come together to create a grammatical conformism, to establish "norms" or judgments of correctness and incorrectness' (Gramsci, 1985, p. 180, Q29§2). It is this notion that learning a language is almost by definition a question of power relationships and cannot be seen as totally free of coercion, regardless of how con-sensual the decision to learn a given language is, that accords well with critics of dominant languages and 'global English' (e.g. Bourdieu, 1991; Phillipson, 1992, pp. 72–6; 107–35, *inter alia*; May, 2001, 2003; Pennycook, 1995).

It almost seems as if Gramsci sets up a dichotomy between 'free' and 'spontaneous' grammar that is separate from power relations and those 'normative' grammars that are the vehicle for coercion and dominant ideologies and cultures being imposed on subaltern or oppressed classes. This would fit his critique of Manzoni and Espe-ranto and may lead to a simplistic rejection of 'global English' in all circumstances. However, Gramsci understands 'spontaneous' and 'normative' grammars to be in a dialectical relationship. Thus, he argues, 'One could sketch a picture of the "normative grammar" that operates spontaneously in every given society, in that this society tends to become unified both territorially and culturally, in other words it has a governing class whose function is recognized and followed' (Gramsci, 1985, p. 181, Q29§2). The supposed 'spontaneity' or unconsciousness of a grammar does not free it from unequal power relations or make it a 'natural' expression of one's being as opposed to the artificial, imposition of a 'normative' grammar that originates from the ruling class.

Quite to the contrary, in various contexts Gramsci regards 'spontaneity' as being the result not of 'free choice' but of the fragmentary, incoherent and ultimately subjugated nature of subaltern conditions. 'In the "most spontaneous" movement it is simply the case that the element of "conscious leadership" cannot be checked, have left no reliable document. It may be said that spontaneity is therefore charac-teristic of the 'history of the subaltern classes', and indeed of their most marginal and peripheral elements; these have not achieved any consciousness of the class "for itself"' (Gramsci, 1971, p. 196, Q3§48). 'Spontaneity' for Gramsci, is not a positive characteristic associated with the ability or capacity to choose for oneself or do what one wishes or decides is best for them. Rather, it is connected with the fragmentary and episodic character of the history of subaltern social groups (Gramsci, 1971, p. 54, Q25§2). Gramsci's advocacy for a 'normative grammar' for Italy is clearly related to his point that 'In acquiring one's conception of the world one always belongs to a particular grouping which is that of all the social elements which share the same mode of thinking and acting ... When one's conception of the world is not critical and coherent but disjointed and episodic, one belongs simultaneously to a multiplicity of mass human groups' (Gramsci, 1971, p. 324, Q11§12).

Here Gramsci is not referring to what we today might call 'diversity', cultural or social, but rather the situation of subaltern groups with 'two conceptions of the world, one affirmed in words and the other displayed by effective action ...' (Gramsci, 1971, p. 326, Q11§12) which entrenches their subordination since the linguistic conception of the world 'is not its own but is borrowed from another group' which is why philosophy becomes divorced from politics (Gramsci, 1971, p. 327, Q11§12), allowing 'traditional' intellectuals to present themselves as above politics (Gramsci, 1971, pp. 7–8, Q12§1) and why subaltern groups hold 'the widespread prejudice that philosophy is a strange and difficult thing just because it is the specific intellectual activity of a particular category of specialists' (Gramsci, 1971, p. 323, Q11§12).

I have argued elsewhere that this is a central dynamic of 'hegemony' explaining how 'consent' is constructed in such a manner that does not define it as the opposite of, or the lack of, coercion, but rather the relation or structuring of coercion and consent (Ives, 2004a, pp. 38–52). It certainly explains why scholars like Phillipson, Sonntag, May and Shannon would find Gramsci's 'hegemony' insightful within the politics of language specifically.

Gramsci's development of a dialectical relationship between 'spontaneous grammars' and 'normative grammars' explains why both the imposition of a language, and its concomitant worldview, works to further entrench inequalities and oppression. Language is not neutral, it is not merely a tool to move ideas from one head to another, but rather is connected to an understanding of the world and the role of speakers within it. Thus, it is futile to hope, as the proponents of 'global English' do, that a hegemony of Florentine Italian in Italy, or the spread of British or American English in the world, could actually act as a vehicle to include subaltern social groups in power structures and democratic processes. In many cases, the very circumstances that provide the incentives for people to 'freely' choose to learn English (economic prospects, political influence, cultural prestige) are the conditions for fragmented, disjointed and episodic 'common sense' where the imposed language, values and concepts will not adequately describe, organize or help them control their daily lives. Learning English may be technically a 'free choice' but it can in fact just further entrench cultural, psychological, economic and political imperialism.

That people may 'freely choose' to devote time and resources to learn English, and not other languages, in a manner that privileges the 'standard' English of so-called native speakers, is a step away from the creation of critical consciousness. Gramsci argues that 'The starting-point of critical elaboration in the consciousness of what one really is, and is 'knowing thy-self' as a product of the historical process to date which has deposited in you an infinity of traces, without leaving an inventory. Now is necessary to make initially such an inventory' (Gramsci, 1971, p. 324, Q11§12).[22] The 'imposition' or supposed 'choice' to learn any dominant language is detrimental to subaltern groups to the extent that it further submerges this starting point of critical consciousness making any such inventory that much more difficult. Thus, it is not the learning of English that is so problematic *per se*, but rather the very circumstances that lead people to make this so-called choice and the psychological, social and cultural fragmentation that it fosters.

There has been much attention given to bi- and multi-lingualism and the rejection of the assumption of monolingualism or homogeneous speech communities within nation-states. Brutt-Griffler, for example, contends that what she calls 'World English' is distinct from the domestic use of languages as well as other instances of language spread or change including international lingua franca such as French or Latin. She argues that international lingua franca are exclusive to socio-economic and intellectual elites and that national languages tend to replace other languages whereas 'World English' creates stable bilingual and multilingual speech communities (Brutt-Griffler, 2002, pp. 107–25). I will not pursue this argument from an empirical perspective with discussions like that of Sue Wright on the characterization of other so-called 'stable' multilingual societies (Wright, 2000, p. 71). Remaining on the theoretical terrain, it is clear that Gramsci's equation of Manzoni's 'solution' to the Italian language question with the project of Esperanto questions Brutt-Griffler's theoretical distinction between English as a national language (of many nation-states) and its use as an 'international' or 'world language'. Gramsci's more detailed socio-logical analysis of social groups provide a more sophisticated understanding than the notion of intellectual and socio-economic elites versus everyone else employed by Brutt-Griffler to distinguish 'world English' from other international lingua franca.[23] More importantly, his equation of Esperanto (as an international artificial language) with Manzoni's plan of 'unifying Italy' linguistically (as a nation-state), gives theoretical weight to arguments like that of Phillipson showing the role of various states, especially the US and England, in creating 'world' or 'global' English (Phillipson, 1992, pp. 137–72). It is only by forcing a separation between the political and the linguistic aspects of language spread and change that Brutt-Griffler can derive her functional distinctions between national and world language on which much of her analysis is based.

That is not to say that the crucial issues involved in the debates on the 'new varieties of English' or World Englishes are not important. On the contrary, Gramsci's focus on the relationship among spontaneous grammars and normative grammars is a terminology developed to focus on the political power dynamics in precisely such situations. Brutt-Griffler's arguments against the monolingual bias of much of sociolinguistic scholarship, her focus on macro-acquisition of languages, her critique of overly individualistic approaches, and her discussions of 'speech communities' are all very useful (Brutt-Griffler, 2002, pp. 126–47). However, if research in these areas begins from her approach of divorcing the political notions from the technically linguistic ones, it will remain quite limited. Moreover, where Brutt-Griffler would rule out Gramsci's analysis of 'national' language in Italy as having little pertinence for our current situation of 'global English', it seems to me that this is far too hasty.

Gramsci's prescription is that a truly 'national-popular' language for Italy be part and parcel of a non-passive revolution that alters the economic, social, polit-ical and cultural fabric of Italy. It is this perspective that is desperately needed in considerations of 'global English'. Gramsci proposes a linguistic 'hegemony' quite different from that which he criticizes. Rather than taking one 'spontaneous grammar'— whether of Florentine Italian or another language like 'standard' English—and imposing it, this national language should be the result of the many spontaneous grammars of all the languages, dialects and idioms throughout Italy communicating together, being coherently organized, their fragmented history being made conscious, and through a slow molecular process inextricable from social, cultural and political developments would create a 'normative grammar' for a truly national-popular language for Italy.

In order for the 'hegemony of English' to be a progressive rather than a regressive hegemony, which truly benefits the lives of the English language learners, it will have to be an English that does not replace their previous 'spontaneous grammars' (nor act as another separate language within an bi- or multi-lingual society). Rather it will have to incorporate the various spontaneous grammars in a process that would include other cultural transformations as well as economic and political changes. It is in this context, that the empirical work on global English*es* is so crucial. If as Kachru and his followers find, there is a proliferation of different varieties of English that are created by, in Gramsci's terms, the existing 'spontaneous grammars' and their interactions with English, then we can answer 'yes' to Sonntag's question about whether English can be a 'counter-hegemonic medium facilitating democratic deliberations ...' as raised above.

Conclusion

This chapter has attempted to bring an analysis of Gramsci's approach to language politics to debates around 'global English' and teaching English as a foreign or additional language. My purpose is not to suggest that Gramsci has some authoritative or privileged approach to the term 'hegemony'. Indeed, Gramsci's entire method of using other thinkers' concepts for his own purposes (Showstack Sassoon, 1990) rejects any such sanctimonious appeal. By addressing Gramsci's own writings on common languages and language education, I hope to have provided some nuance to the understandings of Gramsci's notion of 'hegemony' so that it could be more useful within debates on 'global English'. That Gramsci, in his own context, was in favour of specific means of creating a 'common language' and against others, reinforces the argument that context is crucially important (see all the contributions in Ricento, 2000; and Clayton, 1999). His notions of 'spontaneous' or 'immanent' grammar and 'normative' grammar could be very fruitful to scholars who, like Sonntag and Pennycook, consider both the structural elements of subordination and the possibilities of agency on the part of the oppressed. Gramsci provides some theoretical scaffolding to reinforce Sonntag and Pennycook's insistence that we should neither presuppose that English is, in every context, inherently, an impediment to counter-hegemonic struggle nor should we presume that it is beneficial and an effective tool for individuals to better their conditions. As I have shown, Gramsci developed the concepts of spontaneous and normative grammars in order to achieve precisely such an analysis of his language situation.

Acknowledgments

I would like to thank an anonymous reviewer and Stephen May for comments on this chatper and Peter Mayo for his work on this book.

Notes

1. To make cross-referencing among different English translations easier, I have adopted the standard method of providing both the citation of the English edition used as well as the notebook number preceded by a Q and the section number after §. This also makes it possible to locate the original Italian of the critical addition, Gramsci, 1975.
2. For a discussion of the accuracy and meaning of such numbers, see Holborow, 1999, pp. 54–60. My point here is just to give an indication of the general presence of English throughout the world.
3. De Swaan tries to explain the current 'hypercentrality' of English with quantitative rational choice theory whereby 'People will prefer to learn the language that most increases the Q-value [his measurement of the communication value of a language] of their repertoire' (De Swaan, 2001, p. 21). For more detailed critiques see Phillipson, 2004 and Ives, 2004c.
4. I will use the term 'global English' more or less synonymously with 'English as a world language' and 'the international spread of English'. There are advantages and disadvantages to each label, and important questions of what distinguishes the phenomenon from the international uses of other languages and the use of national languages and local language (often called dialects). I do not wish the term 'global English' to close any of these questions which is why I most often follow Gramsci's method of putting it in quotation marks.
5. Janina Brutt-Griffler makes the opposite contention bemoaning the intrusion of 'political terminology' on what she sees as linguistic issues; she notes that 'hegemony' along with 'dominance', 'imposition', and 'subordination' are 'metaphors chosen [that] are not particularly apt from a linguistic standpoint' (2002, p. 10, see also 64). That Gramsci actually adopted 'hegemony' substantially from Italian linguistics troubles her point here.
6. Tony Crowley initiates some connections in comparison with Mikhail Bakhtin to highlight how important context is (1996, pp. 42–3). This point has been utilized by Pennycook (2000, p. 59). Holborow also shows some awareness of Gramsci's specific writings on language, but makes only sporadic comments about them (1999).
7. This conclusion could be drawn from analyses like that of Ephraim Nimni of Gramsci's inconsistencies concerning nationalism and language despite Nimni's otherwise perceptive analysis (1991, pp. 112–18).
8. My argument has many similarities with those made by Pennycook (1998) and May (2003) in the context of minority language rights. Like both of them, I am interested in strengthening the argument for minority language rights by compelling a closer examination of what language is and how it is connected to the oppression or freedom of language users. So while I concur with the concern over language 'death' or 'genocide' (cf. Nettle & Romaine, 2000; Skutnabb-Kangas, 2000) and the political project of language rights (cf. Skutnabb-Kangas & Phillipson, 1995), I think that Gramsci's framing of these issue has a lot to offer, as will become apparent below.
9. Sonntag is raising some of the criticism of Robert Phillipson's argument about 'linguistic imperialism' as an overly structural approach de-emphasizing the role of resistance and the agency of subjugated people who may use English in their struggles (e.g. Clayton, 1999; Pennycook, 1995, pp. 49–50). Gramsci holds some insight for reframing this debate.
10. 'Hegemony' as developed by Gramsci is obviously a complex concept with layers of meanings. So I should specify here that by 'hegemony of English' I mean the unexamined acceptance that English is and should be the most important language in the world despite or because of the fact that it is connected to 'westernization', 'modernization', British colonialism and

American economic, military and cultural dominance and anyone who wishes to have control over their own conditions of life must speak English and acquiesce to these power structures.

11. Part of Manzoni's argument was that there already existed a high degree of uniformity within the Italian dialects and that Florentine Italian was actually already the Italian language: his theories of language were just revealing this fact (Reynolds, 1950).

12. Elsewhere I have explored Gramsci's counter-intuitive but astute equation of Manzoni's position with Esperanto (Ives, 2004a, pp. 30–33; Ives, 2004b, pp. 58–60).

13. While Gramsci and Bartoli were indebted to Ascoli, their position differed from his considerably (see Ives, 2004a, pp. 25–9). There may also be interesting similarities between Ascoli's and Braj Kachru's approach to World Englishes emphasizing how English is changed, altered and adapted by different communities of speakers (Kachru, 1983; see Bolton, 2005 for an overview). It is also worth noting that Gramsci never explicitly raises the issue of 'diglossia' or the distinction between the 'displacement' of a language in given areas of life as opposed to its total 'replacement' (e.g. Phillipson, 1992, p. 27). Indeed, the linguistic approaches upon which he drew seem to reject implicitly the possibility of stable diglossia (see Ives, 2004a, pp. 24–30). The extent to which the large body of empirical studies in sociolinguistics from the 1960s onwards on code-switching, diglossia and triglossia challenge Gramsci's initial assumptions requires further examination. It may be the case that the 'prestige' of the languages involved supports Gramsci's position but requires a greater degree of complexity than he described.

14. See also Ives, 2004a, 31–7, where I argue that Gramsci's position here is actually more nuanced, if underdeveloped and contradictory in parts.

15. For a somewhat dated but still useful critique of the 'neutrality of English' position see Phillipson, 1992, pp. 78–85).

16. I should note Ngũgĩ's stress that, '[t]hrough translation, the different languages of the world can speak to one another' (1993, p. 40) which is necessary to overcome the oppressive relationship among languages in this struggle for a common language since it is comparable to Gramsci's important and complex focus on translation (see Ives, 2004a, pp. 97–133).

17. For a similar critique of Pogge see May (2003, pp. 103–4).

18. From this perspective, his discussion of 'spontaneous grammars', addressed below, creates greater room for theorizing cultural-linguistic pluralism.

19. While we may want to rejection his distinction here between 'dialect' and 'language' (e.g. Steinberg, 1987, p. 199; Phillipson, 1992, pp. 38–40), Gramsci may also be thinking of the argument made by his professor, Bartoli, that the role of the Sardinian language had been underappreciated in the history of Italian vernaculars. Moreover, Franco Lo Piparo contends persuasively, that Gramsci posits an isomorphic relation between national language and dialect and those of city/country and official culture / folklore (Lo Piparo, 1979, 179–89).

20. This is not the place to rehearse debates about linguistic relativism, but I should note that Gramsci also developed a political conception of 'translation' and does not hold an extreme version of the so-called 'Sapir-Whorf hypothesis' (see Ives, 2004a, pp. 97–133).

21. The answer to this question also responds to Ephraim Nemni's claim of Gramsci's inconsistency in that 'He castigates the Italian bourgeoisie for the same reason that he praises the French Jacobins: the consolidation of a single national-popular collective will in the form of one nation in one state' (1991, p. 112). A closer reading of Gramsci reveals the distinctions between the types of hegemony that he castigates and those that he praises, as will be explained below in reference to a unified language. Nemni's argument here is also tied to his acceptance of Laclau and Mouffe's charge of Gramsci's class reductionism that I have addressed elsewhere (Ives 2005).

22. The last sentence was inexplicably omitted from Gramsci, 1971. Translation my own. Gramsci's point here about the discrepancy between a language in which political consciousness can develop and one which is fragmented and imposed from a different social group's perspective is very similar to Bourdieu's arguments (e.g. Bourdieu, 1991, pp. 81–89).

23. Brutt-Griffler admits that socioeconomic status may not govern access to English in a blunt way but it 'often governs the level of proficiency' which, by implication, has very similar effects (Brutt-Griffler, 2002, p. 125 note 5).

References

Adamson, W. L. (1980) *Hegemony and Revolution* (Berkeley, University of California Press).

Ashcroft, B., Griffiths, G. & Tiffin, H. (1989) *The Empire Writes Back* (London, Routledge).

Bolton, K. (2005) Where WE Stands: Approaches, issues and debate in world Englishes, *World Englishes*, 24:1, pp. 69–83.

Borg, C. & Mayo P. (2002) Gramsci and the Unitarian School, in: C. Borg, J. Buttigieg & P. Mayo (eds), *Gramsci and Education* (Lanham, MD, Rowman & Littlefield).

Borg, C., Buttigieg, J. A. & Mayo, P. (2002) Introduction, in: C. Borg, J. Buttigieg & P. Mayo (eds), *Gramsci and Education* (Lanham, MD, Rowman & Littlefield).

Bourdieu, P. (1991) *Language and Symbolic Power*, G. Raymond & M. Adamson, trans. (Cambridge, MA, Harvard University Press).

Bourdieu, P. & Passeron, J.-C. (1990) *Reproduction in Education, Society and Culture* (London, Sage).

Brutt-Griffler, J. (2002) *World English: A study of its development* (Clevedon, Multilingual Matters).

Buci-Glucksmann, C. (1980) *Gramsci and the State*, D. Fernbach, trans. (London, Lawrence and Wishart).

Buttigieg, J. (1995) Gramsci on Civil Society. *Boundary 2*, 22:3 (Fall), pp. 1–32.

Buttigieg, J. (2002) Education, the Role of Intellectuals, and Democracy: A Gramscian reflection, in: C. Borg, J. Buttigieg & P. Mayo (eds), *Gramsci and Education* (Lanham, MD, Rowman & Littlefield).

Clayton, T. (1999) Decentering Language in World-System Inquiry, *Language Problems and Language Planning*, 23, pp. 133–156.

Coben, D. (2002) Metaphors for an Educative Politics: 'Common Sense', 'Good Sense' and educating adults, in: C. Borg, J. Buttigieg & P. Mayo (eds), *Gramsci and Education* (Lanham, Rowman & Littlefield).

Crowley, T. (1996) *Language in History: Theories and texts* (London, Routledge).

Crystal, D. (1997) *English as a Global Language* (Cambridge, Cambridge University Press).

De Mauro, T. (1986) *Storia Linguistica Dell'Italia Unita* (Rome, Laterza).

De Swann, A. (2001) *Words of the World* (Cambridge, Polity).

Entwistle, H. (1979) *Antonio Gramsci: Conservative schooling for radical politics* (London, Routledge & Kegan Paul).

Eriksen, T. H. (1992) Linguistic Hegemony and Minority Resistance, *Journal of Peace Research*, 29:3, pp. 313–332.

Femia, J. V. (1981) *Gramsci's Political Thought* (Oxford, Clarendon).

Fontana, B. (1993) *Hegemony and Power: On the relation between Gramsci and Machiavelli* (Minneapolis, University of Minnesota Press).

Friedman, P. K. (2005) *Learning 'Local' Languages: Passive revolution, language markets, and aborigine education in Taiwan* (PhD dissertation, Temple University).

Germino, D. (1990) *Antonio Gramsci: Architect of a new politics* (Baton Rouge, Louisiana State University Press).

Giroux, H. (2002) Rethinking Cultural Politics and Radical Pedagogy in the Work of Antonio Gramsci, in: C. Borg, J. Buttigieg & P. Mayo (eds) *Gramsci and Education* (Lanham, MD, Rowman & Littlefield).

Graddol, D. (2006) *English Next: Why global English may mean the end of 'English as a foreign language'* (London, The British Council).

Gramsci, A. (1971) *Selections from the Prison Notebooks*, Q. Hoare & G. Nowell Smith, ed. and trans. (New York, International Publishers).

Gramsci, A. (1975) *Quaderni del carcere*, 4 vols., V. Gerratana, ed. (Turin, Einaudi).

Gramsci, A. (1985) *Selections from Cultural and Political Writings*, D. Forgacs & G. Nowell-Smith, eds; W. Boelhower, trans. (Cambridge, MA, Harvard University Press).

Gramsci, A. (1994) *Letters from Prison*, 2 vols., F. Rosengarten, ed.; R. Rosenthal, trans. (New York, Columbia University Press).

Gramsci, A. (1995) *Further Selections from the Prison Notebooks*, D. Boothman, ed. & trans. (Minneapolis, University of Minnesota Press).

Harris, H. S. (1960) *The Social Philosophy of Giovanni Gentile* (Urbana, University of Illinois Press).

Hoare, Q. & Nowell Smith, G. (1971) Introduction in Gramsci, 1971.

Holborow, M. (1999) *The Politics of English* (London, Sage).

Ives, P. (2004a) *Gramsci's Politics of Language: Engaging the Bakhtin circle and the Frankfurt School* (Toronto, University of Toronto Press).

Ives, P. (2004b) *Language and Hegemony in Gramsci* (London/Halifax, Pluto/Fernwood).

Ives, P. (2004c) *Managing or Celebrating Linguistic Diversity? Working Paper 03/04* (Montreal, Institute of European Studies), <http://www.iee.umontreal.ca/pubicationsfr_fichiers/COLLOQUE-2004/IvesIESfinal.pdf>

Ives, P. (2005) Language, Agency and Hegemony: A Gramscian response to post-Marxism, *Critical Review of International Social and Political Philosophy*, 8:4, pp. 455–468.

Kachru, B. B. (1983) Models for Non-Native Englishes, in: B. B. Kachru (ed.), *The Other Tongue: English Across Cultures* (Oxford, Pergamon).

Kachru, B. B. (1997) World Englishes 2000: Resources for research and teaching, in: L. E. Smith & M. L. Forman (eds), *World Englishes 2000* (Honolulu, College of Languages, Linguistics and Literature, University of Hawaii).

Lo Piparo, F. (1979) *Lingua Intellettuali Egemonia in Gramsci* (Bari, Laterza).

Macedo, D., Dendrinos, B. & Gounari, P. (2003) *The Hegemony of English* (Boulder, Paradigm).

Maiden, M. (1995) *A Linguistic History of Italian* (London, Longman).

May, S. (2001) *Language and Minority Rights* (Harlow, Pearson).

May, S. (2003) Rearticulating the Case for Minority Language Rights, *Current Issues in Language Planning*, 4:2, pp. 95–125.

McLaren, P., Fischman, G., Serra, S. & Antelo, E. (2002) The Specter of Gramsci: Revolutionary praxis and the committed intellectual, in: C. Borg, J. Buttigieg & P. Mayo (eds), *Gramsci and Education* (Lanham, MD, Rowman & Littlefield).

Monasta, A. (2002) Antonio Gramsci: The message and the images, in: C. Borg, J. Buttigieg & P. Mayo (eds), *Gramsci and Education* (Lanham, MD, Rowman & Littlefield).

Morrow, R. & Torres, C. A. (2002) Gramsci and Popular Education in Latin America: From revolution to democratic transition, in: C. Borg, J. Buttigieg & P. Mayo (eds), *Gramsci and Education* (Lanham, MD, Rowman & Littlefield).

Moss, H. (2000) Language and Italian National Identity, in: B. Haddock & Gino Bedani (eds), *Politics of Italian National Identity* (Cardiff, University of Wales Press), pp. 98–123.

Nettle, D. & Romaine, S. (2000) *Vanishing Voices. The extinction of the world's languages* (Oxford, Oxford University Press).

Ngũgĩ, wa Thiong'o (1993) *Moving the Center: The struggle for cultural freedoms* (Oxford, James Currey).

Nimni, E. (1991) *Marxism and Nationalism: The theoretical origins of a political crisis* (London, Pluto).

Parakrama, A. (1995) *De-Hegemonizing Language Standards: Learning from (post)colonial Englishes about 'English'* (New York, St. Martin's Press).

Pennycook, A. (1995) Englishes in the World/The World in English, in: J. Tollefson (ed.), *Power and Inequality in Language Education* (Cambridge, Cambridge University Press).

Pennycook, A. (1998) The Right to Language: Towards a situated ethics of language possibilities. *Language Sciences*, 20:1, pp. 73–87.

Pennycook, A. (2000) Language, Ideology and Hindsight: Lessons from colonial language policies, in: T. Ricento (ed.), *Ideology, Politics and Language Policies* (Amsterdam, John Benjamins).

Phillipson, R. (1992) *Linguistic Imperialism* (Oxford, Oxford University Press).

Phillipson, R. (2004) English in Globalization: Three approaches, *Journal of Language, Identity and Education* 3:1, pp. 73–84.

Pogge, T. (2003) Accommodation Rights for Hispanics in the United States, in: W. Kymlicka & A. Patten (eds), *Language Rights and Political Theory* (Oxford, Oxford University Press).

Quirk, R. (1985) The English Language in a Global Context, in: R. Quirk & H. G. Widdowson (eds), *English in the World* (Cambridge, Cambridge University Press).

Rassool, N. (1998) Postmodernity, Cultural Pluralism and the Nation-State: Problems of language rights, human rights, identity and power, *Language Sciences*, 20:1, pp. 89–99.

Reynolds, B. (1950) *The Linguistic Writings of Alessandro Manzoni* (Cambridge, W. Heffer).

Ricento, T. (ed.) (2000) *Ideology, Politics and Language Policies: Focus on English* (Amsterdam, John Benjamins).

Romaine, S. (1997) World Englishes: Standards and the new world order, in: L. E. Smith & M. L. Forman (eds), *World Englishes 2000* (Honolulu, College of Languages, Linguistics and Literature, University of Hawai'i).

Shannon, S. M. (1995) The Hegemony of English: A case study of one bilingual classroom as a site of resistance, *Linguistics and Education*, 7:3, pp. 175–200.

Showstack Sassoon, A. (1990) Gramsci's Subversion of the Language of Politics, *Rethinking Marxism* 3, 1 (Spring). Reprinted in A. Showstack Sassoon (2000) *Gramsci and Contemporary Politics: Beyond pessimism of the intellect* (London, Routledge).

Simon, R. (1991) *Gramsci's Political Thought Revised* ed. (London, Lawrence & Wishart).

Skutnabb-Kangas, T. (2000) *Linguistic Genocide in Education—or Worldwide Diversity and Human Rights?* (Mahwah, NJ, Lawrence Erlbaum).

Skutnabb-Kangas, T. & Phillipson, R. (eds) (1995) *Linguistic Human Rights: Overcoming linguistic discrimination* (Berlin, Waler de Gruyter).

Sonntag, S. (2003) *The Local Politics of Global English: Case studies in linguistic globalization* (Lanham, MD, Lexington).

Steinberg, J. (1987) The Historian and the *Questione Della Lingua*, in: P. Burke & R. Porter (eds), *The Social History of Language* (Cambridge, Cambridge University Press).

Tollefson, J. W. (2000) Policy and ideology in the spread of English, in: J. Kelly Hall & W. Eggington (eds), *The Sociopolitics of English Language Teaching* (Clevedon, Multilingual Matters).

Tsuda, Y. (1997) Hegemony of English vs. Ecology of Language: Building equality in international communication, in: L. E. Smith & M. L. Forman (eds), *World Englishes 2000* (Honolulu, College of Languages, Linguistics and Literature, University of Hawai'i).

Van Parijs, P. (2004) Europe's Linguistic Challenge, *European Journal of Sociology*, 45:1, pp. 113–54.

Wright, S. (2000) *Community and Communication: The role of language in nation state building and European integration* (Clevedon, Multilingual Matters).

6
Antonio Gramsci and Feminism: The elusive nature of power

MARGARET LEDWITH

My Journey to Praxis

Seamus Milne, in the 1980s, described Gramsci as 'the greatest intellectual influence on the British Left' in a decade (Milne, undated). During that period of rediscovery of Gramsci, I was on my own parallel journey to praxis. Here, I want to trace that journey in its political context before exploring my central, burning question:

> What relevance have the ideas of Gramsci, forged by Sardism, poverty, 'dis'ability and the masculinity of his culture in the early 20th century, to my critical pedagogy as a White British woman today?

True to a philosophy of praxis, as well as to feminist pedagogy, I begin my inquiry in experience. It is short but apt, and traces the role of Gramsci in the development of my own political consciousness. My drive for consciousness came from dissonance in my practice; an inner discomfort that the reality I witnessed around me was not founded on justice and democracy. At that time, I was a classroom teacher who felt a certain discomfort at the young lives acted out before my eyes. I could see that the life chances of the children I taught were determined by their early experience far more than the innate 'cleverness' by which they were judged for academic success by the state. I could also see that the competitive nature of education reinforced a sense of failure in those whose self-esteem already faltered in the face of the harshness of their lives.

Take, for instance, the life of Jennifer O'Leary. Jennifer was a shy, slightly built 10-year-old when I met her. Her father had left the family, and she had lived in the local children's home together with her two brothers since her mother's new partner had made it clear that he did not want the children. In the same schoolroom, Paula Jones assumed superiority. She, by comparison, was the daughter of the house parents in the children's home in which Jennifer was cast into the role of 'orphan', and in that sense had status above Jennifer. Paula needed that status to survive her own oppressions. She was a girl child of mixed heritage in a racist society. Jennifer's brothers, Dermot and Devlin, were in classes older and younger than Jennifer. Every Friday, Dermot would stand on the outer step of the classroom anxiously looking for his mother who had told him that one weekend she would come and get them back. When his classmates taunted him, he screamed abuse, 'You ******, I know she'll come today!'

As a young teacher, in these ways, I witnessed hegemonic forces reaching into my classroom to construct personal lives. Yet, my teacher education had told me that this was an apolitical space, decontextualised from the real world. Jack, a colleague, rubbed his hands together in the staff room at the beginning of each new academic year proclaiming, 'Well that's got that lot sorted out: these will make it, and those don't stand a chance'. Life chances dichotomously reinforced by an agent of the state, acted out unconsciously; Jack played his part well. His words resonated inside me, and my discomfort grew. Teacher education had not provided me with any answers, so I got involved in the beginning of the national adult literacy campaign seeking to address the damage done by schooling (Ledwith, 2005).

Later, I found myself in Scotland working with Vietnamese refugees traumatised by the rejection of the Western world as they floated adrift on the South China Sea. They changed my worldview with their stories of giving birth on rusty landing craft, of being separated from their children, of hope and hopelessness. In my heart, I was desolate in the knowledge that they would be at the bottom of an unjust system, their hopes dashed. As they taught me more about life than I could ever teach them, my search led me to Edinburgh University and a master's degree in community development. It was David Alexander, the adult educator, whose passion in relation to Gramsci and Freire had a profound impact on me. My engagement with both these thinkers touched me on an intellectual and emotional level. What Peter Mayo calls the 'fusion of reason and emotion' (Mayo, 2004, p. 10) contained in Freire touches people in a holistic way that reaches beyond the limitations of the intellect. At this point, I moved closer to a synthesis of action and reflection, of theory and practice, that gave me a glimpse of the potential of praxis to identify the forces of power and disempowerment. The hegemonic function of schooling, which had for so long eluded me, sat in stark relief. My naïveté shocked me; these ideas were so obvious I could not believe that false consciousness had stripped my mind of critical insight. Of course, it is not quite as simple as that. Gramsci emphasised the centrality of popular education in raising consciousness. He recognised that critical consciousness would not erupt spontaneously; false consciousness initially needs an external element to demystify the prevailing hegemony. David Alexander had played that role for me. This not only changed the nature of my understanding of the insidious nature of power, but it changed the nature of my engagement with the world. It was a powerful epistemological-ontological shift. From this point, my involvement in community development and in second-wave feminism expressed a greater unity of praxis (Ledwith, 2005).

The Concept of a Male Hegemony in Relation to Patriarchy

Here I want to acknowledge feminism's intellectual debt to Gramsci. He made an immense contribution to feminism without 'getting it'; such is the elusive nature of power and domination. His insightful analysis of *hegemony*, and the subtle nature of *consent*, offered feminists a conceptual lead on the *personal as political*.

After the Second World War, Simone de Beauvoir's *The Second Sex*, with its thrust on woman as Other, heralded what many feminists see as the real arrival of second-wave feminism in the 1960s, the decade of civil rights and student activism. 1968 saw a watershed in feminist consciousness and activism, which resonated, in my experience, into the early 1990s. In the UK, 'interest in Gramsci emphasized the need for ideological struggle to challenge ruling class hegemony' (Coole, 1993, p. 179) at the same time as Freire's *Pedagogy of the Oppressed*, with its Gramscian influence, brought inspiration to critical consciousness. Freire, on his return to Brazil from exile in 1979, 'began "relearning Brazil" by reading Gramsci and also "listening to the *popular Gramsci* in the *favelas*" ' [Brazilian shantytowns] (Torres, 1993, p. 135 in Ledwith, 2005). The two offered a powerful combination which Paula Allman saw at its most complementary in 'Freire's consideration of the political nature of education and in Gramsci's consideration of the educational nature of politics' (Allman, 1988, p. 92). But as the 1980s progressed, a powerful tide of neo-liberalism, together with feminism's and postmodernism's critiques of metanarratives with their masculinist bias, led Gramsci to fall out of favour. This marked an important shift in which debates around class and patriarchy eventually swayed in favour of feminism's emphasis on cultural identity and difference. Contradictorily, in relation to my debate on Gramsci and feminism, this neglected to integrate the economic nature of gender politics. In the UK, feminism's lack of political vigilance provided a smokescreen for Thatcherism's ideology of individualism, resulting in children and lone mothers imperceptibly replacing older people as most at risk of poverty (Oppenheim & Harker, 1996). Child poverty escalated from 14 per cent in 1979 to 34 per cent by 1996/7 (Flaherty *et al.*, 2004, p. 145), leaving the UK with one of the highest rates of child poverty compared with other countries facing similar economic trends—a situation which persists despite a raft of policies founded on the Blair/Brown government's political commitment to ending child poverty by 2020.

Clearly, there was a need for a more complex analysis which embraced difference but which did not reduce this to a single source of oppression, one which operated from multiple intersecting bases. During the 1970s, Juliet Mitchell began this process by identifying key structures for women's oppression: production, reproduction, sexuality and the socialisation of children.

> By arguing that each structure within the family has a certain autonomy in its capacity to subject women and that these structures themselves rebound on the economy, Mitchell was able to show that women's entry into the workforce would be insufficient to emancipate them since gains (such as working or controlling fertility) are compensated by losses elsewhere (such as renewed emphasis on mothers' socializing role)'. (Coole 1993, p. 180)

By the 1980s, Arnot was arguing that male hegemony consists of a multiplicity of moments which have persuaded women to accept a male dominated culture and their subordination within it (Kenway, 2001). The result is a constructed reality which is qualitatively different from that of men, in which women are diminished and exploited within a *common sense* patriarchal view of the world. Gramsci turned the key to the personal as political with his reinterpretation of the traditional Marxist concept of *hegemony*, opening our consciousness to the public/private divide and the way that domination permeates the most intimate aspects of our being through our interactions in civil society, for example, the family, community, schools and formal religions which remain key sites of male domination. This is the basis for Gramsci's acknowledged contribution to feminist thought which has provided a tool of analysis for understanding the sites of gendered oppression in society. By exploring the nature of consent, we come to see that hegemony is always in process, in continuous struggle, and we begin to see that feminist consciousness is the beginning of questioning the nature of that consent in relation to patriarchy.

These were the ideas that we were working with in community development practice in that period.

Hattersley Women for Change

The 1980s saw my own activism and professional practice informed by both feminism and Freirean-Gramscian thought in relation to popular education. It was a time of grassroots activism in which women came together in leaderless groups to explore consciousness from lived experience. We translated this into collective action for change based on a vision of social justice for all. For instance, in August 1981, a group of women who had never before been involved in political action, marched from Cardiff to Greenham to protest against the siting of cruise missiles in Britain. This was the start of the Greenham Women's Peace Movement, which 'highlighted the development of a new strand of community action' (Dominelli, 1990, p. 119). A praxis began to evolve with emphasis on lived experience as the basis of theoretical understanding.

In praxis, as a community worker, I worked in partnership with Wendy, a Hattersley woman and community activist. We had many discussions about Freire and Gramsci, and likened our roles in Hattersley to that of the *organic* and *traditional intellectual*. She lived the harsh reality of poverty pre-ordained by her working-class roots. Poverty had touched my life in many ways, and as women we shared many life themes, but I had been protected in the long term by my class privilege. Through experiences held in common, differentiated by class, we found a bond and shared a commitment to develop popular education for women in Hattersley. This was the mid-1980s, when the political context in the UK was being dramatically reshaped by New Right ideology under Thatcherism, at the same time as new social movements, and second-wave feminism in particular, articulated a politics of difference. It was a time of activism and alliance, when the Women of Greenham Common and Women Against Pit Closures were supported by a network of local Greenham Support Groups and Miners' Support Groups. It was a time when, on a mission of solidarity, I travelled in Nicaragua, experiencing participatory democracy in action and linking community groups across our different continents. I still feel the fear as I remember being caught up in a Contra raid, where women had been abducted and men were left injured; I still feel the tears of the mothers whose sons and daughters were missing, abducted from their activism in the outstanding literacy and health campaigns inspired by Freire; I still remember the shock of the sonic boom set off by American aircraft every evening over Managua in an attempt to assert the might of capitalism over this little country's bid for true participatory democracy. It was a time of hope and inspiration when Nicaragua and

Nelson Mandela were symbolic of peace and justice in the dawning of a wider political consciousness.

In communities like Hattersley, marked by a *culture of silence*, there was no tradition of meeting in groups. We waded through the apathy and disillusionment of local women. In this predominantly White, working-class community, we were faced with overt sexism, covert racism and vehement homophobia. Culturally, there was immense pressure to conform to working-class norms, which resulted in a denial of difference, at the same time as working-class solidarity was being eroded by individualism. People were pre-occupied with day-to-day survival of the harshness of their lives as poverty increased under high unemployment and the reactionary welfare policies implemented by the Thatcher government.

Wendy began the process by personally approaching women on the streets to set up a writing group as a route to critical consciousness. Local women slowly became more involved in community groups; problematising their everyday reality through a diversity of projects from Hattersley Women Writing to Woodwork for Women, they began to question from a more critical perspective. This was a triumph, but, as Freire (1972) would say, could not claim true critical consciousness unless it emerged as collective action. Moving from successful projects to a coherent movement for change was more problematic. Hattersley Forum, a democratic platform for debate in the community, provided an umbrella organisation for determining action for change. It occurred to me that Gramsci's notion of the *factory council* could be replaced by the community forum as a site of intervention where women could be central to the process of change. Key women activists had positioned themselves on the forum executive, but the forum meeting itself remained a male-dominated context where women in general felt intimidated by male power. We needed a space where women could start from the stories of their lived experience and examine the social, historical and cultural shaping of these narratives.

Gradually, we hit upon the idea of identifying a group of women who were already involved in community projects and inviting them to form a core group at the heart of Hattersley Women for Change. At the initial meeting, ten of us sat round tentatively sharing ideas. Of these, eight decided to meet weekly to explore the issues which were affecting women's lives through a local history project. From this, we would plan a popular education programme for local women. Ages ranged from twenty-three to sixty-eight, and amongst us there were varying differences of ability and ethnicity. At the same time as we were seeking answers to our questions, we were also seeking a strategy for developing critical consciousness on a level which had the potential for releasing the energy for collective change. We negotiated with Hattersley Forum to create Hattersley Women's Room in the community centre. This was a space where women could meet in a women-only environment in *culture circles*. We went out on the streets talking to women wherever they gathered in their community and eventually launched our programme in fine style with food and wine, inviting all women to come and celebrate, which they did! The response was encouraging. By the following week, I faced the realisation that it was not going to be that easy. No new faces had appeared inside the room, despite the fact that many peered in curiously from outside in the community centre snack bar.

As my hopes evaporated, Wendy, in her infinite wisdom, reminded me of the length of the process, of the fact that this sort of coming together was culturally outside their experience, of the need to reflect and perhaps reorganise. She was right of course! Things did not change until there was a critical incident. One morning I had a complaint that the children, left unsupervised, were using the enormous hall, the focal point of the community centre, as a race track, careering into the elderly, sight-impaired residents who were meeting that day. The tedium of yet another conflict situation in a community which raged *horizontal violence* at every tip and turn, exasperated me. As manager of the community centre, I had the responsibility to oversee these incidents, and I strode across determined to restore peace. The group of young mothers who spent most of their days in the centre's snack bar escaping from the harsh reality of their lives were either oblivious to or did not care about the havoc their children wreaked around them. Carole, angered by my perceived power and authority, screamed at her son as I approached, 'Freeze, Anthony, here she comes!'. Furious, and failing in the heat of the moment to locate my actions as political rather than personal, I rose to my full power and delivered a pronouncement about parental responsibility. A hush descended over every corner of this enormous space, and in that silence I pivoted in as dignified a way as I could muster, and left.

That afternoon, Carole appeared in my office for the first time. We talked on a personal level for the first time, sharing our feelings, our hopes, our despair, listening from the heart and soul. She told me that the incident that morning was the first time she had seen my calm exterior ruffled, that it broke the ice and made me human in a way that she understood. We parted friends. So, when I was approached by the local health visitor about concerns that women would not use the local clinic for ante-natal care, the first thought I had was to involve Carole. In dialogue, across barriers, we developed a health project in the community centre where Carole worked in partnership with the midwife. This encounter gave the Women's Room the seal of approval from local women. In relation to Hattersley Women for Change and wider collective action, it took a year to get the breakthrough we wanted. By then, many new women were getting involved in the administration and decision-making. This was just the beginning of women coming together to explore their consciousness through a wide range of activities and projects; a moving out from a core of women activists to extend confidence and understanding on a broader scale in the community. The aim was that, in time, these women would be taking action collectively and linking with others in communities everywhere through the credit union movement, the 'grey power' movement and women's networks. We witnessed the way in which men asserted power over this process using invasion of our women-only space, humiliation and ridicule. We also witnessed the hegemonic ways in which women's lives were put at risk by the public/private divide allowing domestic violence to be beyond the remit of police protection, exacerbated by class prejudice. Hattersley was a place where women 'got what they deserved' in the words of the police. Insight into *ideological persuasion*, and the way in which the dominant ideology reaches through the institutions of civil society into the minds of local people helped me to make sense of what often felt futile.

Patti Lather in her work, at this time in the mid-1980s, drew on Gramsci's notion of a *war of position* and the role of the *intellectuals* in relation to feminist political action. Lather takes Gramsci's emphasis on everyone's innate capacity to be philosophers and considers this in relation to the way that women have documented experience-based knowledge and acted to become prominent in all social institutions, claiming that this constitutes a *war of position*: 'many small revolutions ... many small changes in relationships, behaviors, attitudes and experiences' (Kenway, 2001, p. 59). She places particular emphasis on the role of women as intellectuals in the tide of developing critical consciousness. In Hattersley, we recognised that we were part of women's knowledge in the making, of *women's ways of knowing* (Belenky *et al.*, 1997).

The Changing Theoretical and Political Context

In this section, I move into the changing intellectual and political context which accelerated from the 1980s into the new millenium.

> This interdependent world system is based on the exploitation of oppressed groups, but the system at the same time calls forth oppositional cultural forms that give voice to the conditions of these groups. White male bourgeois dominance is being challenged by Black people, women and other oppressed groups, who assert the validity of their own knowledge and demand social justice and equality in numerous political and cultural struggles ... A major theoretical challenge to traditional Western knowledge systems is emerging from feminist theory, like other contemporary approaches, validates difference, challenges universal claims to truth, and seeks to create social transformation in a world of shifting and uncertain meanings. (Weiler in Holland & Blair, 1995, p. 23)

Paradoxically, the post-structuralist critiques of class metanarratives which laid the foundations for postmodernism from the mid-1980s, dislocated Gramsci in favour of 'mini-narratives rather than metanarratives, multiple identities rather than political identities, positioning rather than repositioning, discourse rather than the politics of discourse, performance rather than poverty, inscription rather than political mobilization, and deconstruction rather than reconstruction' (Kenway, 2001, p. 60). The paradox here is that Gramsci helped to provide the conceptual tools by which this became possible. Here I am mindful of bell hooks' acknowledgment of Freire. She found that Freire offered a structure within which she could define her experience of racism on a global level, when the radical struggle of Black women was not welcomed in the early, White, bourgeois feminist frame (hooks, 1993, p. 151). hooks refers to Freire's 'blind spot' to questions of gender, but acknowledges the ways in which his pedagogy gave her the conceptual tools that offered her insight into the nature of her own oppression as a Black American woman, helping her to see herself as a subject in resistance, thus locating a contradiction between White women and a third-world man (hooks, 1993, p. 150).

In much the same way as metanarratives were derided by White feminists as obscuring male domination, early, White, second-wave feminists were in turn challenged by Black women on grounds of difference. In other words, White feminists stood accused of defining 'woman' from a White perspective, exposing a White power which has the arrogance to overlook other aspects of difference. This is a consequence of what bell hooks (1984) attributes to the either/or dichotomous thinking so central to Western ideological thought, where a concept is only definable in relation to its perceived Other. Early second-wave feminists had defined 'woman' in relation to 'man' overlooking the ways in which 'race', class and gender intersect. These images are 'key in maintaining interlocking systems of race, class and gender oppression' (Hill Collins, 1990, p. 68).

The tide of neoliberalism that engulfed us in the 1980s provided a hothouse for germinating globalisation. Neoliberal globalisation is the 'market-organized and imposed expansion of production that emphasizes comparative advantage, free trade, export orientations, the social and spatial divisions of labour, and the absolute mobility of corporations' (Fisher & Ponniah, 2003, p. 28). This form of corporate capitalism, where the most powerful systems of the West dominate the world economically, invades other cultures with a Western worldview which works on political, cultural, racial, gendered, sexual, ecological and epistemological differences. In other words, in the name of a free market economy not only is labour exploited in the interests of capital (class), but the same structures of oppression which subordinate groups of people according to 'race', gender, age, sexuality, ethnicity, 'dis'ability are being reproduced on a global level.

> Neoloberal globalization is not simply economic domination of the world but also the imposition of a monolithic thought (pensamento unico) that consolidates vertical forms of difference and prohibits the public from imagining diversity in egalitarian, horizontal terms. Capitalism, imperialism, monoculturalism, patriarchy, white supremacism and the domination of biodiversity have coalesced under the current form of globalization ... .
> (Fisher and Ponniah 2003, p. 10)

Wealth is increasingly transferred from poor to rich countries by exploiting the labour and resources of developing countries in order to feed the consumerist greed of the West. The consequences are increased social divisions both within and between countries. This has resulted in complex, convoluted, interlinking and overlapping oppressions which are poorly understood and therefore infrequently challenged. Yet, it is a fragile system, open to abuse as witnessed by the current crisis of capitalism triggered by banking practices, resulting in recession, and maybe full depression.

Clearly critical consciousness which solely looks to class is founded on Western cultural assumptions that subordinate indigenous belief systems. This reflects the cultural dominance that gave moral legitimacy to capitalism and continues to give economic superiority in the process of globalisation. Conversely, ecological thought acknowledges the way that cultures are founded on natural systems, and emphasises that diverse indigenous cultures have evolved in harmony with their natural environments. Cultural diversity thus becomes essential for biological diversity and histories based on local economic development offer alternatives for a future which reflects values other than consumer lifestyles: a harmonious co-existence between social justice and environmental justice.

Eco-feminism's embrace of the environment and sustainability arises from a critical connection between 'death of nature' and the rise of patriarchy, and can be explored through the work of such people as Charlene Spretnak, Carolyn Merchant and Vandana Shiva. The central argument from eco-feminism is that 'a historical, symbolic and political relationship exists between the denigration of nature and the female in Western cultures' (Spretnak, 1997, p. 181). Eco-feminism is rooted in principles of 'harmony, co-operation and interconnection' which challenge the perceived male principles of competition, 'discrimination, extremism and conflict' (Young, 1990, p. 33). This reaches beyond simple ideas of reformism to profoundly challenge capital's competitive worldview; exposing it as a system which elevates men over women and the natural world in ranked order importance, and, as such, is fundamentally corrupt. Eco-feminism calls for an alternative worldview based on harmony and cooperation, non-violence and dignity, a view which embraces both public and private, local and global, humanity and the natural world in equal measure. It reflects women's concerns for preserving harmonious life on earth over time and space. Crescy Cannan stresses that not only is the environmental crisis a crisis for us all, but it disproportionately affects both the poor and the South and so 'intensifies forms of inequality and threatens collective goods—thus it is a human crisis as well as a threat to the entire planet' (2000, p. 365).

In this respect, Fisher and Ponniah (2003) suggest that any counter-hegemony must tread that fine line of embracing a respect for difference at the same time as being able to create a common vision: 'If the global movements are to prosper, they have to produce a vision that allows them to maintain simultaneously both their convergence and their difference' (2003, p. 13).

Gramsci's Continuing Relevance to Feminism

The debate that centres on a view that 'Marxism and feminism are one, and that one is Marxism' has been problematic for feminism (Hartmann, 1981, p. 2). The relationship between capitalism and patriarchy as separate but interrelated systems in which dominant groups have a material interest began in the 1980s and still rages (Ferguson & Folbre, 1981, p. 314). The view that feminism is less important than class or even divisive of class is still argued by Marxists and has risen as a backlash against postmodernism arguing the primacy of class (Allman, 1999, 2001; Hill *et al.*, 1999). Paula Allman (1999), for example, draws attention to the complex ways that global capitalism simultaneously cleaves divisions of poverty and wealth within and between countries and uses individualism as a smokescreen for its necessary illusion of progress, giving legitimacy to this juxtaposition of extremes of wealth and poverty.

In these times when private patriarchy has transcended the divide to public patriarchy giving a distorted vision of equality, Ferguson and Folbre argue: 'as historical factors change the rewards from and opportunities to control these goods and services, men's motives and abilities to control women vary, and the character and degree of patriarchal domination is modified' (1981, pp. 316–326). The contradiction between women's paid and unpaid work remains: 'the way the domestic sphere, the world of work and the state are interrelated dictate a battle on all fronts, a war of position in Gramsci's terms' (Showstack Sassoon, 1987a, p. 174).

Returning to Arnot, 'male hegemony, [she] argues, should be perceived "as a whole series of separate moments through which women have come to accept a male dominated culture, its legality, and their subordination to it and in it ... [which] together ... comprise a pattern of female experience which is qualitatively different from that of men" ' (Arnot, 1984, p. 64 in Kenway, 2001, p. 57).

Sylvia Walby (1992, 1994), in this same vein, argues the dangers of rejecting the centrality of patriarchy. In line with my focus on Gramsci, she sees the limitations of poststructuralism and postmodernism as 'a neglect of the social context of power relations' (1992, p. 16). Her position is that postmodernism has gone too far in fragmenting concepts of gender, 'race' and class, thereby overlooking structures which cleave these divisions. Marxism may have subsumed all forms of discrimination under class, but postmodernists stand accused of fragmenting overarching concepts. Walby emphasises three important issues raised by Black women: racist structures within the labour market; ethnic experience and racism; and locating the intersection of ethnicity and gender as an alternative site of analysis, both culturally and historically.

Walby (1994) offers six causal bases from which to analyse patriarchy: paid work, housework, sexuality, culture, violence and the state. By addressing the interrelationships between these structures, we avoid the trap of reductionism or essentialism. She warns that if we focus on disintegration, we are in danger of missing other patterns of re-organisation which offer insights into new forms of gender, ethnicity and class from a global dimension. For instance, the feminisation of labour in the UK is not only the result of industrial restructuring here, but the British economy depends on the exploitation of Third World women, thus 'there is a strong case for the interconnectedness of the exploitation of First and Third World women by patriarchal capitalism' (1994, p. 232). She cites Swasti Mitter's (1986) case for a 'common bond for women in the newly globalised economy' (Walby, 1994, p. 234) within a recognition of difference.

Peter Mayo points out that 'one has to go beyond Gramsci to avoid Eurocentrism and beyond both Gramsci and Freire to avoid patriarchal bias' (Mayo, 1999, p. 146). In this respect, Weiler refers to Gloria Anzaldua's conception of the *new mestiza* as a postcolonial feminist, warning that feminism can be an invasion of the self, unless patriarchy is critiqued from Western conceptions of *linear rationality, white privilege,* and *assumptions of universal truths.* Antiracist feminists educators have 'stressed that critical and feminist pedagogies, whilst claiming an opposition to oppression, are in danger of taking a kind of imperial and totalizing stance of knowing and "speaking for" those who are to be educated into truth' (Weiler, 2001, p. 72). Weiler rightly raises caution around concepts of *social identity* and *authority* in speaking for silenced others, and this is clearly an issue for global feminism.

In these times of globalisation, in order to avoid falling into a trap of what could be termed 'postcolonial feminism', we need more than ever to develop analyses of the interlocking oppressions of difference, context and level. Based on Walby's (1992, 1994) argument, I put the case for a three-dimensional model through which we can explore the intersections of oppressions, thereby identifying potential sites of liberation. These three dimensions are: i) **difference**: age, 'race', class, gender, sexual identity, 'dis'ability, ethnicity; ii) **contexts**: economic, cultural, intellectual, physical, environmental, historical, emotional, spiritual on another, and iii) **levels**: local, national, regional and global which form a complex set of interrelationships which not only interweave between axes, but which also intertwine on any one axis. (Ledwith, 2001, 2005). The basis of my argument relates to Gramsci's emphasis on critical education, history and culture, knowing who we are and what has shaped our reality on a multiplicity of dimensions in order to act together for change.

A transformative reach, from personal empowerment to collective global action, is vital to any critical analysis. 'The starting point of critical elaboration is knowing what one really is ... as a product of the historical process to date which has deposited in you an infinity of traces, without leaving an inventory' (Gramsci, 1971, p. 324). In this respect, Mo Griffiths' talks about the 'little stories' that link voice to narrative making that vital connection between the deeply personal and the profoundly political ... 'by taking the particular perspective of an individual seriously; that is, the individual as situated in particular circumstances in all their complexity [and linking this] to grander concerns like education, social justice and power' (Griffiths, 2003, p. 81). Griffiths supports the idea that 'little stories' restore self-respect through dignity, mutuality and conviviality—but stresses that this is not transformative until it becomes a collective process.

Similarly, Darder talks about the way she provides learning contexts in which she resists giving answers, but encourages people 'to reach into themselves and back to their histories' (2002, p. 233). Using reflective writing to explore the inner depths of memory and history, she works with her students to analyse these from theoretical perspectives. This offers a past-present-future dynamic, 'moving between present and past with a view to contributing towards a transformed future' (Mayo, 1999, p. 147). At the same time, it offers personal/political and local/global dynamics, such is the complexity of the power that we are struggling to identify with and transform.

It is imperative that this inner-outer movement links people in alliance. My own research with Paula Asgill indicated that autonomy is a precursor of sustainable alliances across difference, in this case between Black and White women (Ledwith & Asgill, 2000, 2007). Without this understanding of who we are and what has shaped our reality, there is no basis for sustained action across difference. This, in turn, links to Doyal and Gough's (1991) notion of personal autonomy as a human need, and as a precursor of critical autonomy and collective action. This thinking connects with Gramsci's *war of position*, moving from personal to critical levels of consciousness and linking a diversity of social groups and organisations in alliance as a collective force for change.

To Return to My Original Question: What Relevance Have Gramsci's Ideas to Feminist Pedagogy Today?

Gramsci's impact on my own political consciousness, most particularly through the concept of hegemony, was profound in its analysis of the insidious nature of power and the role of consent. Retrospectively, I was able to understand schooling as hegemonic, and to see my own role as a young teacher as complicit in this process. Teacher education is conservative, and works well, albeit 'unconsciously', in training agents of the state to maintain the *status quo*. There are many 'Jacks' that it sends out into the formative lives of children. When I eventually discovered Gramsci, he gave me the conceptual tools to make sense of my own life and the experiences which had shaped me and those around me. He triggered my feminist consciousness.

Gramsci provided feminism with the tools with which to make sense of the personal as political through the concept of *hegemony* and female-specific forms of coercion and consent. Ironically, feminism turned on him as metanarrative and dichotomous in thought, provoking major debates between the relationship of patriarchy and capital. But, the insights that postmodern feminism contributed to an understanding of difference holds a tension for transformative action in times when we need to go beyond the self and engage in political action.

We face 'twin global crises of justice and sustainability' (Reason, 2002, p. 3), a context within which action is imperative. A rereading of Gramsci in relation to an analysis of power and difference could contribute to the theoretical foundation for a new-world view. The top-downness of our current system is, I believe, essentially corrupt and incapable of reform. We need to refocus our attention on a horizontal axis, one in which superiority and inferiority are replaced by difference and diversity, and in which humanity and the natural world can co-exist symbiotically.

The enriched insights into difference offered by postmodernism, reconsidered in the context of globalisation, offer immense potential for strategic change with critical education at its heart. This needs to be seen on an inner/outer continuum, which extends from personal to political in analysis, and from local to global in action.

Capital's transition from an industrial to a post-industrial global economy calls for a strongly defined self within a cultural-historical-political analysis which attends to difference and power. I see this as a form of critical autoethnography which locates the person within the power structures which shape experience, and which provokes consciousness of self as the basis of critical consciousness. It is a process which engages with personal autonomy as a precursor of critical, collective autonomy, thus bridging the individual and collective (Doyal & Gough, 1991). Doniger (1998) describes it as looking through the microscope at the thousands of details that bring our stories to life, and through the telescope to see the unifying themes. This was the nature of the identity politics which engaged me with Hattersley women as the basis of wider action for change.

It requires a fundamental shift of analysis to address the complex interconnectedness of a loci of oppressions (Ledwith, 2001, 2005). In these ways, a multiplicity of hegemonies is understood within the complex interrelatedness of oppressions. This not only offers insight into sites of intervention, but offer strategies for uniting 'social agents of unequal power' (Kenway, 2001, p. 58); a *war of position* in which the concept of alliance across difference get us beyond a simplistic structural analysis. In this way, the capital/labour contradiction which Gramsci extended to a 'national-popular', oppressor/oppressed dichotomy is extended to a local/global analysis, but within an analysis of difference which addresses the reach of global power into a diversity of personal lives.

References

Allman, P. (1988) Gramsci, Freire and Illich: Their contributions to education for socialism, in: T. Lovett (ed.), *Radical Approaches to Adult Education* (London, Routledge).

Allman, P. (1999) *Revolutionary Social Transformation: Democratic hopes, political possibilities, and critical education* (Westport, CT, Bergin & Garvey).

Allman, P. (2001) *Critical Education against Global Capitalism: Karl Marx and revolutionary critical education* (Westport, CT, Bergin & Garvey).

Belenky, M., Clinchy, B., Goldgerger, N. & Tarule, J. (1997) *Women's Ways of Knowing: The development of self, voice, and mind* (10th anniversary edn.) (New York, Basic Books).

Cannan, C. (2000) The Environmental Crisis, Greens and Community Development, *Community Development Journal*, 35:4 (October), pp. 365–376.

Coole, D. (1993) *Women in Political Theory: From ancient misogyny to contemporary feminism* (Hemel Hempstead, Harvester Wheatsheaf).

Darder, A. (2002) *Reinventing Paulo Freire: A pedagogy of love* (Oxford, Westview).

Dominelli, L. (1990) *Women and Community Action* (Birmingham, Venture Press).

Doniger, W. (1998) *The Implied Spider: Politics and theology in myth* (New York, Columbia University Press).

Doyal, L. & Gough, I. (1991) *A Theory of Human Need* (London, Macmillan).

Ferguson, A. & Folbre, N. (1981) The Unhappy marriage of Patriarchy and Capitalism, in: L. Sargent (ed.), *op cit.*

Fine, M., Weiss, L., Powell, L., & Mun Wong, L. (1997) *Off White: Readings on race, power and society* (New York, Routledge).

Fisher, W. F. & Ponniah, T. (2003) *Another World Is Possible: Popular alternatives to globalization at the world social forum* (London, Zed).

Flaherty, J., Veit-Wilson, J. & Dornan, P. (2004) *Poverty: The facts* (5th edn.) (London, Child Poverty Action Group).

Freire, P. (1972/82) *Pedagogy of the Oppressed* (Harmondsworth, Penguin).

Goldberger, N., Tarule, J., Clinchy, B. & Belenky, M. (eds) (1996) *Knowledge, Difference, and Power: Women's ways of knowing* (New York, Basic Books).

Gramsci, A. (1971) *Selections from Prison Notebooks* (London, Lawrence & Wishart).

Griffiths, M. (2003) *Action for Social Justice in Education: Fairly different* (Maidenhead, Open University Press).

Hartmann, H. (1981) The Unhappy Marriage of Marxism and Feminism: Towards a more progressive union, in: L. Sargent (ed.), *op cit.*

Hill Collins, P. (1990) *Black Feminist Thought: Knowledge, consciousness and the politics of empowerment* (London, Unwin Hyman).

Hill, D., McLaren, P., Cole, M. & Rikowski, G. (eds) (1999) *Postmodernism in Educational Theory: Education and the politics of human resistance* (London, The Tuffnell Press).

Hooks, B. (1984) *Feminist Theory: From margin to center* (Boston, South End Press).

Hooks, B. (1993) bell hooks Speaking about Paulo Freire—the Man, his Work, in: P. McLaren & P. Leonard (eds), *Paulo Freire: A critical encounter* (London, Routledge).

Kenway, J. (2001) Remembering and Regenerating Gramsci, in: K. Weiler (ed.), *Feminist Engagements: Reading, resisting and revisioning male theorists in education and cultural studies* (London, Routledge).

Ledwith, M. (2001) Community Work as Critical Pedagogy: Re-envisioning Freire and Gramsci, *Community Development Journal*, 36:3, pp. 171–182.

Ledwith, M. (2005) *Community development: A critical approach* (Bristol, Policy Press).

Ledwith, M. & Asgill, P. (2000) Critical alliance: Black and white women working together for social justice, *Community Development Journal*, 35:3, pp. 290–299.

Ledwith, M. & Asgill, P. (2007) Feminist, Anti-racist Community Development: Critical alliance, local to global, in: L. Dominelli (ed.), *Revitalising Communities in a Globalising World* (Aldershot, Ashgate).

Mayo, P. (1999) *Gramsci, Freire and Adult Education: Possibilities for transformative action* (London, Zed).

Mayo, P. (2004) *Liberating Praxis: Paulo Freire's legacy for radical education and politics* (London, Praeger).

Milne, S. (undated) *Fifty Years on, Labour Discovers a Guru* (London, The Guardian).

Oppenheim, C. & Harker, L. (1996) *Poverty: The Facts*, (London, Child Poverty Action Group).

Reason, P. (2002) *Justice, Sustainability and Participation*, available at http://www.bath.ac.uk/~mnspwr/.

Sargent, L. (ed.) (1981) *The Unhappy Marriage of Marxism and Feminism: A debate on class and patriarchy* (London, Pluto Press).

Showstack Sasson, A. (1987) *Gramsci's Politics* (2nd edn.) (London, Hutchinson).

Showstack Sassoon, A. (ed.) (1987a) *Women and the State* (London, Hutchinson).

Spretnak, C. (1997) *The Resurgence of the Real: Body, nature and place in a hypermodern world* (Harlow, Addison-Wesley).

Torres, C. A. (1993) From the 'Pedagogy of the Oppressed' to a 'Luta Continua': the political pedagogy of Paulo Freire, in: P. McLaren and P. Leonard (eds), *Paulo Freire: A critical encounter* (London, Routledge).

Walby, S. (1992) *Theorizing Patriarchy* (Oxford, Blackwell).

Walby, S. (1994) Post-postmodernism? Theorizing Gender, *The Polity Reader in Social Theory* (Cambridge, Polity Press).

Weiler, K. (1995) A Feminist Pedagogy of Difference, in: J. Holland & M. Blair with S. Sheldon (eds), *Debates and Issues in Feminist Research and Pedagogy* (Clevedon, Multilingual Matters/ The Open University).

Weiler, K. (2001) Rereading Paulo Freire, in: K. Weiler (ed.), *Feminist Engagements: Reading, resisting, and revisioning male theorists in education and cultural studies* (London, Routledge).

Young, A. (1990) *Femininity in Dissent* (London, Routledge).

7

Towards a Political Theory of Social Work and Education

(Translated by Florian Sichling with editing by Peter Mayo)

UWE HIRSCHFELD

1.

In order to suggest a political education of social work along the lines of Gramsci's hegemony-theory, this chapter aims to achieve two things:

(1) it seeks to contribute to the development of a political/radical analysis and justification for social work, a profession with a consistent and radical political self-understanding.
(2) on the other hand, it attempts to consciously shape this accepted political component; it tackles the question: by what means can political education be made an integral component of social work?

The chapter attempts to realise these aims within the context of Gramsci's hegemony theory, based on an understanding of the two interrelated areas involved, namely political analysis and theory and the actual practice of social work and political education. In this attempt, the political understanding of social work is grounded in a critical-materialistic theory. In this context, individual and collective formation processes are understood as moments of self performance, what Marx calls, in the *Theses on Feuerbach*, 'revolutionary practice'.

It seems reasonable to provide a rough outline of Gramsci's thoughts at this point. One must keep in mind that Gramsci provided not a *Theory of Hegemony* handbook[1] but repeatedly revised notes; these fragments were not intended to be published but served mainly as a means of self-assurance. His notes therefore are not to be seen as a source for a final theory. Nevertheless his thoughts about a new concept of Marxism as a 'philosophy of praxis' can stimulate an analysis of one's conditions: 'the *prison notes* remain a painful document, not because they provide finished explanations, but because they bring up difficult and unresolved questions and an antidote against self-satisfaction.' (Buttigieg, 1994, p. 554).

Gramsci's initial thoughts focused on the reasons why a revolution did not take place in industrialized and highly developed West-European states. Even economic crises seemed unable to threaten the reproduction of bourgeois society. In addition to traditional Marxist views of the State, Gramsci shed light on the many ways, apart from the use of force, by which the consent of the subaltern classes to bourgeois rule is secured and organised (see Gramsci Gef. 7, H. 12, §1, 1502 and Gef. 4, H. 6, §88, 783).

Refuting simplistic theories of manipulation and conspiracy, Gramsci argues that this established consent is based on the actual *leadership ability* of the ruling class; he argues that the subaltern expect to reap advantages for themselves, and are incapable of exploring and articulating alternatives.

Hegemonic domination is not the prerogative of specific sites. Hegemony is diffuse; it is produced through a wide array of agencies and institutions such as the mass media, schools, churches and associated organisations, street names and architecture. They are as much involved in the construction of hegemony as are such features of social life as philosophical debates, travel agencies, Nobel prize awards, parliamentary debates, the German 'Stammtisch' (synonymous for reactionary political discussions in a pub), military action, scientific publications, corporations' investment strategies, nuclear waste transportation, fast-food outlets, advertising campaigns, medical care provision and organisation, space travel, stock prices, soccer, unemployment and the internet (see Gramsci Gef. 2, H. 3, §49, 374). According to Gramsci all of the above, the list of which is by no means exhaustive, comprise civil society. Within the complex of 'civil society', as conceived of by Gramsci, no part can be *substantially* distinct from others, including such areas as 'politics' and 'economics'. On the contrary, according to Gramsci's understanding, civil society only serves as a heuristic conceptual tool to help one identify its different constitutive elements. It is meant to enable one to comprehend the dynamics of hegemonic domination that entails a *real unity* of 'economics' and 'politics'. It is intended to underline the coherence of the hegemonic process. It reveals how areas where domination does not occur in a *violent form* are implicated in this process. These areas should therefore be subject to critical enquiry in view of their role in supporting the reproduction of social relations within bourgeois society.

The contemporary slogan of the 'private being political' becomes redundant in Gramsci's conceptualisation of hegemony where 'private' and 'public' become one. 'If Gramsci repeatedly talks about the "so called private organizations" of civil society ... , it is to arouse sensitivity to the problematic nature of these old concepts. Within the context of Gramsci's conceptualisation of hegemony, "the private" is not simply the "opposite of the public" anymore' (Jehle, 1994, p. 519).

Within this context *common sense* has a special meaning since it forms 'the starting point for every political movement and therefore [is] to be carefully analysed' (PIT, 1979, p. 65). The battles for 'common sense' and therefore hegemony (hegemony is not limited to common sense) are waged by intellectuals. It is they who organize the 'spontaneous consent' of large masses of people and also the latter's possible refusal of and resistance to alternative concepts. This function is not limited to 'academics', writers or philosophers. Intellectuals, in the Gramscian sense of people engaged in 'organizing and connecting' (Gramsci Gef. 7, H. 12,

§1, 1502), *also* include police officers, union leaders, student representatives, soccer stars—and social workers.

In simple terms, hegemony entails a successful mix of force and moral leadership, of economic structures and a political distribution of power. It also entails a common ideology (around which there is consensus)[2] and the inclusion and exclusion of subaltern groups in a societal process of reproduction under the leadership of one or more classes. The alliance of these groups under the leadership of one or more classes constitutes the *historical bloc*. This is a constellation that provides relative stability in its processes. Within the historical bloc, different societal practices form an organic unit, which is cohesive both in terms of chronology and space. Constituent parts are separated and identified only for analytic and heuristic purposes.

The depth and power of a historical bloc can be determined by how seemingly indisputable terms are being defined. Definitions and constructions of 'objectivity', 'the popular', 'good', 'beauty', 'help', 'welfare', 'health', 'youth' and 'aging', to mention just a few, are related to questions of power. 'The "objective truth" constituted as the societal form of science, therefore is the truth of the ruling/dominating classes, thus a hegemonic effect produced by the balance of power in the historical bloc. Science itself can be regarded as a historically specific manifestation of the coordination of consensus and dissent of what is generally considered and accepted as the truth under the conditions of a "balance of societal conditions" dominated by the bourgeois' (Demirovic, 1989, pp. 84f). If these terms appear to be indisputable and irrefutable, then it is obvious that a certain hegemonic arrangement is in place.

2.

Social work's politicisation is conditioned by changes occurring in the nature of its social responsibilities. This is particularly true of the conceptual changes regarding action-based intervention. For decades social work practice had been seen as a 'politics of passive and active proletarianisation' (Lehnhardt & Offe, 1977). As such, social work practice entailed the integration of 'deviants'. A normalisation exercise was carried out in this regard. Because of this, the area, viewed in both its academic and practical aspects, became the object of much criticism. The area's focus on 'integration' and 'assimilation' came in for much criticism in the course of which calls for the 'client's' autonomy and self-determined lifestyles were made. Recall that these concepts, fashionable in contemporary professional discourse, represented minority positions, in social work practice, at the time.

One would be mistaken to assume that *only* the more reasonable arguments prevailed in these debates and that traditional positions were abandoned simply because of the provision of novel and better insights. The changes in approach to the field in both its academic and practical aspects must be viewed in light of the socio-economic changes that took place during the last twenty years. Once the notion of 'regular employment' began to lose its significance, social work conceptualised and carried out with this purpose in mind became questionable (see Schaarschuch, 1990).

In the first place, the objectives governing both the academic and practical aspects of social work originally emerged to support its 'normalisation' and 'assimilation' orientations. Later these objectives served to provide alternatives to these orientations. These orientations represented not an isolated and unorthodox type of social work but one that was mainstream, reflecting dominant, albeit contested, political tendencies.

One feature of social work practice is that of enabling clients to accept and adjust to a situation of exclusion from paid labour—a *permanent* and not a temporary situation of exclusion. This situation concerns not only individuals (as far as individuals are concerned, this situation had existed in the past) but also and more significantly *whole groups* (e.g. youths). Through pedagogical support, members of these groups are being prepared for a life lived in permanent 'poverty'. The socio-political objective here is to eventually remove such groups from the job market.

The replacement of homogenisation of labour, a characteristic of the former Fordist style of production with its emphasis on 'full employment,' by the present situation of multiple societal fragmentation, has led to a reorganization of social work. Systematic assimilation is no longer the primary goal. The concern now is with controlling the different marginalised groups in order to avoid a threat to the whole system. It is therefore 'not the objective of regulation to impose a very specific type of normality; social policy's *task is the regulation of a fragmented society*' (Schaarschuch, 1995, p. 78).[3]

At this point one needs to keep in mind that opposed to the clearly naïve impression that the target groups of social work are not the 'clients', the 'disenfranchised' or the 'social problems', but as Kunstreich and Peters (1988) pointed out, the economic and political *power groups*, which have very opposing interests in specific societal reproduction modalities, which, translated into social work and— repeatedly argued and changing—are being suitably defined.

According to this understanding social work is not only a *hegemonic battleground* of the different classes and class fractions, but also a room in which groups and projects from *outside* social work are articulated.

Social Work becomes a *central tool* for socio-political action, which *utilizes* the common sense of 'clients' in a specific way. By acknowledging autonomy and self-determination (on a low material level) to those concerned, social work organizes self-understanding within the context of bourgeois domination. Or in other words: social work tries to offer the excluded patterns of explanation, which are meant to interpret the exclusion as opting out, heteronomy as one's own decision, and total dependency as autonomy. With this in mind, social work can only be successful by taking up decisive elements of the common sense of the 'clients'.

3.

One cannot entirely comprehend the emergence of the post-Fordist change in objectives only through the 'Verinselung' ('like being on an island') of certain cultures (Hirsch, 1994, p. 15) and the 'Sozialmanagement der Spaltung' ('social management of division') (Schaarschuch). The changes in production, that amount to higher expectations for workers, who are committed to the process of production but at the same time, do not question the overall purpose of the productive arrangement, facilitate the adoption of (cultural) and social work measures in factories. The dependence of the new production model on the subjectivity of labour and its willingness to entirely give itself up to the factory, calls for a 'protection' of emotional relations and ties.[4] It is obvious that no mechanical nomination is possible here. The production apparatus is actually directly handed over to the passions, the motivation and the intensity of the workers, even if they experience this 'handing over' as discipline. There is no free time for 'breaks' as work occurs within the context of *just in time* production. This production system is highly vulnerable 'even to crises from the periphery' (Revelli, 1997, p. 35)—and periphery in this context cannot be limited to suppliers or economic subsidiary regions, but also includes those personality traits of workers that have a disruptive impact on the production process and high productivity 'from outside'. While Fordism aimed at the 'trained gorilla' (but whose thoughts were believed to be free, or at least independent; see Gramsci Gef. 3, H. 4, §52, 533), the new post-Fordist work processes demand something that the neo-liberal religion of every day life calls 'the total commitment of the whole person'. Examined scientifically, it is a form of self-defined action that is in keeping with the prevailing hegemonic arrangements (see Frigga Haug, 1997).

Simultaneously the gap characterising 'subaltern participation', that occurs between *stimulated* and *satisfied* expectations, between the propagated ideology of creativity and the actual practice of subalternity' (Revelli, 1997, p. 36), widens. Even in Automationsarbeit ('automated labour') there is no participation in tactical corporate decisions, let alone strategic ones. Furthermore in the new trans-national corporate model, the place for strategic decisions occurs apart from the actual place of production. The finance network controls the work network, dictating place and time of production, without ever being in direct contact with the latter. The only connection occurs through the abstraction of capital (see Revelli, 1997, pp. 45ff).

The organisation of the workers' efficiency/productivity, loyalty and identification with the corporation becomes an all-pervasive task. Managing this task will involve the following: company sports teams, festivities, supervisions, minimal capital stock as well as social work intervention taking the form of individual and collective counselling, support and advice.

The tasks, concerning the diverse fragmentations of society, are organized as 'public' social work (the principle of subsidiarity—*Subsidiaritätsprinzip*), in particular, proves to be a concept that suits the various individual groups with their different cultures). The second field, as a new form of corporate welfare/social services/social work, is directly or indirectly under the control and management of corporations.

Furthermore activities and experiences meant to enhance individual social character (and therefore to enhance the value of labour) are of strategic importance for the new requirements of high-tech production. It is immaterial whether these opportunities are offered by private or public organizations: but it is obvious that the customers of social work will have to pay for the use of these services, a process that is already occurring in the educational field. It is obvious, however, that this translates into socially and spatially differentiated opportunities and this brings about greater societal fragmentation.

These indicators of a fundamental change in social work—part and parcel of the (radical) changes characterising the elimination of the Fordist historical bloc—mark unresolved tendencies; there is no automatism in their assertion. Last but not least it is also a matter concerning the still open political shaping of these processes. The theoretical analysis of hegemony (*hegemonietheoretische*) enables one to contribute to this: the investigation of social work cannot be limited to the general statements mentioned before, but has to be examined closely. This process entails an examination of the hegemonic concepts manifest in all relevant fields of practice.

The operation in question and the argumentation brought forward to support it can be completely or partially contradictory: while an official position of the association/lobby group is being presented to the public, the individual street-worker/social worker engages in an everyday social work practice that is at odds with some of the claims made by the social work association or organisation. Regional differences have to be taken into consideration in addition to chronological/time differences. The interior design of a social welfare agency (shabby, confined, dirty or user-friendly) is just as much a target of the hegemonic battles being waged by social workers as the social workers themselves. These extensive investigations would be mechanistic if they are viewed one dimensionally without taking into account the manner in which they are contested, reinterpreted (see Willis, 1991), utilized and altered by those who are directly affected.

The terrain for research is wide and varied.

4.

Even though political/radical education within social work practice (and theory) has to be in sync with the 'policy of the social' (see for example Redaktion Widersprüche, 1997), some principles can still be outlined regardless of that development. These are principles for a process of social work which is conscious of its political/radical elements, thus capable of initiating and supporting individual and collective educational processes.

Political/radical education in social work cannot be seen as taking the form of a course or seminar. Even if in some instances (e.g. youth work) conventional educational methods are being used, this still constitutes the exception. Political/radical education can lead to a change in social work and its impact on society only if the participants *of social work practice* consider political/radical education as a dimension that is integral to their practice. This especially means adopting a critical-research stance with respect to one's practice and to examine whether the very forms of practice, where social work appears to be entirely 'non-political/non-radical,' are practices that support the existing hegemony—practices that serve to consolidate the bourgeois bloc. Long files and missing chairs in the social welfare agency of *Schnödelcity* convey to people, seeking counselling and making claims on the system, clear messages concerning their societal position: they are too many; they are unwanted; 'your claims impoverish us' etc. A critical approach to social work, in this context, contributes to the political self-definition of the ones affected by it. It also constitutes the foundation for further thinking about political/radical education.

If there is no choice regarding whether or not to politically/radically educate, then the decision needs to be made regarding whether this is to be done in a manner that is unnoticed or to a large extent consciously and with a purpose in mind. A coffee maker could be regarded by the visitors as an indicator of the social welfare agency of *Schnödelcity*, something to be welcomed by the employees of the agency.

To consciously carry forward the political/radical education dimensions of their work, social workers require a *consciousness* of their own position and function. This is structurally contradictory, which is why I would like to characterize them as 'fractioned intellectuals' (Hirschfeld, 1998, p. 199) with regard to Gramsci's theory of intellectuals.

In their work, social workers are only effective if they develop a particular relationship with groups of clients and gain the self-confidence necessary to engage critically with their work. These situations appear as moments in which the social workers take over '*objective/tasks* of an organic intellectual', because the social workers are more or less the assimilated intellectuals of these groups—except for those few instances when former users of social services, such as rehabilitated drug addicts, return to the relevant field as professional social workers. Even then, their official position as professionals can separate them from the users of the social services they provide. Their perception of the objectives/tasks of an organic intellectual is only partial—and therefore often instrumental. If someone would—not just partially—but entirely act as an organic intellectual of a particular group, he/she would not only jeopardise his/her own employment (there are numerous examples of this) but also not appear to be 'professional' in the strict technical sense of the term (see Nagel, 1996, p. 82).

This also has implications for the scientific preparatory education of social workers, which, despite the perhaps great efforts of individual faculty members, provides the students with the kind of self-understanding, through the hidden curriculum that places emphasis on 'theory' (isolated from practice) and related humanistic areas, that is typical of *traditional intellectuals* (see Bader, 1987, pp. 13ff). Whether they do so successfully is another argument. Furthermore these studies represent a process of social mobility for the students with respect to their family's social standing (see Maier, 1995, pp. 48ff).

Therefore it seems appropriate to see social workers, generally speaking, as assuming the role of organic intellectuals of a social group—as constituting a cultural milieu of socially mobile educational achievers who are thus distinguished from the 'deviants', 'losers', 'disenfranchised'. At the same time they have a sense of the insecurity/fragility of their career and their position, presenting themselves (and others) as the living embodiment of the current situation characterised by social possibilities, threats and social insecurity (see Nagel, 1996, p. 75; Maier, 1995, p. 48). This assumption ties in with the observation that most social workers today by and large share the basic ideological ideas of their employers, who are loyal to state and economy—despite the increasing cuts in social services, cost-benefit orientation/economisation of social welfare and a deterioration of their own working conditions.

The characterization as 'fractioned intellectuals', as intellectuals who are in a contradictory position, is not the result of individual incompetence, but is rather an inevitable result of different predefined demands, which they usually could not meet.

It is striking that the figure/character of the 'fractioned intellectual' surprisingly correlates with the process of social fragmentation that characterises the terrain in which social work is carried out, its 'Verinselung.' (*See above*) It also correlates with the resulting goals for social work: it exemplarily embodies the kind of social character that is suitable for this society. The 'Abteilungsdenken' (*Thinking according to departments*) with its 'Grenzschutzfunktionen' ('function of defending frontiers') (see Nemitz, 1979, pp. 67ff) as a characteristic of common sense, is professionalised in the person of the social worker. It is generally known that in a class society, individuals '[stabilize] their identity and limited ability to act through establishing relatively individual forms of experience and coping ... this divisional structure of experience and coping allows the ideological subjects a manifold bookkeeping which makes unquestioned approval of contradictory conditions possible' (Haug, 1993, p. 70). Social workers are not simply affected by this as participants in this society. They professionalize this skill/competence—not out of 'stupidity', but because they gain access to their clients by doing so. If they want to develop their social ability to act, they should do so within the borders of a bourgeois society.

Social workers teach their clients the ability to act within the given ideological contexts, by strengthening the 'Abteilungsdenken' (see above), supporting the ability to bear contradictions/tensions or even utilize them sparingly. It is about dealing with contradictions/tensions apparent in certain milieus/'cultures' or rather in the relationship with other social groups. They conduct 'crisis management' in a societal process which, in their view, 'is characterized by crises in its normality' (Nagel, 1996, p. 80) as reflected in the self-understanding of social work as a profession. That the quality of life can be strengthened and improved through these contradictions/tensions, requires a minimum of acceptance of discontinuity and differentiations on the part of the affected. If they seem legitimate or even productive, then they are tolerable to the individual. Two things seem to be necessary for this: (little) self-confidence and a concomitant degree of collective integration. Incidentally the divided convictions of the group provide those contradictions/tensions or rather the strategies for coping with them, with the necessary legitimisation. Therefore it is central to social work practice to stop processes of anomie and/or create new connections (networks etc.).

In addition to the debate concerning the general political role of social work in contemporary society, a clear investigation of the respective organizational context in which it operates, has to be part of the development of a theory of political/radical education in social work. This provides a connection with Foucault's institutionally embodied relations of power.

Critical social work, entailing political/radical self-understanding, has to and is capable of—operating within the contradictions of its objectives and conditions and the occasional liberties that arise from it. Nevertheless there are limits. Those have to be consciously acknowledged (even in the course of professional practice with those affected by social work) and openly discussed. These are to be seen as political frontiers, which are to be the object of critical reflection, but cannot be solved or changed solely through social work. It is important therefore that social workers engage in radical political work outside their professional and institutional boundaries. Even if this also applies to other professions such as plumbers, computer programmers, nurses and salespersons, the political/radical behaviour of (critical) social workers outside their professional contexts would enhance their coherence as social workers. The widespread point of view within social work to limit political/ radical involvement to professional practice can lead to justifiable doubts and a possible sense of mistrust on the part of those with whom they work and with whom they want to engage in political action. This view can also result in there being little resistance to the worsening of one's own working conditions.

5.

One can learn from Gramsci that there are indeed diverse forms of practice of knowledge, those of social workers and their 'clients' among them, but that none of them can claim any *principal* superiority. Even when Gramsci differentiates between common sense and philosophy (as a systemic, coherent body of knowledge), he insists that there is 'no "qualitative" difference, but only a "quantitative" one' (Gramsci Gef. H. 10, II, §52, 1345). The practice oriented forms of knowledge, be they common sense or science, not only do not differ in terms of their subjects (but only in terms of their respective thought operations), but all share the function of Vergesellschaftung ('socialization'). No matter how much the outlooks on life and philosophies of a marriage counsellor and a homeless person may differ, they do not justify any superiority of one over the other. The basic *common achievement* is the Vergesellschaftung of the respective individual/group.

The difference identified by Gramsci lies mainly at the level of its coherence. As for scientific theory, elements of the caveman are very much a part of this type of theory as the principles of the latest and most advanced science. One must avoid prejudice towards all past and local narrow-minded historical times and institutions of a future philosophy, inherent in a globally unified human race' (Gramsci Gef. 6, H. 11 §12, 1376). Karin Priester pointed out that common sense is not just false consciousness but is rather characterised by its incoherence: 'Remains of older traditions of thought, superseded cultural assets, prejudices, etc. are standing next to true/legitimate/rights and in some instances even critical insights' (Priester, 1981, p. 19).

The bizarre 'mixture' that is 'common sense' is anything but the result of the people's 'stupidity'. The individual fragments have long proven to be effective to enable one to function in life. Also one has to consider that the 'true/legitimate/right and in some instances even critical insights' are isolated at the level of reflection, but are united in every day life, so that certain intellectual 'saturations/investigations/ penetrations' of the societal situation can equally result in one's 'being tied' to this state, to use Paul Willis' terms (see Willis, 1979, pp. 183ff).

In the course of this, common sense has to be seen as existing in a subjective universal relationship with the world, as a *worldview* and interpretation. The development of common sense from the spontaneous, bizarre worldview, to a systemic, coherent philosophy is a process which does *not* necessarily *spread* through the 'dissemination' of knowledge. It is not a process that moves from empirical one-sidedness to empirical universality. More so it is primarily marked by a process of the *critical dawning of consciousness of the existing universal relationship of human beings to the world.*

A result of this process, the worldview gains greater coherence, because the *tested/proven/practical functionality* of certain views of common sense is in itself a function. It is therefore contradictory to the totality and the relation of individual fragments/parts to each other: it *is always just a partial functionality*. It correlates with the relation of the individual fragments/parts. The real antagonisms and the real irregularities of society reproduce themselves even in the contradictions of common sense. They are changed in specific ways, condensed and intertwined. We can draw from this the insight that an individual is capable of action but this action occurs (as mentioned previously) in the ideological forms of a class society.

Political/Radical education does not simply attach something new to common sense; it does not add yet another 'political division'. Gramsci stresses 'that it is not about introducing a science ex novo into the individual life "of all", but rather to renew an already existing activity and make it critical' (Gramsci Gef. 6, H. 11, §12, 1382). 'Activity' in this respect is not limited to actual thinking, but it rather refers to those actions that constitute, above all, the lived (and not simply the thought) world view of human beings.

Since common sense contains 'elements of the cave man' as well as 'elements of the latest and most sophisticated science', actions can very much be found in the life of the individual that fit those sophisticated elements. It is about discovering those actions, recognizing them, *realizing* them and *making* them real. By doing so these elements become the focal points in the process of self-awareness: something that already exists is 'renewed', which means it is strengthened by the consciousness/realization of such an action. It can become 'critical,' to use Gramsci's term. *Critical* in this context entails the ability to classify and identify relations (part of the critical culture). It is also a term that expresses the function of this renewed action within the totality of one's individual life, which corresponds with the metaphor of 'critical mass' in the process of nuclear fission.

That this approach to social work exists is also a recognition of the individuality of those concerned with social work. Those personality elements, which are expressed through language, lie at the centre of attention. To social service users, these elements often seem to appear more replaceable, more irrelevant and less important as part of their person/personality, than actions and activities. The preoccupation with practical/everyday life, with the intention to make the subjects discover the consciousness of their action, acknowledges the active personality and at the same time gives the courage and strength to question others, to consider as well as come to terms with emerging tensions/contradictions, and eventually utilize them in a productive manner. Because even a developed, coherent and self-reflecting world view is a combination of theory *and practice*, and has to be implicit in practice.

At a certain point, part of the process of the development of self-awareness, crystallizing around the renewed action, has to be the understanding that *language* is a very relevant medium of *societal action* for the individual. The increasingly reflective debate, examination and analysis of verbal conscience explicated through actions occur in different phases, representing the respective relation between 'talk' and 'action'. 'Even the unity of theory and practice [in the thoughts and actions of the individual] is therefore not a mechanically given fact, but rather a historic becoming. Its basic and primitive phase consists of the feeling of "difference", of "detachment", of an almost instinctive independence [of practice from theory] and which proceeds until a real and total possession of a coherent and universal world view is attained' (Gramsci Gef. 6, H. 11, §12, 1384; see Hirschfeld, 2005).

Although the starting-point for social work should at first lie with the activities of practical/everyday life, social workers need to learn enough (from their 'clients'!) in order to assess the possible results of such an action that is rendered 'critical'. Those bizarre and contradictory elements of a common sense are very valuable to the owner, no matter how old fashioned they might sometimes appear to social workers. These elements (and the structure of their arrangement) have been tested by many in a similar situation. It is these elements that enable persons to cope with the demands that life make on them and they connect individuals with other members of their group, class, region and time. It would be irresponsible to thoughtlessly deprive someone of this foundation. If a (self-)critical process is to be started through the renewal of certain activities, 'elements of the cave-man' and 'local prejudices' etc, cannot simply be condemned. Social workers first have to recognize which *actual problems* are solved through them. Because those problems will not simply go away by doing away with the 'prejudices', which explains why all strategies for unmasking and exposing such elements have failed. In addition to creating insecurity and raising doubts, unavoidable but also productive elements in a process of self-awareness, one has to assist persons in developing problem solving strategies that serve as alternatives to those of the 'cave-man'. These alternatives cannot just be abstract, but have to be at least equal to the old elements in enabling persons to cope with the demands of life; it would be better if they prove to be superior strategies to adopt in practical everyday life.[5] Finally, the personal life style of the social workers is also a matter for critical discussion: their own life experience would enable social workers to examine the extent to which they can vouch for the 'superiority' of self-critical practices.

While at the beginning of this chapter, social workers were portrayed as 'fractioned intellectuals', one can now see the potential that exists in social work for a critical radically democratic social practice. One can easily agree that there are no guarantees for success, which cannot be secured solely by engaging exclusively within the boundaries of social work. It seems to me that there can be no other perspective for a radically democratic practice.

Notes

1. Gramsci wrote about Bukharin's *Theory of Historical Materialism. A Popular Manual of Marxist Sociology* in his prison notebook (7; §29): 'If the doctrine in question has not yet

reached this "classical" phase of its development, any attempt to "manualise" it is bound to fail, its logical ordering will be purely apparent and illusory, and one will get, as with the "Popular Manual", just a mechanical juxtaposition of disparate elements which remain inexorably disconnected and disjointed in spite of the unitary varnish provided by the literary presentation ... . But the vulgar contention is that science must absolutely mean "system", and consequently systems of all sorts are built up which have only the mechanical exteriority of a system and not its necessary inherent coherence' (Gramsci, 1971, p. 434). This observation is still valid about the unlocked character of Marxist theory today.

2. The concept of ideology (as well as the concept of culture) is used, according to Wolfgang F. Haug (1993), to signify different forms of socialisation.

3. 'One shouldn't aim anymore at providing generally binding norms ("normality") as from an ecological point of view one does not draw a distinction between useful plants and pest plants. One should accept every social group the way it is. However, not the groups, but merely the transitions between various social environments and social objectives should be moderate and flexible, for not having to fear the endangering of the complete system.' (Kunstreich, 1996, p. 67)

4. Revelli claims that the 'logic of presents' is eliminating the 'logic of contract'. The relationship of persons cannot be formalized to standards, 'norms' and procedures. It can't, because it's personal ... . That's why the employer-employee relationship which is formed in the postfordistic production model is in some ways similar to pre-capitalistic servitude. (Revelli, 1997, p. 32). On the other hand he articulates, in a later book (1999), that the post-fordistic model cannot reproduce social belongings. He, however, defines the challenge of the left as being not only that of political representation but also of providing a different form of socialisation (for a relevant comment on this topic see Hirschfeld, 2001).

5. It must be emphasized that social workers have to handle responsibly and carefully the problems brought about by social change, especially in times when one cannot identify a nameable, alternative democratic movement for a practical orientation to social integration. The menace of individual separation of the clients, caused by politically-blind social workers and provoked by the fading of cultural connections, is in this situation most hazardous. Particularly the politically interested social worker has to prove that his suggestions are opening an extended view of options for social action for his client that do not serve only his own political will. Sometimes the average or 'normal-bad' social work, trapped in the ken of civil society, is better than a social work fraught with political demands, which can't satisfy itself and harms the client in the end. (Hirschfeld, 1999).

References

Bader, K. (1987) *Viel Frust und wenig Hilfe; Bd. 1. Die Entmystifizierung Sozialer Arbeit* (Weinheim und Basel, Beltz Verlag).

Buttigieg, J. A. (1994) Gramscis Zivilgesellschaft und die civil society-Debatte, in: *Das Argument*, Nr. 206, Heft 4/5 Juli-Oktober, S. 529–554.

Demirovic, A. (1989) Die hegemoniale Strategie der Wahrheit. Zur Historizität des Marxismus bei Gramsci, in: Die Linie Luxemburg—Gramsci. *Zur Aktualität und Historizität marxistischen Denkens* (Berlin/Hamburg, Argument-Sonderband), S. 69–89.

Gramsci, A. (1971) *Selections from the Prison Notebooks*, Q. Hoare & G. Nowell Smith (eds and trans.) (London and New York, International Publishers).

Gramsci, A. (1991ff) *Gefängnishefte. Kritische Gesamtausgabe (z.Z. Bd. 1–7); hrsgg. vom Deutschen Gramsci-Projekt unter d. wiss.* Leitung von K. Bochmann und Wolfgang F. Haug; Hamburg. [Gramsci Gef. in text]

Haug, F. (1997) Gramsci und die Produktion des Begehrens, *Psychologie und Gesellschaftskritik*, 22: Jg., H. 86–87, pp. 75–92.

Haug, W. F. (1993) *Elemente einer Theorie des Ideologischen.* (Berlin/Hamburg, Argument-Verlag).

Hirsch, J. (1994) Vom fordistischen Sicherheitsstaat zum nationalen Wettbewerbsstaat. Internationale Regulation, Demokratie und radikaler Reformismus', in: *Das Argument* Nr. 203; Heft 1 Jan/Feb, S. 7–21.

Hirschfeld, U. (1998) Intellektuelle, Kritik und Soziale Arbeit. Definitionsversuche in Auseinandersetzung mit Walzer und Gramsci, in: U. Hirschfeld (ed.) *Gramsci-Perspektiven*; Hamburg S. 183–205.

Hirschfeld, U. (1999) Soziale Arbeit als Arbeit am Kulturellen. Theoriegeschichtliche Hinweise zur Bedeutung einer materialistischen Kulturkonzeption für Projekte Sozialer Arbeit und demokratischer Politik, in: H. Effinger (ed.), *Soziale Arbeit und Gemeinschaft*; Freiburg im Breisgau.

Hirschfeld, U. (2001) Zur Bedeutung des Kulturellen für die Veränderung der Gesellschaft, in: *Widersprüche—Zeitschrift für sozialistische Politik im Bildungs, Gesundheits- und Sozialbereich*; Heft 80, S. 19–29.

Hirschfeld, U. (2005) Politische Bildung in der Sozialen Arbeit, in: K. Störch (Hg.), *Soziale Arbeit in der Krise. Perspektiven fortschrittlicher Sozialarbeit*; Hamburg.

Jehle, P. (1994) Hegemonietheoretische Defizite der Zivilgesellschaftsdebatte, in: *Das Argument* Nr. 206, Heft 4/5 Juli-Oktober, S. 513–528.

Kunstreich, T. (1996) Das 'Neue Steuerungsmodell' (NSM). Essay über die Hegemonie konservativer Modernisierung, in: *Widersprüche—Zeitschrift für sozialistische Politik im Bildungs, Gesundheits- und Sozialbereich*; Heft 59, S. 57–73.

Kunstreich, T. & Peters, F. (1988) Die 'heimlichen' Adressaten der Sozialarbeit. Ansatzpunkte zur Rückgewinnung des Politischen, in: *Widersprüche—Zeitschrift für sozialistische Politik im Bildungs, Gesundheits- und Sozialbereich*; Heft 28, S. 41–48.

Lehnhardt, G. & Offe, C. (1977) Staatstheorie und Sozialpolitik, in: *Ferber/Kaufmann: Soziologie und Sozialpolitik. KZfSS Sonderheft*, 19, S. 98–127.

Maier, K. (1995) Berufsziel Sozialarbeit/Sozialpädagogik. Biografischer Hintergrund, Studienmotivation, soziale Lage während des Studiums, Studienverhalten und Berufseinmündung angehender SozialarbeiterInnen/SozialpädagogInnen; Freiburg.

Nagel, U. (1996) Krisenmanagement. Über den Zusammenhang von sozialem Beruf und Biographie, in: *Widersprüche—Zeitschrift für sozialistische Politik im Bildungs, Gesundheits- und Sozialbereich*; Heft 59, S. 75–86.

Nemitz, R. (1979) Mut zur Erzihung als Konservativer Spontneismus, *Das Argument*, 113, S. 64–75.

PIT (Projekt Ideologie-Theorie) (1979) *Theorien über Ideologie* (Berlin/West, Argument-Sonderbände).

Priester, K. (1981) Kultur und Politik im Denken Antonio Gramscis, in: *spw—Zeitschrift für Sozialistische Politik und Wirtschaft*, 13.

Redaktion Widersprüche (1997) Zum Stand der Diskussion um eine Politik des Sozialen, in: *Widersprüche—Zeitschrift für sozialistische Politik im Bildungs, Gesundheits- und Sozialbereich*; Heft 66, S. 199–219.

Revelli, M. (1997) Vom 'Fordismus' zum 'Toyotismus'. Das kapitalistische Wirtschafts- und Sozialmodell im Übergang, *Supplement der Zeitschrift Sozialismus* 4, 97.

Revelli, M. (1999) *Die gesellschaftliche Linke. Jenseits der Zivilisation der Arbeit* (Münster, Verlag Westfaelisches Dampfboot).

Schaarschuch, A. (1990) *Zwischen Regulation und Reproduktion. Gesellschaftliche Modernisierung und die Perspektiven Sozialer Arbeit* (Bielefeld, Böllert).

Schaarschuch, A. (1995) Soziale Dienstleistungen im Regulationszusammenhang, in: *Widersprüche—Zeitschrift für sozialistische Politik im Bildungs-, Gesundheits- und Sozialbereich*, Heft 52, S. 73–89.

Willis, P. (1979) *Spaß am Widerstand* (Frankfurt/Main, Campus).

Willis, P. (1991) *Jugend-Stile. Zur Ästhetik der gemeinsamen Kultur* (Hamburg/Berlin, Argument-Verlag).

8

Gramscian Thought and Brazilian Education

ROSEMARY DORE SOARES

A Socialist Project for Public Education?

If we briefly review the great debates concerning public school in Brazil since the 1920s, we see that the Left only took up a socialist project for public education during the 1980s. During the 1920s, anarchism played an important role in the Brazilian labor movement, a consequence of southern European immigration and the transplantation of ideologies in vogue at the time, particularly in Italy, Spain and Portugal (Rodrigues, 1992). The anarchist trend favored locally controlled community schools (Luizetto, 1982, p. 62), but it was against public schools, organized and financed by the government (Luizetto, 1986; Tragtenberg, 1982). Thus, the question of State sponsored education was not contemplated among the ranks of the Brazilian labor movement, nor did it play a decisive role in the political agenda of the Brazilian Communist Party (PCB).[1]

It was a group of liberal intellectuals known as the *Pioneiros da Escola Nova*[2] (New School Pioneers) that advocated public, common and lay schools during this period, a position in direct conflict with the Catholic Church, which favored private education (Dore Soares, 2003; Lima, 1978). The ideas of the Pioneiros were stimulated by an atmosphere of intense industrialization that swept across the country during the 1920s and 1930s, causing the rise of a strong urban industrial base and the dislocation of the agricultural exportation sector, up until then the focal point of the economy (Cohn, 1976; Luz, 1961; Tavares, 1972). The dissolution of agricultural hegemony brought about various economic, social and political crises (Vianna, 1976). Despite the fragility of both the agricultural and industrial factions during this period of volatile transformation, the State managed to intervene and sustain the industrial development of the country. Because of its political and economic impotence, the Brazilian industrial bourgeoisie could not manage to support the educational program of the Pioneers, a position that theoretically favored the modernization and urbanization of the country (Gandini, 1980). The Catholic Church, on the other hand, already maintained ties with the agrarian bourgeoisie, realizing what can be called, in Gramscian terms, a 'concordata' (Gramsci, 1977, pp. 1866–7): an agreement that benefited the interests of the Catholic Church in the arena of education and the general interests of an agrarian bourgeoisie mired in its hegemonic crisis (Bruneau, 1974; Vianna, 1976). It was this spirit of collaboration with the State that permitted the Catholic Church to regain its influence over society (Bruneau, 1974), shattered ever since the republican and liberal movement that accompanied the transformation of Brazil from a monarchy to a Republic (Costa, 1987).

During the peak of its conflict with the Catholic Church, the Pioneers published a *Manifesto*, in 1932 (Azevedo, 1958), which contained its educational program, defending the concept of an active school, present in the European movement, and the idea of a progressive school, inspired by the North American model. The liberal agenda enabled the criticism of conservatism in the oligarchic and elitist Brazilian schools, and helped spread a proposal for democratizing the education system, a proposal in which the State financed its operation. One of the signatories of the *Manifesto* was the educator Paschoal Lemme, who, despite having called himself an 'intellectual independent' (Lemme, 1988, p. 123), is recognized in Brazilian history as a communist. Why would Lemme have signed a document in favor of a school model elaborated by liberals? Was it a political alliance with democratic factions? Yes, but there is another relevant factor: the Brazilian Left did not have a cultural agenda (Mota, 1980; Del Roio, 1990) and, thus, could not oppose, in the educational arena, the progressive framework of active schools.

The dispute of the 1930s resulted in the success of the Catholic agenda, which had a number of its appeals approved in the Constitution of 1934. However, the intent of the Pioneers to strengthen the tie between education and industrial activity also found support in the Government, particularly after Getúlio Vargas took power in 1937 and instituted his program of modernizing Brazil. This was the beginning of a dictatorial period in Brazilian history, known as the Estado Novo, which was characterized by greater government intervention, particularly through the nationalization of the economy, giving a great impulse to industrialization (Vianna, 1976). It was at this time that the State instituted legislation to adapt education to the demands of industrial activity, resulting in a dualistic organizational school structure: on the one hand, secondary education, entrusted to shape the *future leaders of Brazil* (Capanema, 1942), and on the other hand, technical education, directed at 'less privileged classes' (Article 129 of the Brazilian Constitution, 1937), and charged with the task of producing an *army of workers for the good of the Nation* (Capanema, 1937). While the State worked to increase the number of technical schools, private schools focused on general education, academic and college preparation.

In 1945 the Estado Novo entered a state of crises, paving the way for the redemocratization of Brazilian society. Shortly thereafter, a new Constitution was elaborated which proposed legislation (Lei de Diretrizes e Bases) establishing a framework for national education. Debates regarding the formulation and implementation of the law would last for the next 15 years. The Pioneers presented once again a project based on public education, renewing the old confrontation with groups supporting private education. The conflict came to a head at the end of the 1950s when the Pioneers published a new Manifesto, 'Summoned Once Again' (Azevedo, 1960). Who was summoned? In addition to the old Pioneers, representatives of the Brazilian Left, such as Florestan Fernandes, Octávio Ianni, Caio Prado Júnior, and Nelson Werneck Sodré, took up the cause. Once again, intellectuals representing the Brazilian Left were uniting with liberals to combat the movement for private education. Was it merely a political alliance, or did the Left still not have its own proposal for public education?

The sociologist Florestan Fernandes (1960, pp. 219–20) says that his personal position in 'The Campaign in Defense of Public Education' was 'uncomfortable' because, according to his stance as a socialist, he was forced to defend the 'backward values' that corresponded to the 'values of the French Revolution.' But the importance of the Campaign centered on the will of those that wanted to 'set Brazil on the path to modern civilization.' His point of view is that 'economic, social and cultural development is impossible without a parallel integration of schools in the process of social change' (Fernandes, 1966, p. 95).

More than a mere political bloc, the convergence of the Left and the Liberals was made possible because of a shared belief that the transformation of Brazilian society depended on the advancement of a capitalist based economy. For the Liberals, the development of capitalism signified progress and the expansion of industry (Barros, 1960; Abreu, 1963; Lambert, 1959). For the Left, it signified the realization of a democratic-bourgeoisie revolution, a prerequisite for a socialist revolution (cf. Prado Júnior, 1966; Czajka, 2004). Aligned in this perspective, the individuals 'summoned' came to the same conclusion with respect to the forces defending private education: they were rooted in traditional institutional powers that did not want to break the barriers of 'backwardness.' But for the Left, the problem remained the same. It continued to lack a unique cultural perspective with expression in the political arena, and consequently, ended up being subordinate, at least in the educational sphere, to Liberal command.

Despite the mobilization of the progressive factions in favor of public education, in 1961 federal policies were passed which extended, through public subsidies, private sector control in the realm of education (Lei de Diretrizes e Bases da Educação Nacional, 4024/61). The ideological support of the conservative wing of the Catholic Church helped secure the victory for the private sector (Alves, 1979; Lima, 1978; Bruneau, 1974; Martins 1976).

After the approval of these policies, there emerged within the Catholic Church certain movements based on the idea of liberation, sparked by the atmosphere of renovation promoted by the papacy of John XXIII (Bruneau, 1974). One such movement was the Movement for Basic Education, which was the product of a convention between the National Conference of Brazilian Bishops and the Federal Ministry of Education and Culture. The theme of the convention was adult literacy (Kadt, 2003). It was also in the area of adult education that Paulo Freire developed his work, during the presidency of João Goulart (1961–1964). Both initiatives, however, were not presented as national education projects and after the coup of 1964—realized with the help of the national bourgeoisie, the middle class and the military (Toledo, 1997)—both movements were suppressed.

The coup of 1964 was the beginning of a military dictatorship that would institute extreme political repression on all spheres of Brazilian society. During this period the country underwent another intense process of conservative modernization in which the economy grew rapidly, benefiting various sectors, such as the industrial, commercial, communications and energy segments (Singer, 1976). In the area of education, two laws were established to reorganize university and postsecondary education (Law number 5540/68) and high school education (Law number 5692/71), with the objective of meeting the demands of the new economy and the social pressures being exerted on universities because of the expansion of high school education (Dore Soares, 1982).

The military dictatorship suppressed all public debate regarding Brazilian education policy (Cunha & Góes, 1985). It was only after 1974 that the military authorities started to open the country, in a so called 'secure and gradual' manner, and allow more opportunities for the expression of civic and political society. In 1979, political amnesty was granted not only to the politicians and intellectuals that had been in prison or forced to leave the country after the military coup, but also those who were implicated with torture and repression policies during the dictatorship (Magalhães, 1997).

It was in the atmosphere of redemocratization, around 1974, that there appeared in academic circles criticism of the political organization of the school system, encouraged by Louis Althusser's concept (1974), according to which the school system is an *ideological apparatus* of the Bourgeoisie State. Considering the atmosphere of political suppression that had dominated the country, analyses of education that criticized its relation with capitalist society were practically unheard of before the dissemination of Althusser's ideas. His thesis became more influential with the research of Bourdieu and Passeron (1975). In their examination of the French education system, Bourdieu and Passeron developed theories explaining the central role educational systems play in reproducing the divisions of capitalist society.

Although Bourdieu and Passeron found inspiration in a Weberian referential model, (Morrow and Torres, 1995; Cunha, 1979), whereas Althusser based his concepts on Marxism, both theories affirmed a structural paradigm in their analyses of society. They each argued that the role of education is to reproduce social structures through 'inculcation,' of 'habitus' for Bourdieu and Passeron and ideology for Althusser.

The idea that schools realize social and cultural reproduction gave rise to several criticisms (Cunha, 1979), much of which focused on the absence of the category of 'contradiction', a reference to how the scheme of reproduction appears to be done without antagonisms between social classes. If in the approaches elaborated by both Althusser and Bourdieu and Passeron the theory of reproduction admits that the school system has a 'relative autonomy' from the economy, what would such an autonomy be if the school function is supposed only to legitimate social structure?

The research produced by Bowles and Gintis (1976)[3] in North America also proved influential in Brazil during the 1970s. Their theoretical framework was based on a concept that was known as 'correspondence': the superstructure of society, which includes education, is determined by the structure of the economy, which is based on relations of production. For Bowles and Gintis, instead of promoting equal opportunity, the education system perpetuates the forms of consciousness, behavior and personality required for the reproduction of capitalist production relationships[4]. Along this same line of thought, in which schools are antithetical to the interests of common workers, another North American theorist, Martin Carnoy (1977), developed a theory that gained a following in Brazil. In his analysis, Carnoy maintained that formal education constitutes a type of imperialist domination that acts in consonance with the interest of colonizers.

In this climate of criticism of public education, the work of Ivan Illich (1973), which considers schools to be unnecessary organizations, also had a large impact on Brazilian intellectuals and pedagogues. Although he did not adopt the concept of reproduction present in the American and French lines of thought, Illich did maintain that schools reproduce social stratification (Morrow and Torres, 1995). He argued that working-class children, whose failure was produced within the school system, would benefit with the destruction of public schools. Other perspectives calling for the 'deschooling of society' also appeared in Brazil, such as the work of Neil Postman and Charles Weingartner (1971), which accused schools of systematically failing and rebuking children, thus reinforcing inequality, and Reimer (1975), which considered education to be way too important to be left to the whims of public schools.

The idea that the school is a reproductive state apparatus did not generate a project from the Left. However, it did bring up preoccupations from teachers who intended to give meaning to their work, teachers who opposed the idea of being mere 'puppets' of the capitalist State. What should be done? Abandon public schools? Many started doing so (cf. Paiva, 1985a, 1985b, 1986; Gadotti, 1992), a tendency also known as 'reproductivist' (Saviani, 1985), whose effect was to help propel the interests of private school promoters in commercializing education.

The political opening of Brazil during the beginning of the 1980s enhanced the number of social and political protests, and enabled vast sectors of civil society to mobilize and organize in the process of democratically reconstructing the country. During the movement to create a new Constitution, the school system acquired an unprecedented importance. In this context, the work of Gramsci with regard to State and school[5] became an important reference for criticizing the idea that education and culture—parts of the 'superstructure'—are mechanically determined by economic structures. The desire to understand the pedagogical thought of Gramsci generated various research projects (Saviani, 1989; Franco, 1987; Kuenzer, 1985; Paoli, 1980, among others), based on a historic study of the topic of education in the worker's movement. Such work sparked a lot of interest in Brazilian society. Moreover, by giving education and culture an importance never seen before in socialist thought, the ideas of Gramsci helped the Left formulate projects for national education.

In the 1980s, Brazilian educators looked to better understand educational issues in socialist terms, stimulated by the reading of the Gramsci's anthology, *Os intelectuais e a organização da cultura* (1978) [*The Intellectuals and the Organization of Culture*]. But, would they end up advancing Gramscian thought with regard to school, or would they confuse and muddle the premises of his work? To answer this question, one must understand the types of interpretations that prevailed in the historiography of education and in the political struggles to defend the public school, particularly the conceptions of Marx, Lenin and Gramsci regarding education.

Interpreting Gramscian Thought in the Brazilian Context:
Trends and Tribulations

The interpretation of Gramscian pedagogical thought in Brazil was accompanied by a renewed interest in the vague educational perspective of Marx, known in Brazil as the 'polytechnical school'. Consequently, starting in the 1980s, the terms 'unitary school' and 'polytechnical school' were understood in Brazilian educational literature as one and the same.

Marx, however, never properly elaborated a proposal for education. He held up general principles so as to guide the intellectual, polytechnic and physical education of workers (Marx, 1866).[6] The two expressions adopted by Marx, 'technological training' and 'polytechnical training', more than comprehensive educational philosophies represent *methods* of bringing together instruction and work in the formation of specialized professionals, an important objective in an era in which economic production was based on artesanal work. As a reference for his thought, Marx used a model developed by English philanthropists called 'polytechnic schools', which had as its purpose a more generalized form of instruction that trained workers in a range of professions, thereby enabling them to rapidly adapt to innovations in the productive process. Thus, Marx defended the process of converging work and instruction in the education of workers, along with intellectual exercises and physical education.

Lenin and Krupskaya retook Marxist reflections as a reference to confront a different proposal, the 'active school' (or 'new school').[7] It is a concept that even Marx did not know about because it emerged in the field of bourgeoisie theory at the turn of the 20th century. The objective of Lenin and Krupskaya in discussing the 'active school' was to reduce the influence of liberal pedagogy among Russian teachers (cf. Lenin, 1975, p. 64). Still, even after intense debates among Soviet pedagogues, the notions of 'general and polytechnic instruction' and 'common work school' remained very vague, simplified into the notion of factory work (cf. Pistrak, 1981). The work of Lenin and Krupskaya to develop a socialist pedagogy was stifled by two limitations: the backward status of Russian society in the climate of European capitalism, and the influence of economics in the workers' movement, impeding the soviet proposal from expressing a hegemonic vision of a socialist cultural project.

As for the liberal bourgeoisie conceptions of school formulated at the turn of the 20th century, known as the 'active school', its objective was to respond to the crisis of the humanist school, a consequence of the expansion of industrial capitalism and the growing relationship between science and workmanship. The idea of the 'active school' assimilated principles supported by the workers' movement, such as the inclusion of work in schools and the democratization of culture, both under the direction of the traditional hegemonic group. In accordance with the Gramscian conception, the 'active school' deals with a true 'transformism': the incorporation of the 'new' to subjugate it to the 'old' (Dore Soares, 2000). Proposing the democratization of schools, the 'active school' theorists redefine the mechanisms of school social selection in a way that presents it as 'common' (unitary). But the proposal was not able to (and would not be able to in the capitalism system) overcome the expression of social contradictions that divide society into rulers and subjects, remaining in that way a dualist structure: the formation of technical-scientific teams (positions of design and direction) and instrumental teams (positions of execution, subordination).

The reflections of Gramsci on civil society and the State, on the other hand, allow for the clarification of the 'plot' of the 'active school', the *transformism*, and the presentation of a proposal that dialectically overcomes this dilemma (Dore Soares, 2003). The formulation of the 'unitary school' refers to the Gramscian notion of the State and implies a new development of the socialist concept of education that surmounts the idea of 'general and polytechnic instruction' or the 'common school of work'.

Gramsci sought to advance the concept of the State elaborated by Marx and Engels in 1848, taking into account the historical changes since then verified[8]. He understood that the State does not just govern by force through the oppression of workers, which had occurred during the 19th century and impeded any sort of organization on the part of workers. Starting at the end of the 19th century, the laws prohibiting the rights of workers to strike, to form unions, to vote, be elected, to organize political parties and to publish journals began to be invalidated. The dominant class began opening society to its enemies. At the same time it permitted the demonstrations of its adversaries, the confrontation of ideas and positions, the dominant class sought to convince the subordinate classes to submit to its willpower. Gramsci showed that this form of bourgeoisie power had new characteristics compared to the preceding forms of power. One of them was the fight for hegemony.

Hegemony signifies that the Capitalist State does not merely base its power in force, in pure repression of its adversaries. So that the dominant groups obtain societal consensus, they permit the subordinate groups to organize and develop social and political projects. What results is the mediation of the economy and the State which is expressed in civil society: political parties, unions, the press, school. It is a movement similar to what Gramsci, certainly inspired by the reflections of Hegel, understood as the 'private plot', calling civil society the 'private apparatus of hegemony' (Gramsci, 1977, p. 801). Civil society is referred as such because it is within this realm that the struggle between contradictory social and political projects takes place, under the framework of a dispute for hegemony between the fundamental social classes. The power of the dominant group is exercised in a repressive manner, but also in a 'humane' manner, because it seeks the consensus of the subordinate classes. The two dimensions of power are, as Gramsci suggests in a Machiavellian-inspired concept, like the idea of a centaur: half wild, the repression, and half human, the search and dissemination of consensus (Gramsci, 1977, p. 1576).

And, according to Gramsci, the work of the dominant groups to convince subordinate groups to accept the *status quo* does not just occur on an intellectual level. The diffusion of ideas is accompanied by a mode of action. Here becomes clear the dialectical link established by Gramsci between 'theory' and 'practice'. When the dominant class achieves the ability to intellectually direct society, it implies moral direction as well, that is, forms of acting in the world. Hegemony is the exercise of intellectual and moral direction on society. For this reason, Gramsci highlights the importance of an intellectual movement that establishes and disseminates new conceptions of the world, capable of elevating the civil conscience of the masses and of producing new behaviors so that the subordinate groups do not submit under the direction of the capitalist State.

It is under the framework of the dispute for hegemony, however, that Gramsci elaborates his research on the question of culture, which is absent from the theory in which the State is a 'machine' of bourgeoisie repression that needs to be dismantled to overcome capitalism ('Formula of 1848'[9]).

Gramsci's research on hegemony led him to investigate the ways in which popular ideas and beliefs are formulated. This is the period in which he confronts the problem of 'common sense' and its ties to 'customs', in other words, the 'intellectual and moral' dimension that gives support to hegemony. The attempt to formulate strategies to overcome 'common sense', and in turn 'customs', brought Gramsci to the question of education, both in the didactic and organizational point of view.

The didactic point refers to the methods of organizing thought. A mode of thinking, according to Gramsci, is not innate, it is a 'specialization', for thinking is a skill: the 'art of working with concepts'. As a skill, the process of thinking does not derive from raw 'common sense', but depends on education (Gramsci, 1977, p. 2268). Gramsci believed that to learn how to think was just as important as learning how to read or write, considering that the acquisition of a technique for thinking, especially for the children of the working class, was very difficult. For this reason, Gramsci reinforced the importance of the educative roles of schools, particularly for offering the didactic conditions to working class children to overcome the difficulties of learning to think.

As for the question of organization, Gramsci proposed the creation of a 'unitary center of culture'. He drew as a reference on his rich experience editing the magazines of the communist and socialist party, and the accompanying methodological lessons for the educational activity of the masses. In this manner, he suggests that the 'unitary center of culture' be organized as the composition of magazines, like a 'circuit of culture' whose objective is to elevate the level of culture of the great portion of the population that was not able to go to school. This would be a form of helping solve the problem of the organization of culture, though it would not be the only and final solution.

Gramsci wanted to make the 'center of culture' hegemonic. To do this, he proposed two principal lines of action: a general concept of life, whose reference is Marxism, and a school program, that is, 'an *educative principal and original pedagogy* which gives an activity, in the technical area, to the faction of intellectuals that are most homogeneous and numerous' (the professors, from elementary education to universities) (Gramsci, 1977, p. 2047, my italics).

In his reflections on the school, Gramsci sought to develop an educative principle and to formulate the notion of the unitary school. His proposal is associated with the process of 'intellectual and moral reform', and the 'unitary principle' is addressed to the fight for social equality, to overcome the class divisions that separate society into rulers and subjects. Formulating the 'school program' that ought to serve as the guide for organizing a cultural center, integrated in the ideological fight to overcome hegemony, Gramsci affirms that the unitary principle supersedes school as an institution:

> The advent of the unitary school signifies the beginning of new relations between intellectual and industrial work not only in schools, but in the whole of social life. The unitary principle will thus be reflected in all aspects and organisms of culture, transforming them and giving them a new content. (Gramsci, 1977, p. 1538)

For Gramsci, however, the formulation of a pedagogical proposal fits in the framework of his concern that the center of culture would become hegemonic. It was sketched, principally, as an 'organizational schematic for cultural work'.

In Brazil during the 1980s and 1990s, the interpretations most widely spread of Gramsci in the area of education, was shaped by a type of reading that left out the concept of hegemony. It was a reading, that of Mario Manacorda, which confused the concept of 'unitary school' with 'polytechnic'. The Italian historian does not hesitate to affirm that he was responsible for such a confusion while he was in Brazil during the 1980s and disseminating his ideas along with Dermeval Saviani[10], then a professor at the Pontifícia Universidade Católica de São Paulo.

It was during the 1980s that the elaboration of a Constitution was being discussed in Brazil, a Constitution that would be approved in 1988, setting the stage for the debate regarding the new Lei de Diretrizes e Bases for National Education. It was not by chance that during this period the magazine *Revista Sala de Aula*[11] published a report on the 'new polytechnics', those interviewed about the 'polemical' concept of 'polytechnic' that they defended as a policy for national education.

The 'new polytechnics' were readers of Marx and Gramsci and their leader was professor Saviani, for whom 'polytechnic' was a policy for the whole national education system, with an orientating base in work (*Revista Sala de Aula*, 1989, p. 27). According to Saviani, the 'polytechnic' concept was proposed by Marx in 1864 when he was the head of the Association of Workers and thinking of a worldwide socialist revolution. Later, that concept would be incorporated in Gramsci's reflections, which would propose the concept of the unitary and polytechnic school, for it would represent a synthesis of natural sciences and history, the formative base of the new man.

As a reader of Gramsci, Saviani made an analysis of the Brazilian school system during the beginning of the 1980s, and he proposed a 'revolutionary pedagogy', to which he later gave the name 'historical-critical pedagogy'. To formulate such a proposal, he returned to the past, during the rise of the bourgeoisie in Europe, and retook the notion of the humanist school, affirming that the old pedagogy 'had a revolutionary character during the constitution of bourgeoisie power *and still has today*' (Saviani, 1985, p. 67, my italics). For Saviani, the return to the 'traditional school' constituted a strategy to strip away the hegemony of the 'new school' ('active school') and to generate conditions for the rise of a 'revolutionary pedagogy'. Its goal would be to enable workers to acquire cognitive and cultural tools in order to strengthen their battle against capitalist exploration and the conquest of citizenry.

By the second half of the 1980s, Saviani sent a proposal for the elaboration of his project to the Lei de Diretrizes e Bases of National Education based on the concept of polytechnic, which, for him,

> ... involves the articulation of intellectual and manual work and involves an instruction based on social work that develops the fundamental principles that are at the base of the organization of work in our society and which enable us to understand its processes. (Saviani, 1997, p. 19)

The author does not explain the connections between his 'revolutionary pedagogy' and the concept of 'polytechnic', but he asserts that the latter represents the 'mastery of the scientific principles of different skills that characterize the productive process of modern work' (Saviani, 1989, p. 17). Giving examples of the type of activities needed in high school to develop polytechnic skills, he suggests work with wood and metal, arguing that they have 'immense educational worth for they represent ample opportunities for transformation. It involves not only the production of the majority of objects that composes the modern production process, but also the production of instruments with which these objects are produced' (Saviani, 1997, p. 39).

Thus, for the activity of modern production, which starting at the end of the 1970s was characterized by microelectronics and information technology, the author suggests activity with wood and metal, whose introduction in schools dates back to the end of the 19th century in the United States. It was the method adopted to spark the interest of children in work, through the construction of an entire object, useful or ornamental, as explained by the Belgian pedagogue Omer Buyse, whose book *Méthodes américaines d'éducation générale et technique* (1908) was recommended by the Brazilian educator Anísio Teixeira, encouraging its translation into Portuguese (Buyse, 1927). In Brazil, since the 1920s, 'the admirable American methods of elementary education' began to be used by professor Corinto da Fonseca in the then 'Sousa Aguiar Professional School' in Rio de Janeiro. It was considered a desirable method to de-emphasize the instruction of singular skills, and to develop poly skills (Dore Soares, 2000).

Both the 'revolutionary pedagogy' and the 'polytechnic' proposal were presented by Saviani as a return to the past: based at times on the recuperation of the humanist school, a bourgeoisie perspective that was historically overcome, and at other times on the concept of 'polythecnicality', a perspective that became historically defunct with the collapse of socialism, but which the author continues to defend today (cf. Saviani, 2003).

Another reader of Gramsci who, during the 1980s, returned to the past to present an educational plan is Nosella (1986). He does not defend the humanist school, but rather debates Saviani's thesis, affirming that Gramsci criticized the Jesuit humanist school. According to Nosella, the proposal that emerged in the workers' movement came from the Commune of Paris of 1871. For him, the Commune produced a 'new' pedagogy, 'a pedagogical proposal antithetical to that of Adam Smith, by opening freely and immediately education and culture, at its highest levels, to workers' (Nosella, 1986, p. 120). In the meantime, from 1871 to the present, the bourgeoisie challenged the educational plan of the Commune of Paris. Without giving up its 'Adam Smithian flag', the bourgeoisie tried to appropriate and distort the pedagogical concepts that emerged from the workers' movement. Thus, the 'new school' was 'decreasing': the bourgeoisie philosophies 'distort, reduce or dissolve the key concepts of the original education plan of the workers ...' (Nosella, 1986, p. 126). It was in this regard, states Nosella, that Gramsci called attention.

Believing that there exist only two types of pedagogies, respectively related to the two antagonistic types of social classes, the 'traditional'-bourgeoisie and the 'new'-worker, Nosella proposes, in the name of a Gramscian reading of education, to recuperate the proposal of the *communards*. While Gramsci advocated that the unitary school should start to be developed in capitalist society, Nosella argued that the working class should not settle 'for the crumbs of the bourgeoisie table', and, thus, should not accept the type of education outlined by Adam Smith (Nosella, 1986, p. 131), refusing completely the bourgeois school.

According to the interpretation of these authors, however, the existing school, the only one we have historically known, would not develop in our lifetime a concrete premise from which could be formulated a school plan based on democratic and popular interests.

Frigotto is another reader of Gramsci, considered by the *Revista Sala de Aula* one of the major formulators of the polytechnic plan for high school. For him, the polytechnic school 'matches the challenge of modern skills' (Frigotto, 1988).

At the beginning of the 1990s, Frigotto recognized the existing confusion regarding the term 'unitary school' in Brazil. He admits 'misunderstandings' and calls for a deeper understanding of the theoretical concept of the unitary school. Despite making this assertion after the fall of the Berlin Wall, the author continued to argue that the future of the struggle, in the educational realm, ought to be based on 'unitary, technological, omnilateral or polytechnic school' (Frigotto, 1993, p. 41). All of these conceptions, mixed up in this manner, are converted into one sole concept, the unitary and polytechnic school, and constitute Frigotto's reference for developing a decree[12] (Number 5.154/2004) during the government of Luiz Inácio Lula da Silva, instituting 'an educational conception that strives to *overcome the bourgeoisie educational proposal* that allows for the structural transformation of reality' (Frigotto *et al.*, 2005b, my italics).

Frigotto and his colleagues (Ciavatta and Ramos) state that the polytechnic notion was reaffirmed as a school strategy by Saviani (2003), even though such a notion should not be literally interpreted, 'considering that it could signify multiple techniques, a multiplicity of techniques, and in this manner there is the risk of understanding this concept as the totality of different techniques, fragmented, if they are autonomously considered' (Saviani, 2003, p. 140). The term 'technology' would be the most appropriate, but it had been *appropriated by the bourgeois*, and, because of this, the authors adopt the term 'polytechnic', which would be, for them, 'the most appropriate for defining a conception of education based explicitly on the overcoming of social divisions of work determined by a society separated into classes' (Frigotto *et al.*, 2005b). According to Frigotto (2005), Saviani affirms that while the term 'technology' is connected to the bourgeoisie and technocrats, the term 'polytechnic' was 'preserved in the socialist tradition'. In this way, even after the transformations following the fall of 'real socialism', the notion '*polytechnic*' would be, for the group of 'new polytechnics', the most appropriate to set up 'a *technology education* directed at the children of workers' (Frigotto *et al.*, 2005b, my italics).

There are not, however, distinctions between the Marxist conception, that of 'real socialism', and the Gramscian conception. They are understood as being one and the same, independent of the historical contexts in which they were elaborated. In sum, the lack of differentiation between polytechnic and unitary school has marked the predominant reading in the historiography of Brazilian education, constituting a reference for political education projects, even those authoritatively instituted, such as the decree on polytechnic high school education.

But if Marx did not name his idea of education 'polytechnic', where did such a reductionist denomination come from?

Manacorda, as we saw, is partly responsible for the confusion between the concepts of unitary and polytechnic schools in Brazil. The Brazilian group of 'polytechnics', along with the Italian historian, also justified the validity of using the term 'polytechnic' as a reference for an educational project in Brazil, based on the interests of the working class (Ciavatta, 2005). But this does not answer the question: how did 'polytechnic' become the term for the educational conception proposed by Marx? Moreover, why would the term 'polytechnic' express an 'omnilateral' formation just because it was 'preserved in the socialist tradition'?

Certainly, Manacorda's reflections on 'polytechnic' were welcomed in Brazil. His studies on the types of pedagogy adopted by socialist countries were realized in the 1960s, when he[13] represented the cultural commission of the Italian Communist Party (PCI) and directed the journal *Riforma della scuola*. During this period, Manacorda developed a trilogy on socialist education. The first book covers the thoughts of Marx, Engels and Lenin (Manacorda, 1964), the second the Soviet school experiment (Manacorda, 1965), and the third one the educational experiments in the socialist nations (Manacorda, 1966). His thesis is that the three sources that constitute the socialist pedagogical experiment, in complete or partial form, are the 'Marxist analysis, the Soviet model, and the national reality' (Manacorda, 1966, p. 5). According to his research, 'the Marxist pedagogy' was 'filtered and reflected in the Soviet experience' (Manacorda, 1966, p. 6), and it was this already codified interpretation that was transmitted to the countries that would become socialist after the Second World War. In this way, a certain schematization of the Soviet experience was exported to the new socialist countries, without the necessity of Marxist pedagogy 'being discovered and discussed again, as in the first years of Soviet power' (Manacorda, 1966, p. 6).

Manacorda criticizes the educational program during Stalin's rule. He argues that, although the terms 'polytechnic' and 'omnilaterality' were adopted, they lost their significance. Polytechnic came to signify.

> ... a multiplicity of professional preparations, the ability of the worker to complete different tasks in cases of technological advancements, silencing

(although not excluding) the theme of intellectual formation, the acquisition of scientific fundamentals and theories in addition to the practical
capacity to use industrial tools, in sum, the link between science and
work. (Manacorda, 1966, p. 7)

Nevertheless, Manacorda argues that, after Khrushchev denounced the crimes
committed by Stalin (XX Congress of the Communist Party that took place in
1956), there was a reorientation of the Soviet educational policies. Thus, 'the truer
meaning of Marxist indications' would be recuperated, that which, for the author,
'suggests not so much manual work (which is certainly suggested), but more
productive work, *the work of the factory, because the factory is the typical mode of modern
production*' (Manacorda, 1966, p. 8, my italics). In Manacorda's interpretation, in
accordance with Marx, 'instruction should not be based so much on assuming the
tradition of the past, but more on inserting the present perspective. This objective
process *creates the new factory instruction ...*' (Manacorda, 1966, p. 8, my italics). In
this way, it is this idea of 'polytechnic' linked to 'factory instruction' that constitutes,
for Manacorda, the socialist model which was adopted in all of the countries of the
Soviet bloc, from 1956–1961.

In his educational policies, Lenin (1919) did not adopt the term 'polytechnic'
separately, but rather connected it to general education, calling it 'general and polytechnic instruction'. In addition, he thought about the formation of leaders, an
aspect that was left behind by real socialism, whose phraseology of the 'omnilateral'
man did not stop the Soviet Union from asphyxiating every movement towards
liberation, as it did in Hungary in 1956, in Poland in 1956 and in Czechoslovakia
in 1968. In these countries, there also occurred the polytechnic and 'omnilateral'
experience, which Manacorda considers a 'Marxist pedagogy'. But if for Manacorda 'polytechnic' represents the link between 'instruction and factory', an economic dimension of school instruction, what would be 'omnilateral' development?
This is a point that the Italian historian does not develop in his studies and that is
not approached in the authoritarian experience of real socialism. The direct link
between Manacorda and the positions taken by the PCI allied to the Soviet Union,
even after the denunciations of Stalinism, lead him to state that the Hungarian
and Polish revolts of 1956 were 'muddled calls for a more civil development in
the direction of socialism, for patriotism, *and for nationalist anti-Sovietism*' and
'*open hopes for capitalist restoration*' (Manacorda, 1966, p. 11, my italics).

Was it from this experience on the notion 'polytechnic', in which attempts for
social and political emancipation were cruelly suffocated, that Manacorda made
conclusions about Marxist education based on development and 'omnilaterality'?

'Real socialism' was marked by the absence of democracy and by policies of
repression not only in terms of attempts to 'liberalize' socialism, but also in terms
of preventing innovation and the development of workers associations and
exchange between qualified workers and scientific researchers (Blackburn, 1993,
p. 162). In the cultural and philosophical realm, the negation of civil and political
rights was reflected in the cultural 'inertia' of the communist countries, where
the lack of critical debate prevented the birth of new ideas, favoring the diffusion

of an already outdated and dogmatic Marxist philosophy. For these reasons, school organization in 'real socialism', known as 'polytechnic', cannot be considered an experience that expresses Marxist thought on the development of 'omnilaterality'.

Manacorda's synthesis of the notion 'polytechnic', however, was not realized with a basis in the Gramscian reflection on unitary schools, but rather in accordance with the Soviet model, which lacks perspectives on hegemony and the formation of leaders. In his trilogy on socialist pedagogy, Manacorda (1964, 1965, 1966) does not even refer to Gramsci[14]. For this reason, it is strange that the idea 'polytechnic' would come to constitute, in the 21st century, a theoretical referential to formulate educational proposals for Brazilian education, as has been the case with the 'new polytechnics'.

Final Considerations

Certainly, the diffusion of Gramscian ideas in Brazil, starting in the 1980s, contributed to the resurgence of the importance of public education, which was devalued after being considered an 'ideological apparatus' of the State. However, this did not signify the understanding and advancement of Gramscian pedagogical thought. Rather, it ended up that the notion of 'polytechnic school' was considered the same as 'unitary school'.

Nevertheless, there are no documents in which Marx considers education solely as 'polytechnic', for, as we saw, this is for Marx merely one aspect of education, along with intellectual and physical education. The confusion between Marx's and Gramsci's educational ideas can be traced to the supposed theorists responsible for the diffusion of Gramscian thought in Brazil during the 1980s, and the failure to place each proposal in its specific historical and political context. The majority of Brazilian educators that read Gramsci did not understand that his notion of the State was a rupture with Marx's notion of the State and that this rupture was also expressed in civil society, and thus, in the realm of education and its relationship to the State. Gramsci sought to present suggestions for organizing schools in such a way as to respond to the contextual demands of the beginning of the 20th century, which was after Marx's time. To respond to the contemporary problems of education it will be necessary to part with the Gramscian notion of school and update it. Initiatives in this direction are problematic because they do not take into account that the concept of unitary school is part of the complete theory of Gramsci on the State, which goes beyond the 'formula of 1848', be it from a tactical point of view or from a strategic point of view. To present a 'polytechnic' proposal as a political guideline for organizing school in the 21st century is to continue to defend the 'formula of 1848' in the cultural realm.

Notes

1. The Brazilian Communist Party (PCB) was founded on March 25, 1922, a development shaped in the aftermath of the Soviet Revolution that happened in 1917. After the rise of

Stalin, the PCB adopted an economic and fatalist interpretation of communism, according to which the triumph of socialism would be an inevitable consequence of the fall of capitalism (cf. Secco, 2002). The PCB had periods of legitimacy and illegitimacy, and after the changes in Eastern Europe, it underwent a profound crisis, finally being dissolved in 1992 by its own members.

2. This name refers to Brazilian educators who had launched the *Manifesto para a Reconstrução da Educação Nacional* (*Manifesto for the Reconstruction of National Education*), in 1932, inspired by the 'New School' (or 'Active School') movement spread throughout North America and Europe since the beginning of the 20th century.

3. Bowles and Gintis's sociological research also devoted its attention to the ways in which social institutions, including education, served to reproduce inequalities in larger society (Bowles & Gintis, 1976).

4. The theories of Bowles and Gintis were criticized in the United States by authors such as Apple (1979) and Giroux (1983), who sought to develop a perspective of 'resistance' (cf. Morrow and Torres, 1995, pp. 318–9). The criticisms made by Apple and Giroux, however, only began to be published in Brazil during the 1980s, and became more widely recognized during the 1990s.

5. Before the tightening of the military dictatorship, there was a fledgling movement to publish and spread some of Gramsci's work, an effort made by the Brazilian Civilization Editor, mainly editor of Brazilian Left wing writings during the initial years of the military regime (Czajka, 2004; Vieira, 1996). A *Dialectic Conception of History* and *Letters from Prison* were published in 1966, *Intellectuals and the Organization of Culture* and *Literature and National Life*, *Macchiavelli, Politics and the Modern State* in 1968. These works, however, were only reedited at the end of the 1970s, during the period of political amnesty and the return of political exiles. It was at this time that Gramscian thought began to influence the State in a way that broke with Althusserian interpretation, up until then dominant.

6. In the 'Instructions for the Delegates of the Provisional General Council (1866)', Marx writes at the end of August 1866:

    By education we understand three things.

    Firstly: *Mental education.*

    Secondly: *Physical education*, such as is given in schools of gymnastics, and by military exercise.

    Thirdly: *Technological training*, which imparts the general principles of all processes of production, and, simultaneously initiates the child and young person in the practical use and handling of the elementary instruments of all trades. [The German text calls this 'polytechnical training.' *Ed.*]

    A gradual and progressive course of mental, gymnastic, and technological training ought to correspond to the classification of the juvenile laborers. The costs of the technological schools ought to be partly met by the sale of their products.

    The combination of paid productive labor, mental education bodily exercise and polytechnic training, will raise the working class far above the level of the higher and middle classes. (http://www.marxists.org/history/international/iwma/documents/1866/instructions. htm#04)

7. The different educational conceptions regarding 'The New School', debated internationally, gave rise to a doctrine that became the principal policy underlining successive school reforms occurring in the West since the beginning of the 20th century (cf. Dore Soares, 2000).

8. Gramsci refers to the 'Formula of 1848' as a concept of a violent Revolution against the capitalist State, conceived as a 'committee' of the bourgeoisie. See Marx and Engels' concept of the State in *Manifesto of the Communist Party*, published in 1848, which says: 'The executive of the modern state is but a committee for managing the common affairs of the whole bourgeoisie.' See also the conception of revolution as a direct confrontation with the State: 'Finally, in times when the class struggle nears the decisive hour, the progress of dissolution going on within the ruling class, in fact within the whole range of old society, it assumes such

a violent, glaring character, that a small section of the ruling class cuts itself adrift, and joins the revolutionary class, the class that holds the future in its hands. Just as, therefore, at an earlier period, a section of the nobility went over to the bourgeoisie, so now a portion of the bourgeoisie goes over to the proletariat, and in particular, a portion of the bourgeois ideologists, who have raised themselves to the level of comprehending theoretically the historical movement as a whole.' Or: 'In depicting the most general phases of the development of the proletariat, we traced the more or less veiled civil war, raging within existing society, up to the point where that war breaks out into open revolution, and where the violent overthrow of the bourgeoisie lays the foundation for the sway of the proletariat' (Marx and Engels, 1969, http://www.marxists.org/archive/marx/works/1848/communist-manifesto/).

9. See preceding note about the Manifesto of the Communist Party of 1848 (Marx and Engels, 1969).

10. Referring to his influence in Brazil, Manacorda stated in a letter from April 2001, addressed to Dore Soares: 'In fact, I believe that it was I, perhaps along with Dermeval Saviani, who was responsible for this confusion [between the Gramscian and the Marxist conception of education], with my lectures in 6 universities, one of which in Minas Gerais (Belo Horizonte) and with my books *The History of Education: From Antiquity to Modern Times*, translated by Cortez in 1979, and *Marx and Modern Pedagogy*, translated by Iniciativas Editoriais, in Lisbon in 1975' (Dore Soares, 2004, p. 4).

11. The *Revista Sala de Aula* (1989) produced a piece on the 'new polytechnics', entitled 'The Word is ... Polytechnic. A synthesis of science, skill and humanism. With this word, a group of educators want to revolutionize education in Brazil'.

12. The authors excuse themselves in a way for having contributed to the application of a decree, which is an authoritarian measure, stating that if they had not acted in this way, 'conservative forces would have occupied the space to impose their interests, both in the National Education Council and in Congress' (Frigotto *et al.*, 2005a).

13. In *Perchè non posso non dirmi comunista* (2000), Manacorda remembers his participation as director of Edições do Rinascita, 'the entity within the PCI Press that was responsible for culture, which primarily translated the Marxist classics'.

14. In Italy, Gramscian thought only began to be published and spread after the fall of fascism. The first volume of his work was only published after the crisis of 1956 (The XX Congress of the Communist Party) (Santarelli, 1991, p. 13). Moreover, in the Italian Communist Party the reading of Gramsci was filtered by the interpretation of Togliatti. According to Lucio Magri (2001), the diffusion of Gramscian ideas during the 1950s was shaped by Togliatti's political objectives of remodeling the Party and maintaining ties with the Soviet Union. In this way, he advocated a fragmented reading of Gramsci's *Letters from Prison*, realizing that the Gramscian reflection went beyond the PCI's positions, and even contradicted them.

References

Abreu, J. (1963) Educação e desenvolvimento: uma colocação do problema na perspectiva brasileira, in: *Revista Brasileira de Estudos Pedagógicos*, 40:91, pp. 6–28.

Althusser, L. (1974) *Ideologia e aparelhos ideológicos do Estado* (Lisboa, Presença).

Alves, M. M. (1979) *A Igreja e a política no Brasil* (São Paulo, Brasiliense).

Apple, M. W. (1979) *Ideology and Curriculum* (Boston and London, Routledge).

Azevedo, F. (1958) A Reconstrução Educacional no Brasil. Manifesto dos Pioneiros da Educação Nova, in: F. Azevedo, *A educação entre dois mundos* (São Paulo, Melhoramentos, obras completas), Vol. XVI, pp. 59–81. The *Manifesto dos educadores de 1932* was also published in the *Revista Brasileira de Estudos Pedagógicos*, 34:79, July/Sept., 1960, pp. 108–127.

Azevedo, F. (1960) *Mais uma vez convocados: manifesto ao povo e ao Governo*, in: R. S. M. Barros (ed.), *Diretrizes e bases da educação nacional* (São Paulo, Pioneira), pp. 57–82. The same document was also published in the *Revista Brasileira de Estudos Pedagógicos*, 31:74, April/June., 1959, pp. 3–24.

Barros, R. S. M. (1960) *Diretrizes e bases da educação nacional* (São Paulo, Pioneira).

Blackburn, R. (1993) O socialismo após o colapso, in: R. Blackburn *et al.* (eds), *Depois da queda: o fracasso do comunismo e o futuro do socialismo* (Rio de Janeiro, Paz e Terra), pp. 107–215.

Bourdieu, P. & Passeron, J. C. (1975) *A reprodução: elementos para uma teoria do sistema de ensino* (Rio de Janeiro, Francisco Alves).

Bowles, S. & Gintis, H. (1976) *Schooling in Capitalist America: Educational reform and contradictions of economic life* (New York, Basic Books).

Bruneau, T. C. (1974) *Catolicismo brasileiro em época de transição* (São Paulo, Loyola).

Buyse, O. (1908) *Méthodes américaines d'éducation générale et technique* (Charleroi, France, Establissement Litho de Charleroi).

Buyse, O. (1927) *Métodos americanos de educação geral e técnica* (Salvador, Imprensa Oficial).

Capanema, G. (1942) Exposição de Motivos da Lei Orgânica do Ensino Secundário (Decree Number 4244, April 1, 1942). Ministério da Educação. Serviço de Documentação (Folheto n. 8). Lei Orgânica do Ensino Secundário (Rio de Janeiro, Imprensa Nacional), pp. 33–42.

Capanema, G. (1937) Discurso, in: *Panorama da educação nacional* (Rio de Janeiro, Ministério da Educação e Saúde).

Carnoy, M. (1977) *La educación como imperialismo cultural* (México, Siglo Veintiuno).

Ciavatta, M. (2005) A formação integrada: a escola e o trabalho como lugares de memória e de identidade. *Trabalho Necessário*, Ano 3, n. 3, (available at http://www.uff.br/trabalhonecessario/MariaTN3.htm Accessed: 3 April 2006).

Cohn, G. (1976) Problemas da industrialização no século XX, in: C. G. Mota (ed.), *Brasil em perspectiva* (São Paulo, DIFEL).

Costa, E. V. (1987) *Da Monarquia à República*: momentos decisivos (São Paulo, Brasiliense).

Cunha, L. A. (1979) Notas para uma leitura da teoria da violência simbólica. *Educação & Sociedade*, I:4, Sept. (São Paulo, Cortez & Moraes/CEDES), pp. 79–110.

Cunha, L. A. & Góes, M. (1985) *O golpe na educação* (Rio de Janeiro, Jorge Zahar Editor).

Czajka, R. (2004) Redesenhando ideologias: cultura e política em tempos de golpe (Redesigning Ideologies: Culture and politics at the time of a coup). *História: Questões & Debates*, 40, (Curitiba, Editora UFPR), pp. 37–57.

Del Roio, M. (1990). *A classe operária na revolução burguesa*: a política de alianças do PCB (1928–1935) (Belo Horizonte, Oficina de livros).

Dore Soares, R. (1982) *Formação de técnicos de nível superior: do engenheiro de operação ao tecnólogo* (Belo Horizonte, FaE/UFMG) (Master's dissertation).

Dore Soares, R. (2000) *Gramsci, o Estado e a escola* (Ijuí, Unijuí).

Dore Soares, R. (2003) A pesquisa educacional no Brasil sobre o programa da escola nova: notas teóricas e metodológicas, in: L. A. Gonçalves (ed.), *Currículo e políticas públicas* (Belo Horizonte, Autêntica), pp. 63–104.

Dore Soares, R. (2004) Entrevista com Mario A. Manacorda, *Revista Novos Rumos* (Encarte), 19:41, pp. 1–23.

Fernandes, F. (1966) *Educação e sociedade no Brasil* (São Paulo, Dominus/Edusp).

Fernandes, F. (1960) Análise e crítica do Projeto de Lei sobre Diretrizes e Bases da Educação Nacional, in: R. S. M. Barros (ed.), *Diretrizes e bases da educação nacional* (São Paulo, Pioneira), pp. 217–306.

Franco, A. C. (1987) *A escola do trabalho e o trabalho da escola* (São Paulo, Cortez).

Frigotto, G. (1988) Formação profissional no 2º. grau: em busca do horizonte da Educação Politécnica, *Cadernos Saúde Pública*, 4:4, pp. 435–445 (Available at: <http://www.scielo.br/scielo.php?script=sci_arttext&pid=S0102-311X1988000400012&lng=en&nrm=iso>. Accessed: 4 March 2006).

Frigotto, G. (1993) Trabalho e educação: formação técnico-profissional em questão. *Universidade e sociedade* (5) (São Paulo, ANDES), pp. 38–42.

Frigotto, G. (2005) Escola pública da atualidade: Lições da história. in: J. C. Lombardi, D. Saviani & M. I. M. Nascimento (eds), *A escola pública no Brasil: história e historiografia* (Campinas-SP, Autores Associados) (Available at: http://www.classiserra.com.br/cid/51arq.doc Accessed: 22 January 2006).

Frigotto, G., Ciavatta, M., Ramos, M. (2005a) A política de educação profissional no Governo Lula: um percurso histórico controvertido, *Educação & Sociedade* [online], 26:92, pp. 1087–1113 [cited 22 January 2006]. Available at: http://www.scielo.br/scielo.php?script=sci_arttext&pid=S0101-73302005000300017&lng=en&nrm=iso).

Frigotto, G., Ciavatta, M. & Ramos, M. (2005b) A gênese do Decreto N. 5.154/2004: um debate no contexto controverso da democracia restrita, *Trabalho Necessário, Universidade Federal Fluminense*, 3:3 (Available at: http://www.uff.br/trabalhonecessario/MMGTN3.htm. Accessed: 20 February 2006; Also available at: http://www.diaadiaeducacao.pr.gov.br/portals/portal/institucional/dep/fc_genesedec5154.pdf Accessed: 20 February 2006).

Gadotti, M. (1992) Estado e educação popular: educação de adultos em São Paulo (Brasil), in: Adult Literacy: An international urban perspective: issues, strategies, and challenges, United Nations Headquarters August 3–6, 1992—New York City (Available at: http://www.paulofreire.org/Moacir_Gadotti/Artigos/Portugues/Educacao_Popular_e_EJA/Estado_educ_pop_1992.pdf Accessed: 22 January 2006).

Gandini, R. P. C. (1980) *Tecnocracia, capitalismo e educação em Anísio Teixeira* (Rio de Janeiro, Civilização Brasileira).

Giroux, H. (1983) *Theory and Resistance in Education: A pedagogy for the opposition* (South Hadley, MA, Bergin and Garvey).

Gramsci, A. (1978) *Os intelectuais e a organização da cultura* (Rio de Janeiro, Civilização Brasileira).

Gramsci, A. (1977) *Quaderni del carcere* (Turin, Einaudi).

Illich, I. (1973) *Sociedade sem escolas*, L. M. Endlich Orth, trans. (Petrópolis, Vozes).

Kadt, E. (2003) *Católicos radicais no Brasil* (João Pessoa, Editora Universitária/UFPB).

Kuenzer, A. (1985) *Pedagogia da fábrica: as relações de produção e a educação do trabalhador* (São Paulo, Cortez).

Lambert, J. (1959) *Os dois Brasis* (São Paulo, INEP).

Lemme, P. (1988) *Vida de família*: formação profissional, opção política, Vol. 2 (Brasília, Cortez).

Lenin, V. I. (1919) The Basic Tasks of the Dictatorship of the Proletariat in Russia (Source: Lenin's *Collected Works, 4th English Edition, Progress Publishers, Moscow, 1972 Volume 29*, pp. 97–140. Available at: http://www.marx.org/archive/lenin/works/1919/mar/x02.htm Accessed: 26 January 2006).

Lenin, V. I. (1975) Carta a Maximo Gorki, escrita non mas tarde del 8/02/1916, in: V. I. Lenin, *La instrucción pública* (Moscow, Progress Publishers), p. 64.

Lima, D. (1978) *Educação, Igreja e ideologia* (Rio de Janeiro, Francisco Alves).

Luizetto, F. (1982) Cultura e educação libertária no Brasil no início do século XX, *Revista Educação & Sociedade*, 12, pp. 61–79 (Campinas, São Paulo, Cortez & Moraes/CEDES).

Luizetto, F. (1986) O movimento anarquista em São Paulo: a experiência da escola moderna n° 1 (1912–1919), *Revista Educação & Sociedade*, 24, pp. 18–47 (Campinas, São Paulo, Cortez & Moraes/CEDES).

Luz, N. V. (1961) *A luta pela industrialização do Brasil* (São Paulo, Alfa-Omega).

Magalhães, M. D. B. (1997) A lógica da suspeição: sobre os aparelhos repressivos à época da ditadura militar no Brasil, *Revista Brasileira de História* [online], 17:34, pp. 203–220.

Magri, L. (2001) Il Gramsci di Togliatti, *La Rivista del Manifesto*, 20, September (Available at: http://www.larivistadelmanifesto.it/archivio/20/20A20010917.html Accessed: 2 March 2006).

Manacorda, M. A. (1964) *Il marxismo e l'educazione* (Testi e documenti 1843–1964), Vol. 1, *I classici: Marx, Engels, Lenin* (Roma, Armando Armando).

Manacorda, M. A. (1965) *Il marxismo e l'educazione* (Testi e documenti 1843–1964), Vol. 2, *La scuola sovietica* (Roma, Armando Armando).

Manacorda, M. A. (1966) *Il marxismo e l'educazione* (Testi e documenti 1843–1964), Vol. 3, *La scuola nei paesi socialisti* (Roma, Armando Armando).

Manacorda, M.A. (2000) *Perchè non posso non dirmi comunista: una grande utopia che non può morire* (Valentano, Scipioni) Available at: http://www.logosfreebooks.org/pls/wordtc/ecommerce. stampa_scheda_1?hcodice=67551&hlingua=IT Accessed: 23 February 2006).

Martins, W. V. (1976) *Liberdade de ensino: reflexões a partir de uma situação no Brasil* (São Paulo, Loyola).

Marx, K. (1866) Instructions for the Delegates of the Provisional General Council (1866), (10/09/2005) (Available at: http://www.marxists.org/history/international/iwma/documents/ 1866/instructions.htm#04 Accessed: 22 February 2006).

Marx, K. & Engels, F. (1969) Manifesto of the Communist Party, in: *Selected Works*, Vol. 1 (Moscow, Progress Publishers), pp. 98–137 (Available at: http://www.marxists.org/archive/ marx/works/1848/communist-manifesto Accessed: 23 February 2006).

Morrow, R. A. & Torres, C. A. (1995) *Social Theory and Education: A critique of theories of social and cultural reproduction* (Albany, NY, SUNY Press).

Mota, C. G. (1980) *Ideologia da cultura brasileira (1933–1974)* (São Paulo, Ática).

Nosella, P. (1986) Educação tradicional e educação moderna: debatendo com Saviani, *Educação & Sociedade*, I:4, pp. 79–110 (São Paulo, Cortez & Moraes/CEDES).

Paiva, V. (1985a) Estado e educação popular: recolocando o problema, in: C. R. Brandão (ed.), *A questão política da educação popular* (São Paulo, Brasiliense), pp. 79–87.

Paiva, V. (1985b) Que política educacional queremos? *Educação & Sociedade*, 8:21, pp. 121–140 (São Paulo, Cortez & Moraes/CEDES).

Paiva, V. (1986) Introdução, in: V. Paiva (ed.), *Perspectivas e dilemas da educação popular* (Rio de Janeiro, Editora Graal), pp. 15–60.

Paoli, N. I. (1980) *Ideologia e hegemonia* (São Paulo, Cortez/Autores Associados).

Pistrak (1981) *Fundamentos da escola do trabalho* (São Paulo, Brasiliense).

Postman, N. & Weingartner, C. (1971) *Contestação: nova fórmula de ensino*, A. Cabral, trans. (Rio de Janeiro, Ed. Expressão e Cultura).

Prado Júnior, C. (1966) *A revolução brasileira* (São Paulo, Brasiliense).

Reimer, E. (1975) *A escola está morta*: alternativas em educação, A Thompson, trans. (Rio de Janeiro, Francisco Alves).

Revista Sala de Aula (1989) 'A palavra é ... politecnia. Uma síntese de ciência, técnica e humanismo. Com ela, um grupo de educadores quer revolucionar o ensino no país', 2:13, pp. 26–30.

Rodrigues, E. (1992) *O anarquismo na escola, no teatro, na poesia* (Rio de Janeiro, Edições Achiamé Ltda).

Santarelli, E. (1991) L'eredità politica e la fortuna letteraria di Antonio Gramsci, in: E. Santarelli (ed.), *Gramsci ritrovato (1937–1947)* (Catanzaro, Abramo), pp. 9–80.

Saviani, D. (1985) *Escola e democracia* (São Paulo, Cortez).

Saviani, D. (1989) *Sobre a concepção de politecnia* (Rio de Janeiro, Fundação Oswaldo Cruz).

Saviani, D. (1997) *A nova lei da educação (LDB): trajetória, limites e perspectivas* (Campinas, S.P., Autores Associados).

Saviani, D. (2003) O choque teórico da politecnia, *Trabalho, educação e saúde. Revista da EPSJV/ FIOCRUZ*, 1, pp. 131–152 (Rio de Janeiro, Ed. FIOCRUZ).

Secco, L. (2002) *Gramsci e o Brasil. Difusão e recepção de suas idéias* (São Paulo, Cortez).

Singer, P. (1976) *A crise do milagre* (Rio de Janeiro, Paz e Terra).

Tavares, M. C. (1972) *Da substituição de importações ao capitalismo financeiro* (Rio de Janeiro, Zahar).

Toledo, C. N. (1997) *O governo Goulart e o golpe de 64* (São Paulo, Brasiliense).

Tragtenberg, M. (1982) *Sobre educação política e sindicalismo* (São Paulo, Cortez, Autores Associados).

Vianna, L. W. (1976) *Liberalismo e sindicato no Brasil.* (Rio de Janeiro, Paz e Terra).

Vieira, L. R. (1996) *Consagrados e malditos: os intelectuais e a editora Civilização Brasileira* (Brasília, Tese (Doutorado em Sociologia). Instituto de Ciências Humanas. Universidade de Brasília).

Index

Pri